Advance Praise for

The Healing Heart ~ Families

Stories are truer than the truth. They have the power to transform without
resistance because they do not threaten as statistics and beliefs do. As a surgeon,
I have learned wordswordswords can become swordswordswords which, when used
properly like a scalpel, can cure diseases. Every life is a story which needs
to be told, from beginning to end, so healing can occur.

—Bernie Siegel, MD, author *Love, Medicine & Miracles and Prescriptions For Living*

Both children and adults, sick or well, need the embrace of soulful storytelling.
They need to witness and be witnessed, for it is in this state that healing occurs. This labor
of love by David Albert and Allison Cox weaves magical connections. If newscasters were to
read aloud each night to their listeners for 1001 nights one of the stories from this treasury,
we would all be healed and lose our fear, recapturing real security in our homeland.

—N. Michael Murphy MD, author, *The Wisdom of Dying*

An extraordinary work. *The Healing Heart ~ Families* hits the bulls eye by providing
both process and practice. Thought provoking and insightful theory is intertwined with
appropriate stories for direct application. It makes clear that story can be a powerful
catalyst for change, giving eloquent voice to what many of us have known for
some time but have been unable to express. What a gift for those who
work with families! I can't wait to see the one on Communities.

—Elizabeth Ellis, co-author of *Inviting the Wolf In: Thinking about Difficult Stories*

With an effective blend of traditional tales, personal reminiscence, model programs, and applications, this fine book serves as an inspiring read, as well as a handbook for those using stories in healing. A ground-breaking work.

— Gay Ducey, former Chairperson of the National Storytelling Network and co-founder and director of the Bay Area Storytelling Festival

The Healing Heart

~ Families

The Healing Heart

~ Families

Storytelling to Encourage Caring and Healthy Families

Edited by Allison M. Cox and David H. Albert
Foreword by Nancy Mellon

NEW SOCIETY PUBLISHERS

Cataloguing in Publication Data:
A catalog record for this publication is available from the National Library of Canada.

Cover design by Diane McIntosh. Image: Artville, illustrator: Lisa Zador.

Printed in Canada by Friesens.

Paperback ISBN: 0-86571-466-5
Library Binding ISBN: 0-86571-467-3

*Some of the authors of this book have offered their stories for other tellers' oral use. These stories are indicated by an asterisk in the table of contents. Please credit the author when you use these stories.

If this symbol(*) does not appear with a story, please contact the author to request permission before telling his or her story (contact information is given with the author biographies at the back of the book). Audio recording or reprinting of any material in this book requires permission from the authors.

Inquiries regarding requests to reprint all or part of *Healing Hearts* should be addressed to New Society Publishers at the address below.

To order directly from the publishers, please add $4.50 shipping to the price of the first copy, and $1.00 for each additional copy (plus GST in Canada). Send check or money order to:

New Society Publishers
P.O. Box 189, Gabriola Island, BC V0R 1X0, Canada
1-800-567-6772

New Society Publishers' mission is to publish books that contribute in fundamental ways to building an ecologically sustainable and just society, and to do so with the least possible impact on the environment, in a manner that models this vision. We are committed to doing this not just through education, but through action. We are acting on our commitment to the world's remaining ancient forests by phasing out our paper supply from ancient forests worldwide. This book is one step towards ending global deforestation and climate change. It is printed on acid-free paper that is **100% old growth forest-free** (100% post-consumer recycled), processed chlorine free, and printed with vegetable based, low VOC inks. For further information, or to browse our full list of books and purchase securely, visit our website at: www.newsociety.com

NEW SOCIETY PUBLISHERS   www.newsociety.com

Dedication

To my parents, who opened the door to all — Madonna, who taught me to speak with feeling, and Allan, who always laughed the loudest. And to my grandparents — Jeanette, who spun the best stories, and Basil, who listened deep and long. This book is woven with memories of nights around your kitchen tables. —A.M.C.

To my Indian Amma Krishnammal Jagannathan, the greatest storyteller I have ever met (and all the stories are true!), who, when asked how many children she can care for, always replies, "How many are there?" —D.H.A.

Contents

*Authors have offered their stories for other tellers' oral use. Please credit the author when you use these stories.

See copyrights page (vi) for more details.

Foreword

NANCY MELLON

FROM TIME IMMEMORIAL the paths of story-tellers and healers have tangled together. As we face our immensely challenging new century, it is not surprising that much attention is being given to the fact that even a one-minute story can change both tellers and listeners for the better.

Perhaps you who are reading this book are part of the growing throng of individuals and groups who are telling stories with a healing intention. A few years ago Allison Cox, a creative health educator and storyteller, and David Albert, a public health planner and author, recognized that people in a multitude of different professions were experimenting with this mode of purposeful storytelling. They sensed with sturdy compassion and an ear to the wind that the time was right for creating a set of books that shared the many ways that stories can open doors for individuals, families, and communities.

They summoned storytellers involved in this work. Back came a ripple of response, followed by wave upon wave of confirmation from around the United States and abroad that storytelling can be healing medicine for a huge range of troubles.

The book you have in your hands was created through Allison and David's inspired vision and leadership. *The Healing Heart ~ Families: Storytelling to Encourage Caring and Healthy Families* and its companion volume, *The Healing Heart ~ Communities: Storytelling to Build Strong and Healthy Communities*, pay tribute to the growing number of pioneers, many as yet unacclaimed, who have listened for a good story to illuminate perplexing dilemmas. Having once successfully trailed a mysterious narrative through to new light, they have celebrated with humble wonder — and then tried again. At home or in school, hospital, or treatment center, whether addressing a minor or major problem, these experimenters often have taken time to attend to the results of their storytelling sessions.

Why such growing attention in recent years to healing through the spoken word? One reason is the difficulty we have retaining the nuances and multisensory experiences that happen during direct contact between people, but not through computer communiqués or television or movies. As our powers of listening have clouded over and our speech has been spirited into an array of mechanical devices, we have become increasingly awakened to the need for more gratifying and direct communication. Beyond generating information, storytellers provide a sense of soul exchange as they share reliably coherent narratives. Listening to well-turned phrases spoken with wonder and affection by a storyteller primes the natural poetry in our souls and ignites our creative courage for life.

As health professionals and families cultivate storytelling, individual and communal immune response are enhanced. Storytellers can choose their intent for delivering any sort of story. They can find opportunities to share their passion with an audience — or to deliver thoughts and moral perspective with intellectual fervor. They can engage personality and heart through sharing stories of many cultures to fascinate and entrance. Whether a folktale, a personal story, an invented tale, a grand myth, or a good joke, stories can be styled and delivered with loving care in the intimate service of another.

The story offerings and commentaries contained in the two volumes of *The Healing Heart* are generally of this sort. Selfless and devoted attention to the needs of others can lead beyond intellectual understanding to a feeling of being rooted in the cosmos. Through such storytelling, as these books demonstrate, the restorative wisdom that creates words and imaginations can be felt with complete humility. As words and movement inherent in the words flow together, they can offer ingeniously creative perspectives on depressing and alarming conditions. As story lines dart and flash, they can dive into bogs between the rocks and hard places and leap to celestial resonances — all in the same breath. They can stir creative juices for the joyously abundant life that brings about healthier perspectives and attitudes.

The two volumes of *The Healing Heart* represent a lively, robust leap forward. They are a generous and encouraging contribution to the growing art and science of storytelling. They indicate that, in answer to the needs of our time, a very healthy body of work and methodology is now evolving.

Acknowledgments

THE FOLLOWING PEOPLE championed the birthing of this book:

The Healing Heart finally got rolling when community members of Tacoma, Washington, planned a conference: Storytelling For Prevention, Building Wellness In Our Communities. Many thanks for the hours dedicated by the planning committee, above all Gene Uno, Sheri Badger, and N.C. Griffith, and to Louie Thadie for asking the question, "Who wants to learn more about storytelling?"

My appreciation goes to fellow workers at the Tacoma Pierce County Health Department who encouraged and validated my work in storytelling — especially Merle Hemphill and Sue Winskill. And particular recognition must be given to the "Odyssey Ladies," Willie Goble and Ruth Jeynes, as well as the wonderful teachers and students who welcomed us into their lives every week.

Kudos to my professors at the University of Washington's Public Health Graduate Certificate Program, who expressed interest in my efforts to apply storytelling to health promotion/disease prevention and allowed me to begin compiling *The Healing Heart* books as my practicum project.

My heartfelt thanks to the storytelling organizations of western Washington that have repeatedly welcomed me to their stages, allowing me to delve into new story frontiers: the Mount Tahoma Storytelling Guild, Seattle Storytelling Guild, Olympia Storytelling Guild, Story People of Port Angeles, and Storytellers Network of Longview. I am grateful for the friendships that have been forged through these alliances and all the encouragement that was offered.

The storytellers of the Vancouver Society of Storytelling and the Vancouver Storytelling Festival gave me vital feedback while offering endless enthusiasm and inspiration — special thanks to Nan Gregory, Melanie Ray, Kira Van Deusen, and Catherine Racine for opening up their homes and hearts to me. And my gratitude to Merle Harris, Sandy Byer, Barb Gale, Nancy Duncan, Gail Catlin, Joan Stockbridge, Josephine Pedersen, Frances Feist, and all the others who believed strongly enough in my work to invite me to travel across Canada and the United States to share these tales and speak of the healing applications of story.

The members of Texas Women's University's Storytell listserv offered guidance on countless occasions during my search for tellers and stories to include in these pages. The Healing Story Alliance listserv and board members rallied to help, especially Cristy West, who kept urging me on, and Gail Rosen, who acted as my patient sounding board on all those late-night phone calls. Kind words from Steve Sanfield and Merle Davis gave me courage. I am grateful for all the storytellers, health workers, teachers, and other community members who told me they were eager to read this book and cheered me on along the way.

I could not have completed the work without Madonna Sturmer, who washed dishes and cooked meals while I typed. And Allan Sturmer, who planted, weeded, and watered the gardens while I typed. And Mark Bassett, who built the fire, kept the computer running, and rubbed my shoulders — sore from all that typing.

I am grateful to the Brimstone Foundation for a grant that supported my work on this book, and to the staff at New Society Publishers for sharing the vision. The credit goes to my co-editor, David Albert, for suggesting this book in the first place and for keeping the dream alive.

And finally, I offer my deepest thanks for all those marvelous listening faces in the audience, hugs in the grocery aisles and school hallways ("Look, Momma, it's the storyteller!"), and parting smiles in the detention centers, shelters, recovery clinics, community centers and at the elder meal sites. Each time you ask "Will you please come back again?" — I want to tell these tales all night long and would be willing to start this book from scratch. This book, above all else, was inspired by you.

Allison M. Cox
Storytelling crosses over all boundaries
for it speaks the language of the heart.

Thanks —

- to the members of Olympia Friends Meeting, who have taught me to find stories in silence;

- to the people of Bread & Roses, who have taught me to find stories in service, and to seek out the particulars;

- to all my wondrous friends in India, who first taught me — confirmed city dweller that I am — to find stories in the earth;

- and to my family — Ellen, Aliyah, and Meera — who've put up with the fact that I am often a notoriously slow learner.

David H. Albert

HEALING
THROUGH
STORY

⧼The Tale-Teller⧽

LESLIE SLAPE

*Long, long ago, in the time of lords and ladies, castles and kings,
monsters and dragons and magical rings, there was one who told,
to young and old, tales of all these things.*

The tale-teller traveled from village to village with his leather satchel over his shoulder, telling tales in exchange for a hot meal and a place to sleep ... and perhaps a new tale or two to take with him when he left. For tales are meant to be shared. If they're not told, they crumble into dust.

On the night my story takes place, the townspeople were rejoicing at the news that the tale-teller was coming. The lord of the manor had opened the Great Hall and declared a feast day, and all the people from miles around came to eat and drink and listen.

Among the listeners was a young maiden — a peasant girl — who was collecting food in her apron for her sister lying sick in bed at home. They lived alone, their parents having died.

When the tale-teller entered the hall, the people cheered. "Tell us a story! Tell us a story!"

The old man smiled and set his leather satchel down on a table. He opened it, and those who were nearest could see it was filled to the brim with polished stones.

"I've prepared a new one for you," he said, and picked up a stone from the top. Grasping it in his right hand, he pressed it against his heart, closed his eyes, and took a long, slow breath. He opened his eyes.

"Once upon a time there dwelt a father and three sons ..." he began. His hand never left his heart.

The listeners leaned forward, hardly breathing, not wanting to miss a word. It was a story of a thrilling adventure, and when the tale-teller finished, the listeners cheered. The tale-teller took the stone away from his heart and replaced it in the satchel.

"Another! Another!" the people shouted. "A funny one!"

"Here's one you'll like," said the tale-teller, choosing a small red stone from the satchel. He placed it over his heart as before. "One day in the forest a fox met a bear ...."

Soon the listeners were weak with laughter. When the tale-teller finished, they shouted, "Another! Another!"

"Do you have a love story?" asked a young couple nearby. The tale-teller smiled and said, "Of course." He reached into the satchel and pulled out a silver stone shaped like a teardrop.

"A long time ago there lived three sisters ...."

As he told this tale, tears formed in the eyes of his listeners, for the lovers had to undergo many trials to test their love. But there was one listener whose eyes were not wet.

This man was a thief, and he had come to the feast for the free food, not the stories. But when he saw the silver stone, his interest in this tale-teller grew.

Easily, like a snake, he slithered through the crowd until he stood beside the table where the satchel lay. His practiced eyes scanned the stones within.

These were no ordinary stones!

He would have to have a jeweler appraise them, of course, but he'd be willing to wager that he was looking at carnelians, opals, jade, amber, lapis lazuli, and other semi-precious stones.

He hadn't even noticed that the tale-teller had finished his tale. The old man set the teardrop-shaped stone in the satchel right before the thief's eyes.

It was solid silver!

A stone like that would bring a good price, thought the thief, and he waited for his chance. Suddenly it came.

"My friends, I must go slake my thirst ... but I will return shortly," said the tale-teller. He left his satchel, still open, on the table.

The thief snatched the silver stone and slipped it into the leather bag that hung from his belt. He glanced around, grabbed a handful of other stones, and slithered into the night.

The tale-teller, returning with a frosty tankard, saw him go. He stroked his beard and sighed.

Soon the thief arrived at the home of a jeweler.

"What would you give me for this?" he asked, reaching into his pouch. Feeling the largest stone, he pulled it out.

"Nothing," said the jeweler. "Common stones such as this can be found alongside any road."

"What?!" said the thief. He peered at the stone in the candlelight. He could have sworn it was silver, but now it looked like an ordinary rock.

He turned the pouch over and dumped out all the stones. Every one of them was a common pebble.

"I don't understand," said the thief. "In the tale-teller's hands, these stones were different!"

"Ah, so that's what happened," said the jeweler. "These are story stones. They can't be sold. Did you listen to the stories?"

The thief shook his head.

"Without the stories, they're completely worthless," said the jeweler. "Go on your way. I'm going to bed."

Back at the hall, the tale-teller had returned and the listeners were again begging for a tale. What to tell? His eyes scanned the room and met the eyes of a young maiden with an apron full of food. I know what she needs to hear, he thought. Ah, here's the perfect stone ... a heart-healing tale.

"In a certain time, in a certain place, there lived a peasant girl ...."

His eyes never left those of the maiden.

"She needs this story," he realized. "She needs this story even more than I do."

When the tale was done, the girl moved through the crowd until she stood before him.

"Would you come to my house and tell my sister that story?" she begged.

He looked at her a moment, then picked up the stone again and placed it in her hand.

"I think you need to be the one to tell it," he said.

The girl hurried home, with her apron full of food and the stone clutched tightly in her hand. Her sister was lying in bed, feverish and weak.

"I've brought you something wonderful," said the girl, opening her hand.

Oh no! This was a plain, ordinary rock!

Quickly she closed her hand to hide it. She would have to pretend. She placed her hand over her heart and took a deep breath.

Suddenly her mind was flooded with images, feelings ... everything that had been in the story.

"In a certain time, in a certain place, there lived a peasant girl ...."

She stumbled over some of the words, but the images remained, and she found new words. Her eyes never left her sister.

When she finished, her sister's face was radiant. "Oh, what a beautiful story. Could you tell it again?"

"Of course." The girl put the stone over her heart again, and again the images washed over her. The words came easier this time.

"This is better nourishment than food," said her sister. "Again ... please?"

Through the night, the story was told again and again, each time more smoothly. When the morning sun came through their window, it shone on two sleeping girls.

And in the hand of one of them was a stone of bright, shining gold. 🙦

Once upon a time, there was and there was not …

(Traditional folktale opening)

ALLISON M. COX

THE WINDS OF CHANGE were blowing through my life again … The health department where I worked had just acquired a new director, who informed the employees that most of the programs that met "one on one" with the public would be ending. "The health department," he told us, "needs to be *population based*" (which meant that, to be cost-effective, we needed to be getting our message out to the population at large instead of working with individuals). "Our future focus will be *prevention oriented*, so we can strive to avert health risks before they happen rather than intervene after the fact. "And," he said, "we need to employ methods that have been *tested and proven effective*."

Given these parameters, I realized that my job (counseling pregnant women) was about to come to an end. But rather than focusing on imminent unemployment, I couldn't stop the director's list of priorities from running around in my head … until an idea sprang to life.

I quickly wrote up a proposal and waited impatiently for a requested meeting with the director. When we finally met, I took a deep breath and proposed, "You say that you want our work to be population based, prevention oriented, and tested to prove effectiveness — then what you really want is storytelling!

"*Storytelling is population based*. I can tell stories to many people at the same time and each one will have their own personal interaction with the tale while sharing in the group experience as well.

"*Storytelling is prevention oriented*. The audience can try on new behaviors and adopt fresh ways of perceiving the world when listening to stories. The 'cautionary' tale is a standard story motif used around the world to warn others of what could happen.

"*Storytelling has been tested through time and proven to be effective* not only in getting a message across, but also in keeping the message in the minds of the listeners, which is why the shamans, healers, and great leaders through time have told stories (Muhammad, Buddha, Jesus, Mahatma Gandhi, Martin Luther King …). People relax into the safe and known environment of story, while they often raise their defenses when they listen to a lecture."

I talked about my background in counseling psychology and how my teachers had often spoken of the power of metaphors to support behavioral change. I even added a few categories of my own for our future work in public health. "We work in a port city with diverse people from around the world. I haven't met a culture yet that doesn't have stories. Our ethnic communities will be comfortable and fluent in storytelling. We keep churning out literature to educate the public, but over a third of our residents cannot read the pamphlets! Storytelling puts everyone on equal footing — it's the language of community."

It happened, it did not happen, it perhaps could have happened in the tents of our neighbors ...

(Traditional folktale opening)

Well, even though I was laid off, I was awarded a two-month contract to "come up with as many stories as you can that the health department could use in its work." I was also given a shopping list of subjects: violence, substance abuse, suicide, teen pregnancy — many of the issues that you hear about in the daily news — and also a list of attributes that we wanted to encourage through story: respect for others, resiliency, adaptability to change, examples of positive role models, etc. I was to collect as much material as I could find and then present a selection of these tales, along with suggestions for applications, to the health department.

Towering piles of books surrounded my chair as I wandered through an ancient forest of folktales, myths, legends, and literary tales, searching out stories that would tackle difficult subjects and offer possible choices that encourage healthy outcomes. I plied my local librarians with queries and I contacted authors, storytellers, and publishing houses, asking permission for the health department to use their stories.

At the end of my allotted time, I had collected and gained permission to use 112 versions of folktales and literary stories on a myriad of health-related subjects. I was amazed at the generosity of others. Storytellers called me long-distance and sent me their tapes. Authors sent lists of other books they had written that I might want to use as well. One publisher sent an entire catalogue and said, "Let us know what else interests you." I had told them all that the health department wanted to tell these stories to the people in the community who most needed to hear them, and they had opened their hearts and given freely.

One of the authors I contacted was David Albert, who had written an environmental tale, inspired by historical events in India, (see "Gaura Devi Saves the Trees" in *The Healing Heart ~ Communities: Storytelling to Build Strong and Healthy Communities*). I found this story to be an ideal example of how community members can combine efforts to protect their ecosystem and their homes.

I was surprised to learn that David lived only 40 miles away. When I called, he was enthusiastic about my project and immediately agreed that we could share his story through our health education and community outreach efforts.

"What you don't know about me," David explained, "is that I am the senior health planner for the state board of health. If you tell me when you're presenting your project to the health department, I will come and tell them that they should hire you back to tell stories for health promotion." And that's exactly what he did — even though we had only talked briefly on the phone. David appeared, just like the little brown gnome that suddenly emerges on crossing pathways in the woods of the fairytales, bearing gifts of valuable advice.

In olden times, when wishing still helped ...

(Beginning of "The Frog Prince" from the Brothers Grimm)

Above the noise and beyond the lunch crowd surrounding us at the food court of the shopping center, David Albert and I were making a wish.

"We could write a book about storytelling," David mused between sips of tea, "about telling stories to families…"

"And using story in community building too!" I added excitedly.

"Stories that would encourage resiliency."

"The book could include stories that focus on specific social health topics … and articles about the array of possible applications of this storytelling work. I would love to get the word out to more people!"

We had just come from my presentation to the health department, and we were already talking about writing a book together. We'd only just met! But something had clicked. We both understood storytelling is a compelling medium that can reach out to listeners and create a sense of community through shared experience and deepened understanding. We saw storytelling as a time-tested craft that could tackle the challenges confronting our culture and carry important messages of hope.

But as we talked about all the projects we were currently involved in, we looked at each other and wondered when in our busy lives we would ever get this book written.

"When it's time, it will happen …" David said cryptically, reminiscent of those talking animals in folktales that suddenly say something enigmatic, and then remain silent for a long time.

A great while ago,
when the world was full of wonders …
(Traditional fairytale opening)

It took the health department a year to hire me back as a health educator. In this position, much of my work was done through storytelling. I taught storytelling to outreach workers, who passed the talent on to families with young children. As part of a team of health educators/storytellers, we developed an adolescent pregnancy prevention project that revolved around students in Grades 3, 4, and 5 sharing stories. I told teens across the county tales about violence, substance abuse, sexuality, and rites of passage in an uncertain world. Substance abuse recovery groups welcomed my storytelling with open arms since the 12-Step programs encourage clients to share their personal stories. I trained volunteers of an asthma and allergy prevention project to use stories of other people's experiences when offering information to their clients. I told stories with the women and children in the domestic violence shelter and at meal sites serving elders from various ethnic groups. Stories were even featured at community gatherings to encourage involvement in neighborhood health assessments.

When my co-workers and I presented a short workshop on storytelling at a local prevention meeting, fellow prevention workers from across the county were so excited about the possible applications that they proposed we organize a conference on the subject. After months of planning, applying for funding, and networking with local agencies and storytelling guilds, we sent out a brochure advertising our conference — Storytelling for Prevention: Building Wellness in our Communities. One of the first responses I received was a phone call — David Albert suddenly reappeared, a fairytale king commanding an impossible task.…

"I just received the brochure for the storytelling conference — this looks great! And now that all these storytellers are coming together for this purpose, it's the perfect time to write that book we talked about. I can write up a request for submissions. We need a name for this project —

let's call it *The Healing Heart!*" It had been four years since our conversation and poof! — here we were again as though no time had elapsed.

I explained to David that while this did indeed *seem* like the perfect time to start the book, I had just received a scholarship from the federal Centers for Disease Control and Prevention to return to school and pursue another graduate degree, this time in public health. So now I was enrolled full time in graduate school, which meant studying on the weekends and evenings — whenever I wasn't working full time at the health department. "When," I asked David, "could I possibly have the time to work on a book on top of all this?"

David was not fazed a bit. "Well, most of these programs require some kind of practicum project. Why not propose that the compilation phase of *The Healing Heart* will be your project. I can be your mentor in the field if you need one." David was right — I was supposed to be working on a practicum and was required to have a site supervisor who was a specialist in that field to oversee my work. And to my continued disbelief, the university team overseeing my studies supported my proposal of compiling the book with enthusiasm. I was working 40 hours or more each week, taking full-time graduate studies, and compiling a book, all at the same time. I was simultaneously accomplishing what I considered to be three incredible tasks, like the town fool in the old stories who battles the three-headed giant and lives to tell about it ....

It all happened long ago, and believe it or not, it is all absolutely true ...

(Traditional Irish opening)

Little did I realize how long it would take to bring all these efforts to fruition. I was about to wear thin my own pair of iron sandals, akin to the heroine in those folktales of long journeys to bring back what was almost lost. Initially it didn't occur to me what a demanding task it might be to reveal an oral art on the written page. I sometimes found myself having to convince tellers that they really were engaged in healing work, even though they did not have professional credentials. In the end, the biggest challenge became choosing from the scores of wonderful stories and articles sent in by the many tellers who are applying storytelling in their work toward a healthier world. There was so much valuable material that it became apparent this venture would have to become two books: *The Healing Heart ~ Families: Storytelling to Encourage Caring and Healthy Families* and *Communities: Storytelling to Build Strong and Healthy Communities*!

In June 1999 I was approached at the National Storytelling Conference and asked, "Would you like to join the Healing Story Alliance, a special interest group of the National Storytelling Network?" I immediately sang out "Yes!" When I was asked, "Do you know of anyone else who may be interested?" I had to laugh. "Yes," I said again. "There are so many…"

And now we are coming together to share our combined wisdom to further our knowledge and advance this field. It is my sincere hope that these books will encourage even more people to start rethinking the place that story has in our lives and the possible applications for the transformative healing that can occur.

These two books are a collective effort containing the thoughts and expertise of 66 storytellers. Essays include information on why storytelling works; approaches for sharing stories in various settings; suggestions on how to encourage others to tell and how to process stories through song, art, games, improvisation, community projects, and discussion; and a bibliography of more stories to consider. Chapters in the books cover a myriad of health topics: healing through story; coping with grief; sexuality; heart disease; hypertension; asthma and allergy education; substance abuse intervention; cancer; character development; domestic violence; early childhood interventions; disenfranchised youth; homelessness; elder health; children with medical problems; working in schools and hospitals; violence prevention; countering prejudice; programs for incarcerated adults and adolescents; spiritual healing; oral history; cultural identity; environmental health; community development; and peacemaking. Whew!

During the four years of editing these books, David Albert would suddenly materialize in my e-mail, an enchanted bird singing encouragement, strewing bread crumbs along the path to storytelling. He once sent me a quote from Martin Buber: "All our stories are true, whether they happened or not." May the thoughts, stories, and layers of truth in these books open new doors for you and widen the scope of possibilities in building stronger and healthier families and more vibrant and resilient communities.

In a place, neither near nor far, and a time, neither now nor then …
(*Traditional folktale opening*)

Let the storytelling begin …

꩜ Gold-Tree and Silver-Tree ꩜

JAN ANDREWS

> *There was once a king who had a queen called Silver-Tree and a daughter*
> *called Gold-Tree. Now it happened on a day of days that Silver-Tree*
> *and Gold-Tree went walking, and they came to a little glen,*
> *and in the bottom of that glen there was a brook.*
> *In the brook there was a fish.*

"Oh, troutie, troutie, my bonnie troutie," said Silver-Tree, "am I not the fairest one in all the world?"

"No," said the fish, "you are not."

"Who then?" asked Silver-Tree.

"It is your daughter, Gold-Tree," said the fish.

Silver-Tree went home straightaway and climbed into her bed and said that she was sick unto death. When the king came home, the servants sent him to her.

"Is there nothing that I might do for you?" he asked her.

"Gold-Tree and Silver-Tree" is adapted from Alan Garner's *Book Of British Fairy Tales* (London: William Collins Sons & Co. Ltd., 1984).

"Only that I should have the heart and liver of my daughter, Gold-Tree, to eat, for without them I will die."

As chance would have it, a prince had come from over the seas to ask for Gold-Tree's hand in marriage. The king gave his permission at once, so the prince took Gold-Tree back to his kingdom where the king thought she would be safe. The king also sent his servants into the hills to kill a goat and bring back its heart and liver. When the servants returned, the king gave the heart and liver of the goat to Silver-Tree and said that they were her daughter's. Silver-Tree devoured them both, leapt from the bed, and cried out that she was cured.

A year went by and again Silver-Tree went walking. Again she came to the little glen and to the brook. Once more she saw the fish.

"Oh, troutie, troutie, my bonnie troutie, am I not the fairest one in all the world?" she asked it.

"You are not," the fish replied another time.

"Who then?" asked Silver-Tree.

"It is your daughter, Gold-Tree," the fish answered as before.

"She is dead and I have eaten of her heart and liver," Silver-Tree insisted.

"No," said the little fish. "She lives yet, across the waves."

Now, Silver-Tree went straightaway to the king.

"Give me a ship of your fleet," she demanded of him. "I must sail away to see my darling Gold-Tree, my darling daughter, for it has been so long."

The king gave Silver-Tree the ship and she steered it with her own hand. On the day when she was to arrive at Gold-Tree's new home, the prince was out hunting. Gazing from a window of the castle, Gold-Tree saw the ship and recognized it.

"It is my mother come to kill me," she cried out.

"We will not let this be," said the servants. "We will keep you from her. We will lock you in a room."

This they did. Silver-Tree got down from the ship and went running through the castle.

"My darling daughter, my darling Gold-Tree, will you not come to greet me?" she called.

"I cannot," Gold-Tree answered. "For I have been locked up."

"Would you not at least put your finger through the keyhole so I might kiss it?" begged Silver-Tree.

Gold-Tree did. She put her finger through the keyhole. At once, Silver-Tree stabbed it with a dart of poison so that Gold-Tree fell down as if dead. Silver-Tree returned to the ship and sailed away.

When the prince came back, he was so distressed that he said Gold-Tree was not to be buried but laid upon a bed and left where she was as if she were asleep. For a while his grief was terrible, but he was a prince and so at last he took a second wife. He trusted her and loved her and gave her the keys to all the castle, but he said she must not use the key to that one room. Time passed and again he was out hunting. His second wife was curious.

"My husband is a good man," she thought to herself. "He can have nothing terrible to hide."

She went then to the room and put the key into the lock. As the door swung open, she saw what seemed to her to be a beautiful young woman sleeping. She went to wake her, but as she did so, she moved Gold-Tree's hand and the dart of poison fell forth. Gold-Tree came to herself. She was quite recovered.

The prince returned home, but he seemed sad at heart.

"Is there nothing I might do for you?" the second wife demanded.

The prince shook his head. "Only that you would bring my darling Gold-Tree back to life again," he said.

"Go to the room that was locked," the second wife told him. "Go there and you will see."

The prince went to the room. He found Gold-Tree and he took her in his arms with joy. As he held her, he heard a noise behind him. Turning, he saw the second wife.

"I must go away from you," she said, "for this was your first wife."

"No," said the prince. "Let us live happily, all three of us together."

That then is what they did. But again Silver-Tree went walking, and again she came to the glen and the brook, and again there was the fish.

"Troutie, troutie, my bonnie troutie," demanded Silver-Tree, "am I not now the fairest one in all the world?"

"You are not," said the fish.

"Who then?" Silver-Tree asked.

"It is your daughter, Gold-Tree," came the answer.

"Gold-Tree lies dead, for I have stabbed her with a dart of poison."

"Gold-Tree lives yet, across the waves."

Silver-Tree went to the king once more. "Give me a ship of your fleet — a ship that I might sail to see my darling Gold-Tree, for it has been so long," she said again.

Just as before, the king gave her that ship. Just as before, she steered it with her own hand. Again

as she approached the land where Gold-Tree lived, the prince was out hunting. Looking out from the castle window, Gold-Tree saw the ship. She knew who to be expecting.

"It is my mother — my mother come again to kill me," she called out.

The second wife spoke this time. "We will not let this happen. We will go to the beach together to meet her," she declared.

Gold-Tree and the second wife went to the beach and waited. When Silver-Tree had steered the ship to shore, she came from it carrying in her hands a chalice of fine wine.

"My darling daughter, my darling Gold-Tree, will you not drink this wine that I have brought you?" she burst out.

Gold-Tree would have taken the wine, but the second wife would not let her. "In our country it is the custom that whoever brings the wine shall taste it first," she said.

Silver-Tree sipped the wine, meaning to hold it in her mouth. The second wife pushed her so she choked and swallowed it down. Of course, the wine was poisoned and Silver-Tree fell dead upon the shore. There was nothing for it but that the sailors should carry her body back to the king and her own land.

Gold-Tree and the second wife went back to the castle. When the prince came home, the three of them rejoiced together. And they did live the rest of their days in happiness. They lived — the three of them — as happy as may be and happy as might. 🐚

Entering in

Jan Andrews

A HEALING STORY? If, when I first came on "Gold-Tree and Silver-Tree," someone had asked me to name my top ten healing stories, I would certainly not have put that one on the list. I loved the ingenuity and generosity of spirit evidenced by those two wives in the face of an impossible situation, but I also saw problems. I knew some members of my audiences would find the eating of the heart and liver unbearable. I was fairly certain I was going to have feminists rising up in protest at yet another example of a prince of a man — who after all is always absent when anything needs doing — getting altogether more than his just desserts.

When I started telling the story, however, I found personal epiphanies to be almost zinging through the air for my listeners. At a weekend retreat, one of the participants commented: "That's me. Me and my mother. I stick my finger through the keyhole every damn time for her. I see now she'll always stab it. I see I have to take responsibility for not giving her the chance."

I use the story in a role-playing exercise in my workshops for beginning storytellers. This exercise is a means of helping students find personal connections and come more easily to the storyteller's chair. The process is simple. I explain that, since a story told is nothing until those who are there to listen take it into themselves and see it

— having it for themselves and re-creating it in their own being — each listener is, in fact, all of the elements of the tale.

"You are the king and the queen; you are the first wife and the second; you are the prince and the ship and the castle; you are the goat and the heart and the liver; you are the glen and the brook," I say of "Gold-Tree and Silver-Tree."

I then lead those present in a guided meditation in which they start out by choosing that one element which comes to them most immediately as especially theirs. Through the meditation, I try to help them find the shape and feel of what they have chosen. The meditation over, I offer the opportunity to name the element selected and say "I am ... ," to speak through the voice of that element, letting whatever presents itself emerge. The results are always powerful.

Once, when I was in a school, an eleven-year-old boy came forward. "I'm the first wife," he said, "and I feel so stupid. I let everyone else do things for me and I never do anything for myself." Before returning to his place, he picked out all the moments in the story where Gold-Tree waits passively. As he did so, his look of satisfaction grew more and more intense. "He has learning disabilities," his teacher told me. "He's just named his whole problem. He wants everyone else to do the work for him and, of course, no one else can."

In another school, a shy boy whom I was not expecting to speak got up. "I'm the fish," he announced. "I have golden scales and a gold chain about my neck. I know things. I know who's the most beautiful in the world. I know that people are alive across the seas even. I feel wonderful." His whole demeanor suggested he had found a resource within himself he had not seen before.

Adults respond equally well. "I'm the first wife and the second," a woman concluded. "There's a poisoned part of me. I've left it for dead but it isn't. The older me needs to be waking the younger one up."

I believe that such "epiphanies" represent important insights into the ways of the psyche. I know that insights are not in themselves enough for the achievement of "healing." I believe that healing most often requires action, but I also believe that the insights offered to us by the stories may function as signposts pointing the directions for further exploration or movement along a healing path.

I believe we all need to be concerned with that path because we all have wounds and scars of one kind or another. We all wander lost. We will never be fully and finally "healed" — not one of us. Life is too various, too dark and dangerous, too exciting and unexpected for that.

I recognize there are people who have faced abuse and terror, loss and trauma far beyond the boundaries of ordinary experience. I do not wish to trivialize what has happened to them. What I do wish is to establish firmly that, when it comes to the stories, there are insights to benefit us all.

When I say "the stories" I am referring to the old traditional folktales and fairytales, for it is there that I find all the age-old wisdom. It is to those old stories that I frequently turn for new strength. The folktales and fairytales seem to me to contain all of everything within them. They are like a complex and beautiful Celtic knot around us, binding us loosely together, giving us arches to dance in and out of, offering themselves to us at every twist and turn. My work with "Gold-Tree and Silver-Tree" leads me to conclude no one of them is more innately healing than another. They all have much to give us if we will only put ourselves in the way of their gifts.

How to do that, though? How to be there for the tales so they can open those "epiphany" doors for us? There with our whole beings, with what we are needing and feeling at the deepest level — most likely without even knowing it — in the moment, right now.

Sometimes we can manage this by paying attention, listening, relaxing into the story's events and images, being open to whatever comes. Sometimes it is a matter of carrying the story on with us, allowing it to float to the surface of our minds when it appears again vividly for us in some other situation in years to come.

The role-playing provides us with one more means of entrance. At the very least, we can give ourselves the chance to live in the story longer. There is more to it than that, though, for the role-playing works as the stories themselves do. It reaches into our subconscious on some level beyond understanding and reasoned thought. It lets us speak the awareness, hopes, and fears we have hidden from ourselves. It gives us the opportunity truly to listen to what it is we have to say.

And we can do the role-playing on our own behalf. The guided meditation is a useful introduction, but it is not necessary, although I would suggest that a quiet time and space will be a help. The important thing is to focus on the "I" and not get lost in connections and explanations and retellings of the tale. It is also important to know that although healing may require action, this is the part of the journey where you are merely looking for map and compass. This part requires letting go. If you try to impose your will, if you approach the activity with a rigid agenda, you will only be creating blocks for yourself and for the tale.

"Gold-Tree and Silver-Tree" is here — all ready for you to get started the minute you want to. When I thought of the sea that carried the ships and imaged its pictures, I found myself writing:

I am the waves and the winds that lash them. I am the surface and the depths. I am the changing colors of sunlight and moonlight and gray rain times. I am the bitter salt and the buoyancy. I am the connecting link between the lands.

What did that say to me? It said I have poetry in my soul and I had better not forget it. I had better stop rushing hither and yon and trying to get a million things done. I had better give the poetry some room for growth. Maybe not an earth-shattering discovery, but one that I needed on that day — something which for that day was gift enough.

Guidelines for healing work

CRISTY WEST

MOUNTING EVIDENCE SUGGESTS that stories and the storytelling process can promote recovery, inspire hope, trigger insight and personal growth — in short, "heal." And a growing number of storytellers feel challenged to work outside of entertainment venues, in prisons, hospitals, homeless shelters, and with individuals in crisis and/or with special needs. What are some basic issues to be considered here? How can this work best be accomplished? The following very preliminary guidelines are offered not as hard-and-fast directives, but rather as a supportive overview to help individuals think about their role and responsibilities. Keep in mind, too, that storytelling can be deeply therapeutic when not necessarily offered as a form of therapeutic treatment.

1. **Understand your role.** Storytellers can be described as therapists only when they are trained as such (i.e., as a certified mental health professional such as counselor or social worker). Storytellers will want to be clear about what they can and cannot offer. Those storytellers who are not trained therapists are urged to refrain from impinging on relationships between listeners and members of a treatment team. And even if you are not a trained professional, it makes sense to develop your own rationale for the work you are doing and how it may be effective.

2. **Set flexible goals and refer back to them.** It's a good idea for tellers to develop a set of goals as well as strategies for accomplishing them. Through the ongoing process of observation and conscious evaluation, storytellers may modify and reformulate these goals, thereby raising their work beyond the realm of vague good intentions to become more effective and articulate practitioners.

3. **Create safe space.** "Safety" can include both physical and emotional aspects of the storytelling event. This includes issues like confidentiality, encouragement of mutual respect among group participants, appropriate choice of material, sensitivity to dynamics within the group, and care to achieve a sense of closure within the session.

4. **Foster staff involvement.** Whenever possible, storytellers should try to work with staff in order to determine the rules and customs of the setting as well as the goals for the storyteller's work. In this way they can complement and enhance the ongoing work of the treatment team. Frequently, staff who are unfamiliar with storytelling in these settings may have unrealistic expectations about what the storyteller can accomplish.

5. **Determine group needs.** Storytellers will want to be sensitive to the emotional and developmental level of individuals they work with and to choose stories and story processes accordingly. If in doubt about how to do this, tellers are urged to enlist support from more experienced tellers and those familiar with the treatment audience.

6. **Assess materials carefully.** While storytellers cannot know how a story will be heard, they will want to attempt in advance to evaluate possible harmful effects a story might produce. At the same time, understanding that listeners will use defense mechanisms to "take what they need" from a story, it's best that storytellers not probe listeners for alternate meanings or insist on a given interpretation.

7. **Practice self-assessment.** Storytellers will want to develop an understanding of their own inner dynamics. What issues do stories touch in their own lives? Is there a particular type of story they tell repeatedly, and if so, why? What intuitive processes are at work? Storytellers should not attempt to work in a healing situation when their own physical or emotional condition might be a detriment to their effectiveness.

8. **Monitor personal boundaries.** While a degree of emotional involvement with listeners is inevitable, especially in longer term work, storytellers should maintain an appropriate sense of boundaries. For example, it would be a mistake for storytellers to consider it their job to "rescue" listeners, and they should be wary of trying to promote any personal agenda that would be outside their stated purpose.

9. **Keep process notes.** It is a good idea for storytellers to keep a written record of their work, especially for longer term residencies. Here they can assess their own processes and reactions, and comment on what works or doesn't. They may also remark on the progress of various individuals or evaluate responses of the group as a whole in terms of goals they have set. A written record can document an ongoing learning experience, serving, too, as a basis for research and possibly a model for others. It can also be a creative and fulfilling accomplishment on its own!

10. **Strive for an informed perspective.** The more storytellers know about the basic issues and needs of specialized groups, the more effective their work will be. Obviously one cannot become an instant expert in, say, drug abuse prevention, but some basic knowledge can influence the multitude of intuitive decisions a storyteller will make. At the same time, those who hire tellers or work with them will greatly enhance their input by learning more about the art and craft of storytelling.

11. **Seek a mentor.** Applied storytelling demands sensitivity and ongoing reflection. Apart from on-site direction from staff, storytellers are urged to find a mentor or consultant with whom to discuss the complexities of this work. The Healing Story Alliance hopes to develop a list of experienced individuals who are willing to offer this kind of guidance (see below).

12. **Trust the power of storytelling.** With a sound, informed judgment as the underlying basis for therapeutic work, remember that the healing process originates with a love for the stories told and the joy of sharing them with others. Have fun! The spirit of creative play between teller, story, and listeners carries with it a richness of possibility.

These guidelines focus on work with traditional tales — folktales, fairytales, and myth. Slightly different issues may pertain where the emphasis is on personal narrative. My hope is that, as a knowledge base develops, more tellers will feel inspired to seek out challenging new opportunities and that they will then share their experiences with the broader community.

The guidelines were originally developed in consultation with other members of the Board of Directors of the Healing Story Alliance: Gail Rosen, Allison Cox, Colin McNaughton, Diane Rooks, Laura Simms, and Diane Wyzga. Thanks, too, for additional input from Karl Hallsten, Peggy Kenny, Staci Marinelli, Erica Meade, Mary Medlicott, Elisa Pearmain, and Fran Stallings.

"Storytelling as a Healing Art" is the focus of a special interest group of the National Storytelling Network, which hopes to encourage discussion and the exchange of information about this kind of work, sometimes referred to as "applied storytelling." For more discussions of some of the ideas touched upon here, I recommend visiting the Healing Story Alliance website (www.healingstory.org).

HEALTH PROMOTION AND DISEASE PREVENTION

The breath of life

ALLISON M. COX

ASTHMA IS THE MOST common chronic disease among children, causing the deaths of approximately 200 children each year in the United States. Asthma is also the number one cause of students chronically missing school and the most common reason for pediatric emergency room visits. Hospitalization rates for asthma continue to rise. This disease usually shows up in children by age five. The symptoms may decrease as children get older, only to reappear later in life. Often asthma is diagnosed in adults in their 30s, although up to ten percent of new asthma cases are also found in seniors who are 65 and older. Asthma has been linked to increasing societal costs of missed work and to financial losses for both families and businesses. An estimated 75 to 85 percent of people with asthma have some type of allergy, which can play a major role in aggravating the condition.

To promote asthma and allergy education in Washington State's Puget Sound area, the American Lung Association has joined forces with local public and private health agencies to organize asthma support groups with great success. They have also developed volunteer programs to help educate the public cost-effectively. Volunteers in the Master Environmentalist Program receive 40 hours of comprehensive training. These volunteers visit homes in the community to perform a HEAL (named after the Home Environmental Assessment List that they carry to check for possible asthma and allergy triggers). During a 1½-hour home visit, the volunteers educate families about common triggers for asthma and allergies such as cigarette and wood smoke, dust mites, mold, pet dander, cockroaches, toxic products, and ozone.

As a health promotion specialist, I was asked to help train the Master Environmentalists by telling them how to use stories to teach their clients. I explain that storytelling can offer survival tools to the community. By including sensory descriptions that match people's everyday experience, audiences come to understand how it feels to have asthma and allergies. I suggest participants look for those universal experiences that everyone would share from simply walking around in the human body. For example, everyone has probably at some time sneezed, gasped for breath, and had watery eyes or itchy rashes. As people listen to stories, they create sensory images that are stored in the memory as symbols and that lead to greater recall of the information than occurs from reading informational pamphlets. Since storytelling lends narrative structure to events that might otherwise seem random, I encourage the Master Environmentalists to gather story snippets of different incidents that clients have shared with them, describing their discovery of asthma and allergy triggers.

My mother always ran the humidifiers when I had a cold as a child. She said that it would help me breathe, so when I had kids I did the same thing. Imagine my surprise when I discovered in the Master Environmentalist training that the moist air from the humidifier promotes dust mite infestation and mold!

Tony had been told by his grandmother that it was all in his imagination that he felt sick whenever he visited. But Tony's coughing would get so intense that he had to stop visiting his grandmother at her home. Now, after allergy testing, he realizes that it was all those dogs and cats that Grandma had that caused him to cough, and NOT his imagination!

Shannon couldn't understand why she would sneeze and wheeze each time she went to work on her computer. The volunteer asked to observe Shannon as she worked on her computer and Shannon agreed. Before walking back to her office, Shannon flicked on the fan that was perched on top of a bookcase at the end of the hall, pointed at her office door. "It keeps my office from getting too stuffy" she explained. The volunteer stood on a chair to look at the top of the tall bookcase and discovered that it was covered in dust. Each time Shannon turned on that fan for better ventilation, she sent a dust storm in her direction.

When they hear these stories of others' experiences, people are less likely to become embarrassed or to feel that they are being lectured or that they should have known better. These examples let families know that this is a problem that lots of other people share. Experience has shown that using little teaching tales enhances people's ability to remember information compared to what they absorb from lists of facts and statistics.

I designed the following story to illustrate some of the causes of asthma and allergies in a format that was fun and would help people remember at least some of the common triggers (dust, mold, pollen, insect sting, poisonous plants, smoke, specific foods, poor ventilation, cosmetics, etc.). Before I tell this story, I talk with the audience about what it is like for me to grow up and live in the world with asthma and allergies. I tell them, "I was often embarrassed by the sounds that I would make as a result of my sniffling, sneezing, wheezing, and coughing in school, at work, in the library, in church, or anywhere that people were trying to be quiet. So I thought it would be fun for all of us who have had this happen to make these noises on purpose — and really loud! The rest of you can help too. Of course, these are little asthmatic and allergic pigs — so we have to throw in a few snorts as well." I tell the audience that whenever I bring my hands up to cover my nose and mouth and say that the pigs are beginning to sniffle, snort, wheeze, and cough (indicated by italics in the text) ... it is time for them to join in with their best sniffles, snorts, wheezes, and coughing.

The Three Little Pigs
of Hog Holler Swamp

ALLISON M. COX*

*Long ago, in the deep South, there lived three little pigs right
in the middle of Hog Holler Swamp.*

They lived in the swamp with their Ma, just as all their family had for generations. But right around the springtime, life was always hard on those three little pigs, 'cause when the skunk cabbage started to bloom, those piglets became miserable. Wheeza, who was a girl piglet and the spitting image of her Ma, and her two little brothers, Sniff and Snort, would begin getting itchy skin and watery eyes. They'd get a high-pitched whistling sound in their chests, and snuffly noses. And at night — well, *Sniff sniffed, Snort snorted, Wheeza wheezed, and all three of them began to cough something fierce.* In fact, those pigs raised quite a racket with all their coughing.

Well, one day those piglets wiggled up to their Ma, and Wheeza, the oldest, said, "Ma — we've decided it's time we start out on our own and find another place to live."

"But my dear piglets," said their Ma, "why leave? Hog Holler has been the family ancestral home for as far back as we can remember!"

"That may be true," Snort replied. "But if we stay here this place will be the end of us."

"That's right, Ma," Sniff explained. "This swamp's just too hard on our breathing! In the

dry season there's dust. In the growing season there's pollen. In the wet season there's mold. There's poison oak in the backyard and poison ivy in the front and more stinging insects than a pig can shake a tail at!"

"Yeah, Ma," said Snort. "I'm tired of colds that never go away and waking up every night coughing."

Well, their Ma could see that they had a point, so she packed them up some vittles, hugged and kissed each one, and said, "Just don't forget to come visit now and then ... and be careful out there!"

"We will, Ma! Goodbye!" Wheeza, Sniff, and Snort called as they went off to find their new home. It felt good to climb up out of the swamp, where the fresh air blew. And in no time at all they found a nice little home in the middle of a meadow that looked as though it was woven just like a bird's nest.

"How pretty!" Wheeza said. "Let's move in here."

Being swamp pigs, they did not realize this home was an old hollow haystack. They liked the dappled light as it shone through the wall and all the fresh air that blew through the cracks. But by nightfall they began to sniffle and itch and cough and wheeze.

"Oh no!" said Sniff. "I'm allergic to our new house."

"Me too!" said Snort.

And before Wheeza could answer, they heard a third voice respond, "Well, then, come on outside into the fresh air!"

"Who was that?" Wheeza whispered to her brothers. They got their answer momentarily, for as the breeze wafted in from the front yard, *Sniff sniffed, Snort snorted, Wheeza wheezed, and all three of them began to cough something fierce.* Their watery eyes met. If there was one thing that the Hog family was allergic to — more than anything else — it was wolf fur! So they clung to each other and tried to keep quiet.

"I said come on outa' there. I know there's someone in there!"

"Nobody in here but us crickets," Wheeza lied.

"Ooooooh nooooo! I smell those three little swamp pigs. I'm sure I do!"

Just then, Snort began to sneeze again.

"I knew it!" sang the wolf. "Just when a wolf gets hungry! How nice of you pigs to move into the neighborhood. Now let's see — what's the best seasoning for swamp pigs?" The wolf reached into his pocket and pulled out some dried plants and herbs and began huffing and puffing and blowing that seasoning right through the cracks in the straw walls and all over those piglets.

Sniff sniffled, Snort snorted, Wheeza wheezed, and all three of them began to cough something fierce. There was garlic powder and parsley flakes flying everywhere.

"And now that you are properly seasoned, IT'S SUPPER TIME!"

The wolf huffed and puffed some more and more and more ... until he blew the door in! He

ran in to find — that those piglets had escaped out the back door and were nowhere to be found. Lucky for those pigs, this wolf was not the sharpest knife in the drawer. Meanwhile, those three little pigs had to hide in a hollow log that night, and you can imagine how hard it was for them to keep quiet as they gasped for breath after running away from that wolf. Their little hearts were beating fast.

Finally, when the daylight came, they carefully stepped out of hiding and went searching again for a better place to live. On the edge of the forest they came upon an unoccupied house that appeared to be made of sticks. Snort sniffed at the house cautiously.

"Well, this one doesn't seem to make me sneeze."

Sniff and Wheeza sniffed carefully and nodded. Wheeza went inside and declared, "It's got the same dappled light and fresh air as the last house."

"I think it's sturdier," said Sniff.

Well, they decided to give it a try. So they moved in, had a wonderful dinner of collard greens and black-eyed peas that their Ma had packed for them, and were just settling down for their evening rest when ... *Sniff sniffled, Snort snorted, Wheeza wheezed, and all three of them began to cough something fierce.* They were coughing all around until they heard —

"Aha! I did find that little pig scent after all. They don't call me the super sniffer for nothing. So come on out, little pigs! IT'S SUPPER TIME FOR WOLFY!"

Those little pigs held their noses to prevent them from smelling that wolf any more than they already had.

"Not coming, eh? Well, let me see if I can help you. Hmmm — how do I like my bacon? Oh yes — SMOKED!"

And with that said, the wolf reached into his pocket and pulled out a cigar. He began huffing and puffing on that nasty-smelling thing and blowing it right through the cracks of that stick house. *Sniff sniffled, Snort snorted, Wheeza wheezed, and all three of them began to cough something fierce.* Those poor little pigs were coughing up a storm!

The wolf was hungry and in a hurry, so he kept up on the huffing and puffing until he blew in the door! Luckily for the pigs, that wolf was dumber than a box of hair, so they were able to escape again through the back door. They spent another miserable night in that old hollow log. By now, everything in that end of the woods smelled like cigar, so the wolf was unable to track them. The poor little pigs lay hiding, wheezing, and shaking all night.

By the next morning those pigs had resolve. They had purpose. They were also very stiff from spending two nights in a hollow log.

"That does it!" said Snort. "I've had it with that wolf, dust, pollen, smoke — all of it! Let's find ourselves a place that's safe and helps us feel good too!"

So the pigs searched all day until they finally came across a sweet little rental that was clear of the woods, but outside of the city. It was built of brick to keep out the dust, smoke, pollen, and mold, but it had windows all around to let in the fresh air whenever they wanted. Inside was perfect. No carpet or blinds to hold dirt and dust. No mold in the kitchen or bathroom. There weren't even any leaves to rake around the house or grass to mow — just evergreen trees that never lose their leaves, and ground ivy that was definitely not the poison kind!

"We'll take it," Wheeza told the landlord. The three little pigs moved in and set up housekeeping. They were so happy to have finally found a home where they felt good.

Every week they took turns washing the sheets, blankets, curtains, and throw rugs to keep away the dust. They dusted the house and vacuumed too. They cleaned the bathroom and kitchen to keep the mold away. They would air out the house on clear days and keep the windows shut during hay fever season. Yes, life was good and those pigs were happy. Until one day, who should happen along while they were out back, hanging the wash to dry (since sunlight kills the dust mites), but that mean old wolf.

"Well, well! If it isn't my old friends, the three little pigs. I'm going to have to be sneaky this time if I want to catch all three of them."

So that wolf went on down to the Goodwill and got himself a disguise. He picked up a pink dress, pink shoes, and a pink hat. He even invested in some smelly powders, perfumes, and soaps. He got himself all dressed up and knocked on the door.

"Who's there?" called Wheeza.

"Oh" (the wolf caught his deep voice and sweetened it up) "I mean, Oh — it's the Mary Fay lady, dear. I have some beauty products here you will just love." Well Wheeza was mighty excited, seeing as how neighbors had yet to come a-calling, so she opened the door. The wolf played it cool and began to show Wheeza one smelly beauty item after another. *Wheeza began to sniffle and wheeze and cough ....*

Sniff and Snort heard voices, sniffed the air as pigs are known to do, and ... Sniff sniffled. Snort snorted.

"Do you smell that?" Snort asked. Sniff nodded. It was sort of a sweet, gooey, powdery smell all mixed up with ...

"WOLF!" they both shouted. Those pigs went barreling around the side of the house, knocking the wolf right over and dashing inside, pushing Wheeza along with them. They slammed the door and locked it.

"Well, I didn't want to buy that smelly stuff, but did you have to be so rude?" Wheeza demanded.

"I'll show you rude!" Sniff squealed. "C'mon!" They ran to the upstairs window and looked down. There was the wolf, tearing off all those pink clothes as he circled the building, searching for a way inside.

"What'll we do?" Wheeza cried.

"He can't get in," assured Sniff.

But they began to hear a scratching, scraping sound.

"He's climbing up on the roof!" Snort exclaimed.

"The chimney!" Wheeza shouted. "He's going to come down the chimney."

"Not if we can help it!" Snort insisted.

Snort ran down the stairs and began throwing all of their wooden spoons, mops, and brooms — anything that would burn — into the fireplace. Then he started crinkling up bags and shoving them in there, too, and he lit a match.

"Are you trying to cook him?" Sniff whispered, horrified. After all, they were strict vegetarians.

"No," said Wheeza. "I know what he's doing! Think, Sniff — what's the one thing that really gets us coughing besides wolf fur and tobacco..."

"Wood smoke!" Sniff interrupted.

"Thaaaat's right!" Snort beamed, and he closed the fireplace doors to trap all the smoke in the chimney.

And no sooner had they said that than the sounds started. *They heard a sniffling ... and wheezing ... and coughing ... and what a racket — even howling!* Well, by morning they finally opened the fireplace and looked, but there was no sign of the wolf anywhere. Word spread of the three brave little pigs, and soon all kinds of animals came by to visit and thank them for getting rid of that nuisance wolf.

Some said that the wolf must have died of smoke inhalation. Others heard that he had run off to another forest and was last seen running from a woodsman with an axe. Whatever the story, you can bet that those three little pigs breathed a lot easier after that. Yes, they slept sounder and lived happily ever after in their little brick house (except of course during the rainy season, when they headed down to Arizona for the winter — but that's another story). 🌸

ACTIVITY FOR ASTHMA EDUCATION

Health educators may use the following exercise to help their audiences understand how it feels to have asthma or allergies. For this exercise, I use the thin straws that are usually used to stir coffee. My co-workers have found that fast-food chains are often willing to donate these once we explain our purpose. While handing out the straws, I tell the audience that anyone who has asthma or allergies does not have to participate since they already know how it feels — and it may be too difficult for them to breathe!

Then tell your audience — "Take a long deep breath and feel the air fill your lungs."

"Now, when I count to three, we are going to run in place for one minute while holding our noses and breathing only through these thin coffee straws." (Be sure to explain to children what "running in place" means or you will have kids shooting off in all directions during the next step.)

"Okay, one, two, three, go!" Run in place along with them and offer encouragement, such as "That's it — a little bit longer. Remember to hold your nose. Keep running in place. Okay, stop!"

Have someone walk around collecting the straws, as you ask the group, "How do you feel?"

Audiences of all ages will have comments like: "I felt dizzy." "I couldn't get enough air into my lungs!" "I had to sit down."

Tell your listeners, "That's how it feels when you have an asthma attack, and some allergy flare-ups are like that too! People who have allergies and asthma cannot take the straw out of their mouths to feel better. Asthmatics have to take medicine and someone with allergies may have to move away from whatever is causing the allergic reaction."

This is a great way to begin a discussion on asthma and allergies. For more information on this subject, contact your local American Lung Association office or visit the ALA website (www.alaw.org). Another helpful source of information is the Asthma and Allergy Foundation of America (www.aafa.org).

There is a balm in Gilead: Storytelling as a Healing Resource for African-American Women

JoAnne Banks Wallace

There is a Balm in Gilead
To make the wounded whole...
— African-American spiritual

My professional work and personal journey have convinced me that storytelling is one of the greatest gifts we have been given as people. I am a storyteller in the tradition of African-American storytellers. I am also a nurse-scientist. For the past eight years, I have been learning about the types of stories African-American women tell (and don't tell), the methods used to share stories, and the function of these stories in our lives. It is out of these experiences that I am developing my ideas about storytelling as a healing resource. I hope that sharing my experiences will inspire others to explore the healing power of the oral tradition.

Storytelling and healing: Reflections on my research

During my second semester as a doctoral student, I took one class on nursing theory and another about nursing therapeutics. I was required to develop my own nursing theory in the first class and a therapeutic intervention in the second. The therapeutic I chose to study was storytelling. This choice was the result of an experience I had while sitting in class listening to my instructor talk about what we needed to do to successfully complete the assignment. In the midst of class, I was transported back to Flint, Michigan. I had not lived there since I was six years old, yet I saw myself walking to the elementary school I had attended. I sat down in the library and waited anxiously for the weekly storytelling session to begin. A feeling of immense peace and joy flooded me.

Then I was back in class, listening to my instructor again. At the end of the class period we were to share with our classmates the therapeutic we were planning to study. When my time came, I said I wanted to explore storytelling as a nursing therapeutic. I remember vividly the look of disbelief that passed across my professor's face. However, she gave me unwavering support and feedback that helped clarify my initial thinking about storytelling. Since that time, I have been blessed with the opportunity to study storytelling as both a storyteller and nurse-scientist. I have come to understand that the healing power of storytelling resides in the ability of stories to get past the barriers we erect consciously or unconsciously, allowing us to communicate spirit to spirit.

Wading in the water: Beginning research

Despite a growing interest in storytelling, I had no intention of making it the focus of my dissertation. However, my plans changed while I was analyzing data from a focus-group study in which I was the co-principal investigator exploring why African-American women were reluctant to participate in research. A preliminary review of the transcripts from the sessions revealed that women spent considerably more time engaged in storytelling than in directly answering the questions raised in the focus groups. This was consistent with earlier findings regarding the use of storytelling by clients in a therapeutic situation.

The power of storytelling was epitomized by an incident that occurred during one of the focus groups. The women were in the process of determining important issues that needed to be included in our final session when a participant declared that she was tired of the racist treatment she had endured in the United States and just wanted to go home. Her story was the turning point for the group. The women stopped what they were doing and began sharing stories about the importance of resisting oppressive situations and developing solidarity. The following story was the first to be told. It marked a shift away from women being simply co-participants to becoming comrades in a common struggle.

The Ashanti people have a symbol called the golden stool. And they feel that the golden stool represents the soul of the Ashanti people. During colonialism, the Queen of England wanted to sit a white man on the golden stool, which would symbolize that she held the soul of the Ashanti people. The men of Ashanti were tired, didn't want to fight anymore. They said, "They want the stool? Give them the stool." And the warrior Queen Mother said, "Ught ugnh. They can have our bodies, we cannot allow them to have our soul!" And she bared her breast, and she and the women smelted rifles out of gold and went to war for the Ashanti people. And the Europeans never got the golden stool, nor the soul of the Ashanti people.

As part of the research, I analyzed 115 stories drawn from the focus-group transcripts to examine the role storytelling served in promoting health among the women who participated in this study. I identified six major functions:

A. To provide contextual grounding
B. To provide a means of bonding with other participants
C. To provide a means of validating and affirming women's experiences
D. To provide a means of catharsis
E. To provide a means for resisting oppression

F. To provide a vehicle for educating other participants

Reaching deeper: Storytelling as a therapeutic intervention

My earlier experiences led me to explore storytelling as a tool for assisting women in managing their hypertension. During the first session, two women shared the following personal stories about their experiences with hypertension:

I don't know where to begin. I wanted to be brief. I wanted to get through this without being really emotional, but one thing I know I need to do is get rid of old baggage. We all know that comes when we start something or learn something new. Sometimes we bring baggage and, unfortunately, the baggage sometimes is so heavy that it stops you from moving around, from what you need to do. I want to be able to become educated so I can help others who have gone through tragedies and losses, and to know how to move on and get beyond them because you can carry so much weight, so much guilt. Like I said, that can stop you from doing what needs to be don e... And then my health has been battered. Struggling with high blood pressure and taking all this medication. And unfortunately, it spaces me out. You know that's reality, so I want to come off some of the meds.

When I was growing up, my father died when I was 14. My mother had five of us and my mother has high blood pressure because she thought she could do it alone. I mean, I'm a Black woman! I was taught to be strong and I think that if my mother had died, there were plenty of people to help my father out with five children. But my mother was expected to do it alone. And she thought that was what she was supposed to do and she didn't ask for help. And now I'm growing up and thinking that I'm supposed to do the same thing, I can do it alone. If people don't call me and say, "Do you need help?" I wouldn't call them and say, "I need help!" And I've learned over the last year that I've got to be able to reach out in order to get back.

I was struck by how deeply ingrained the myth of the "Strong Black Woman" was in the psyches of many of the women who participated in the study. This myth provided the foundation for many survival habits. Paradoxically, these survival habits have historically been critical to the well-being of the African-American community, while at the same time being detrimental to the health of women who subscribe to them.

When I was a post-doctoral fellow, I completed a study that let me explore more directly how storytelling could affect health behavior decision making. The purpose of this pilot project was to examine whether storytelling as an intervention could decrease the risks of either developing hypertension or manifesting the secondary negative outcomes of hypertension. Group storytelling was the cornerstone of this ten-week intervention. The intervention focused on helping women understand the factors influencing self-care behaviors that could help decrease the risks of developing hypertension or maximize their health. Specifically, I wanted to evaluate the value of storytelling for helping women —

A. analyze self-care behavior related to hypertension,

B. examine cultural norms regarding women's roles and their relationship to personal behavior, and

C. expand their knowledge regarding alternative strategies for living with hypertension or diminishing risks for developing it.

During the study, women shared a variety of personal stories, folktales, literary tales, and their own fiction creations. Story topics included:

- **The meaning of being a woman of African descent at this point in history.** These stories resulted in tears and laughter. I shared a story about healing from an abortion I had as a teenager. Afterwards, one of the women talked about her own abortion and healing. Women noted that they appreciated my story, as it conveyed important information about me and helped strengthen group bonds. I healed a little more this day!

- **Common behaviors or beliefs within African-American communities.** Much of the information here related to the impact of "Strong Black Woman" stories that we had grown up with and held dear.

- **Specific aspects of living/dealing with high blood pressure.** These produced some very powerful stories and lots of journal reflections.

Guest storytellers shared stories for 30 minutes at the beginning of our sessions during even-numbered weeks. These storytellers were all African-American women with established reputations within both the local storytelling and African-American communities. Storytellers were invited to share stories from African, African-American, or other cultures throughout the African diaspora. Stories could be from any genre, as long as they were stories the teller personally found meaningful for her own life. (One of the storytellers was Debra Harris-Branham, who told the story "Yonjwa Seeks a Bride," which follows.)

Each week, 20 to 30 minutes were allotted for examining technical or conceptual issues related to storytelling. Topics included: selecting stories to tell, distinguishing among story genres, storytelling in African and African-American culture, influencing coping strategies and health through storytelling, reclaiming your voice as a prerequisite for health, and uncovering cultural ideology in stories and popular media. These discussions were followed by a storytelling exercise. The exercises gave the women an opportunity to practice creating or sharing stories, to examine directly the impact storytelling can have with respect to perceptions, and to explore the value of stories as an education tool.

Storytelling proved to be a wonderful tool for helping women examine their lives and health behaviors. The quotes shared in this section are recorded verbatim from the women's journals. Initially, the women were unsure how storytelling could help them manage their lives and hypertension. However, as the weeks passed, they became thrilled at the possibilities for storytelling as a healing agent.

Last week I questioned how storytelling would aid in lowering my blood pressure. This week, I found myself looking forward to and being excited to come and hear stories from our culture! The guest storyteller put the study into perspective for me when she said that her craft is a way for her to release tension! Just watching her as she dramatized the stories was exhilarating, yet relaxing. I thoroughly enjoyed her!

These sessions have truly opened my eyes to the beauty and richness that storytelling, especially oral storytelling, brings to our culture and everyday outlook on life. I am encouraged to study African-American storytelling more closely. I've found that sharing truly does soothe me.

The journal entries provided further support for the six functions of storytelling identified in my earlier work. The folktales, literary tales, and poetry shared by guest storytellers were especially beneficial for validating or affirming the beauty and worth of African-American women and culture.

The storytelling settled my mind and eased my headache — I barely feel any discomfort. My mind was filled with the beauty of the "Creation Story." There is healing in beautiful stories that lift you up and take you away from the hassle and stress of a day's work.

Guest storyteller Debra Harris-Branham swooped in and out of this session in a blaze of fast-talking, hand-clapping storytelling! Her interactive style of storytelling was refreshing! I love the fact that women in African folktales are big, and considered beautiful!

Personal stories were most effective in assisting women to examine the context of their lives and the impact of specific behaviors. In particular, these stories caused women to re-examine the myth of the "Strong Black Woman" and its negative influence on their ability to be healthy. Sharing personal stories was also a cathartic experience, allowing women to vent built-up frustrations, anger, and hurt.

The stories were again uplifting and shifted my mood from feeling overwhelmed to feeling light. The transition was needed in order for me to continue forward. It is imperative that I do some serious shifting in my schedule. Before I explode into little pieces. I don't feel like I am honoring myself or the people in my life that I love and hold dear to me. There isn't enough of me to go around. There are my children, my companion, my friends, my co-workers, the tutors, the students, the parents, classmates, advisor, instructors, others who are interested in getting to know me — all of these wonderful people are seeking something from me. I feel as though I want to run and hide, and I equally feel I want to be available to everyone because that is what my spirit desires. Reality of course has said for me to back up and pick only a few of these groups and slowly incorporate others as time and my well-being permits. Okay — I feel better now — I will take one — hour at — a time and make the best of it. Sharing my spirit and just being there for others as deemed necessary. I believe that all my concerns will fall into place. Venting sure helps.

Tonight as our group discussed "what's on top" and shared our stories of living with hypertension, I kept thinking of how privileged I feel to know such strong black women. I thought about the characteristic that is commonly used to describe black women, "strong." It occurred to me that, at this point in my life, I have strength enough for only one person: Me. I'm so used to being the pillar that everyone leans on, and don't get me wrong, I reveled in the role of the strong one! It made me feel good, knowing that I was a strong black woman. But I'm also coming to realize that I don't have to stand alone to be strong. To be a strong pillar, I need to have a firm, solid foundation. I'm realizing I have that in my family and my friends. I have people to lean on! That's comforting. That's enough to keep my blood pressure from skyrocketing!

The pilot project reaffirmed for me what I in fact already knew. As people, we may stumble through life. We make the same mistakes over and over again. We may suffer pain and hardship.

We look for love in all the wrong places. We may reject or ridicule the wisdom of elders and our peers. All the while we may be crying out, begging for help, for love, for direction. I would posit that we already have what we need to be whole, to be healed. Sharing our stories with each other and our children can provide the foundation for moving into that fuller, richer life we crave. Our stories act as a road map and lamp, guiding us through the dark, sacred night, all the while letting us know we are not traveling alone.

I would like to recommend reading and/or listening to the following authors and storytellers who have helped shape my research and development as a storyteller: Patricia Hill Collins, G. Etter-Lewis, H.L. Gates, L. Goss and M. Barnes, C. Estes, M.A. Gillespie, L. Goss and C. Goss, V. Hamilton, G. Howard, Zora Neale Hurston, J. Lester, N. Livo and S. Rietz, A. Lorde, E. Mishler, D. Polkinghorne, Bernice Johnson Reagon, G. Sarris, Yvonne Kesho Scott, L.M. Silko, Terry Tafoya, and Alice Walker.

⇒ Yonjwa Seeks a Bride ⇐

A FOLKTALE FROM THE CONGO
RETOLD BY MARGARET READ MACDONALD*

THIS IS A SMALL PART of the Congolese epic of Lonkundo and his sons. For more of the adventures of Yonjwa and Eyonga see Jan Knappert's *Myths and Legends of the Congo*.

Knappert points out that among the Nkundo, the ideal woman is one of strength and stature. In further episodes, Eyonga becomes the mother of the Nkundo people.

> *Yonjwa went courting.*
> *Yonjwa was the son of a chief,*
> *Son of Lonkundo, that famous hero.*

For such a man a bride must be fine.
No skinny little weaklings for Yonjwa.
A large, strong woman he needed for a wife.
Yonjwa traveled far.
Many villages he passed.
Many women he saw.

But all were too weak ... too skinny.
None worthy of a chief's son.

Then one day Yonjwa met a man on the road.
This man was covered with oil,
greasy from top to bottom.

Reprinted from *The Storyteller's Start-up Book* by Margaret Read MacDonald (Little Rock, AR: August House, 1993) with the permission of the publisher.

"What on earth happened to you?" Yonjwa asked.

"Oh, I did a foolish thing.
In this next village down the road there is a girl called Eyonga.
She is the chief's daughter.
That Eyonga is so strong.
She is large.
She is handsome.
She is *beautiful*.
Everyone wants to marry Eyonga.
But she won't marry any man.
When a man comes to court her ...
that Eyonga makes him *wrestle* with her!
If she can throw him down ...
he has lost.
But that's not all.
She makes him wrestle her in a pit of *oil*.
Her father is so rich.
He has palm oil plantations.
That oil is expensive.
But her father fills a pit with palm oil.
And she wrestles standing in that oil.
She rubs that oil all over her body.
She is so slippery.
You can't get a grip on her anywhere.
I tried to throw her.
Look at me.
She threw me down in that oil.
Everyone laughed.
They ran me out of the village.
It was the most foolish thing I ever tried.
What a fool ... to think I could beat that woman."
When Yonjwa heard this he thought, "At last I may have found a woman worthy to be my bride!"

Yonjwa went at once to that girl's village.

When he entered he saw a group of girls talking together.

All of them were large, and all of them were beautiful.
But one of those girls was larger and more beautiful than the others.
She was *gorgeous*!

Yonjwa went right up to her.
"Are you the famous wrestling champion?"

She deigned to look at him,
"I might be."

"Then I have come to *marry* you."

"Oh is that so.
Well, come back tomorrow and we'll *talk* about it."

"No. I have come to marry you ... *today*."

She looked at him more closely, then turned and walked away.
"Who *is* this person?"

Yonjwa followed her into the village.
He went right up to the village elders.
"Sirs, I have come to marry this woman of yours."

"Oh? Well, come back tomorrow, young man, and we will *talk* about it."

"No. I have come to marry her *today*."

"Who is this young man?" they asked.
But to Yonjwa they said, "Her *father* isn't here."

Yonjwa was bold. "Then fetch him."

They sent for that girl's father, and when he came, Yonjwa spoke.

"Sir, I have come to marry your daughter."

"Well, come back tomorrow, young man. We will *talk* about it."

"No. I have come to marry her ... *today*."

"Who *is* this young man?" asked her father.
But to Yonjwa he said, "We have a test here."

"Get it ready," said Yonjwa. "I will take the test."

Her father ordered the vat filled with palm oil.
Eyonga jumped into the oil.
She threw palm oil over her shoulders.
She rubbed her face with palm oil.
She was ready.

Yonjwa jumped into the oil.

The oil came up to Eyonga's waist.
The oil came up to Yonjwa's waist.
She was tall.
He was tall.

She was the daughter of a chief.
He was the son of a chief.

She waited.
She watched for her chance.
Eyonga grabbed Yonjwa around the waist.
She lifted him over her head.
"*Aaaaaaannngh!*"
She *threw* him into the oil.

Yonjwa jumped up.

Oil was streaming down his face.
He was grinning.
"*I like this woman!*"

She grabbed him again.
She lifted him over her head.
"*AAAAAAANGH!*"
She *threw* him under the oil.

Yonjwa came up again.
Oil was running from his hair.
He was laughing.
"I've got to *have this woman!*"

She grabbed him again.
This time Yonjwa was ready for her.
Yonjwa got a hold around Eyonga's neck.
He would not let go.
She twisted this way and that.
She tried to throw him ... both went down beneath the oil.

When they came up, Yonjwa was still holding on.
He clung to her like a vine to a tree.
Wherever she turned ... there was Yonjwa, hanging fast.
Then... Yonjwa got his footing.
Slowly ... slowly ... he began to push Eyonga down.
Down ... down ... until she touched the bottom of the vat.
He had *thrown* her!

Those two leapt up.
They were *smiling*.

Eyonga said, "At *last*! A man *strong enough* to be my husband!"

Yonjwa said, "At *last*! A woman *strong enough* to be my *bride*!"
Her father said, "Yes. It is a good match. Tomorrow I will send eight men to bring back the bride price from your village."

Yonjwa said "*Eight* men? You had better send *eighty* men! This woman is worth a *lot* of bride price!"

And on the next day Eyonga's father sent eighty men to Yonjwa's village.
There Yonjwa filled their baskets so full of bride wealth that they could scarcely stagger home.

Such was the price of a good strong woman in *those* days.

A story of a strong woman

Debra Harris-Branham

Prior to publication of her book *The Storyteller's Sourcebook*, Margaret Read MacDonald gave me a copy of "Yonjwa Seeks a Bride." When I read it, I knew this story was mine! It grabbed me instantly — my reaction was ecstatic. Imagine beauty being determined by the size and strength of a woman! A story featuring a large and "in charge" woman, now that's my kind of tale. Being descended from a long line of African-American women, with ample hips and thighs, I relish every minute of telling this spirited, energetic story. I especially love the reactions of audience members' faces, primarily women, when a realistic standard of beauty is defined and glorified through the telling of this tale. Knowing smiles, nodding and reared-back heads, hand-clapping, and laughter fill the air as the audience joins Yonjwa in his pursuit of the perfect soul-mate.

Yonjwa's bold search, looking for that beautiful woman of strength and size, needed to be emphasized in the telling. Thus came the chant that I added to the tale:

He walked here — he walked there,
He couldn't find her anywhere!
He looked here — he looked there,
He couldn't find her anywhere! He couldn't find her anywhere!

Along with the chant, I add a rhythmic stomp and clap that I learned years back from a toe-tapping group of first graders. The chant is interspersed throughout the story as Yonjwa journeys to find that special woman. At the end, the last line changes to:

He found the right one, right there. He found the right one, oh yeah!

≈Kimo's Heart≈

RANDY LANDENBERGER

I WORK AS A HEALTH professional as well as a storyteller. I wrote the following story to illustrate the potential for healing that comes from telling the right story at the right time. The inspiration for this story came when I lived in Maui, Hawaii, and my neighbor, Steve, was an echocardiographer, someone who uses ultrasound to view people's hearts. Steve told me how, in the dark, with the machine humming and with the echocardiographer's hand holding the transducer on the patient's chest, his patients often feel like they are on the therapist's couch.

"People open up and tell you their story. It amazes me," Steve said. "These huge local guys, whose wrong side you would want to avoid, sometimes begin to cry and tell me about how hurt they are emotionally."

When Steve asked me about my own profession as a storyteller, my girlfriend piped up, "Randy uses stories to help open people's hearts." To which Steve replied, "And I look into them to see the stories that already exist."

Special thanks to Nyla Fujii-Babb for her help in editing the Hawaiian dialect.

Steve opened the room shades and gazed out to the tall palms holding their own in tropical trade winds. The west Maui mountains reluctantly released the clouds that gathered around them. A gentle shower would be blowing through soon, leaving a rainbow trail in its wake.

"Rainbows, like babies, are good for the heart," Steve always said. "You can't look at one without feeling wonder and showing a smile." He glanced at the chart for the next appointment: Kimo Haiku, 52-year-old Hawaiian male, with chest pains. A commotion stirred in the hall outside the door.

Steve watched the scene from a respectful distance. A very large, stout man with graying hair and moustache, arms as thick as a beef roast, legs dark and sturdy as a Koa tree, was surrounded by his family. They argued fiercely, which made the man's lava-black eyes burn.

"So what you here for, anyway?" Kimo yelled in the local pidgin dialect to a well-dressed man who seemed to be a younger version of himself by two decades.

"I just want to see you get mo betta, Papa. It's for your own good."

"You just wanna see me gone!" Kimo snorted. "Den you goin' sell da family land and dey put up condos on our graves. Damn kids, you fight me all your life, you nevah like learn Hawaiian ways. Now you can't wait fo sell-out to developers. Go on, get outta here, I be gone soon enough."

"Oh, you, Kimo, why you always start dis?" His wife pleaded with him. "You know you da kids love you," Two women in their 30s joined in the arguing while the younger man stood tight-lipped, arms crossed and staring back at his father through equally dark eyes. Together they stood as sure and stout as a eucalyptus grove.

Tugging on Kimo's shorts was a plump three-year-old, his other hand in his mouth, his eyes swamped with tears.

"Tutu Kimo," he called to his grandfather with every tug. Kimo reached down and pulled the child up into a warm cuddle in his giant arms, and the verbal assaults became no more than wind through the trees. Steve watched as a soft smile spread over Kimo's face as he kissed the child tenderly and whispered in his ear, then gently put him back on the floor. As soon as his hands broke contact with his grandson, Kimo was once more the erupting volcano.

"Go on then," he yelled to everyone. "Get the hell out of here." Then he turned to his wife. "Mama, you take Kawika," he pointed to his grandson, "wait for me in da truck. Kawika stay with us again tonight. No good son, no can take care of his own kid," he pointed an accusing finger at the young man, "but want all my land for get rich. Go on, I don't want none of you hanging around here." Kimo turned his wide back to them and tromped up the hall toward Steve.

"Hey," he huffed, "you da doctor guy, supposed for give me test? I don't understand none of dis stuff. Let's get it done, tell me when I goin' die."

"I'm the cardiac tech," Steve answered. "I'm going to do an echocardiogram of your heart. It's ultrasound, just like looking at a baby in the womb. It won't take long, but you'll have to wait for your doctor to give you his diagnosis. Come on in, take off your shirt, and lie on your left side here on the table."

Kimo removed his sun-bleached shirt, revealing an intricate pattern of Polynesian tattoos across his shoulders and chest. Beside the bed, Steve seated himself in front of the ultrasound machine. In his hand he held what appeared to be a small electric shaver, which he covered with a blue gel.

"This is the transducer," Steve explained. "I'm going to move this around on your chest and a picture of your heart is going to appear on this screen. We look at how the valves and muscles move, and how big the chambers are. The exam is videotaped and recorded by the machine."

"You gonna see my heart with that thing on the outside?"

"Yes, sir. It uses sound waves to make a picture, like sonar, and we can look right inside. Just watch this screen, and you can see your own heart beating."

Kimo tried to keep up his stoic stare, but Steve could detect the apprehension as he placed the transducer probe over Kimo's chest and adjusted the knobs on the machine. Kimo's eyes widened as the shadowy image of his heart pulsed on the monitor. Steve broke for just a moment to speak some technical jargon into the microphone, then continued to move the probe and adjust the machine until an image began to take form.

"Are you nervous?" he asked Kimo. "Your pulse is a bit fast."

"Dis is pretty scary stuff, looking at my own heart. I afraid I goin' see it stop, den I be dead, eh?" He laughed nervously. "It only strained 'cause I angry all da time now. You heard dose kids, didn't you? Can't wait for see me gone. Dat's what's giving me problems wit my heart. My *keiki*, my own children, breaking it by giving up Hawaiian ways. Dey want sell out to developers. Even my daughters argue wit me now. But dis land sacred, we already lose all our culture. My *keiki* no can even speak Hawaiian. Only grandson, *opuna*, speak Hawaiian because we, *tutuwahine* and me, teach him." Kimo paused with a saddened but still smoldering look. "So what you see in there, doc?"

"Well, it looks a little enlarged," Steve replied. "It's had to push one big load. Do you have any family history of heart disease?"

"My own papa, he die young. But he one mean old man, die from always stay grumpy. Always tell me I'm wrong, always try fight with me, never listen, never try help me. Dat's how my kids gonna kill me; dey turn me into one big grump. Tutu Kane, though, my papa's papa, he live long, raise me real Hawaiian way, strong but gentle. He teach me protect da land, no let business guys or government take it away. He one wise-kine Tutu, always find way for make things work. He try for make my papa go easy, laugh a little, but Papa no would listen. So Papa die young and grumpy, fight with me till the end.

"Dat's why I try teach Kawika. He my last hope dis family stay strong in Hawaii, no let this island turn into Disneyland. Damn kids all ready for give it away, say we no can afford for keep it, better for sell it while we can. I say dey should work it, protect it, but dey no like get dey hands dirty. Afraid of a little honest work, afraid government take it for taxes." Kimo shook his head in disgust. "Den what happens for da land and da money?" Kimo continued to vent. "Mo houses, mo people — and no Hawaiian people either, only rich *haoles* can afford new house here. So developers make money, government get money, and da *keiki* want da rest for spend on new cars, clothes, and fancy go-out-eat dinner. Dey no have nothing left for Kawika and da other *keiki* when dey grow up. Dey no do nothin' for Hawaiian people. No wonder my heart failing.

"You know," he continued more calmly now, as though this minor eruption released enough pressure to keep him from blowing, "Tutu Kane learn me how for play slack-key guitar. He sing beautiful, like Gabby Pahanui. We would play and sing for hours and hours. I try for teach my own kids, but like everything else Hawaiian, they like listen, but no for like learn. When little babies, I play and sing them to sleep every night. Now I get so angry, no can play anymore. Hawaiian songs, you know, dey almost all about happy things, sometimes maybe sad songs about love or losing our 'aina, but never angry songs, not like rock and roll, boom, boom, boom kind crap, kids listen to." He paused for a brief moment. "How 'bout you, Steve, you like play music?"

"Yeah, as a matter of fact," Steve replied, "I do play a little guitar. I started taking slack-key lessons, too, but the teacher didn't have much patience. I'd love to learn if I could find someone who would be more tolerant of a beginner."

"Well, I tell you; slack-key used secret tunings. Every family's little different, and dey no like nobody steal dey sound. Dey no share with anyone — even other Hawaiians. That's one thing I think maybe a good thing for share. Maybe mo people play Hawaiian music, dey feel Hawaiian spirit and quit screwing over Hawaiian people."

"Exactly," agreed Steve. "They say music soothes the savage breast. I use this transducer to put sound into your heart. But you can use your guitar to put music into our spirits. I wish I knew a way to encourage you to play again."

"Yeah, me too," Kimo paused briefly with a deep sigh. "So what you see in dare, doc?"

"Here's an interesting part." Steve pointed to an area below one of the heart valves fluttering on the monitor.

"What, you see something wrong?"

"You see this little spot here? This is a real special place, and it looks like it's growing."

"No! You mean I got some kine cancer?"

"Not at all. See how bright this is? This is the spot where your Tutu Kane lives. It's healthy and growing. And here's another spot," Steve pointed to the monitor, "where your grandson Kawika, lives. It's healthy and strong too. Hey, and there's one for your wife."

"Hey, you kidding me, yeah?"

"No sir, Kimo. You got one good heart here, just overstressed from all the burdens you carry. These are the people and places that are holding your heart together, keeping you strong so you can share all the good things that have been through it."

"What kind stuff you talking about?"

"You said your Tutu Kane was wise and tried to get your papa to lighten up. He loved you and raised you Hawaiian way. Now you're doing the same with your grandson. But you're like your own papa with your kids. Maybe you need to laugh and sing with them, not fight so it kills you. Teach them like your Tutu taught you. Use Kawika as the bridge to them."

"How I do that? I say keep da land, dey like sell."

"Maybe you can do both. If you can't afford to keep it because of the taxes, maybe there's a way around selling it so that you can still keep it for all Hawaiian *keiki*. Maybe now that you know where it is," Steve pointed to the glowing spot on the monitor, "you can go to this spot in your heart where your Tutu lives, where the true Hawaiian spirit lives, and ask for wisdom and guidance. Like you said, he always found a way to make things work. Now that you've seen it here on the monitor, take this memory and visualize it glowing bright and strong when you need help talking to your kids. You're a good man, Kimo, and your heart's still plenty strong. I'd hate to see you die like your father, young and grumpy."

"Humph, maybe you right. Tutu would know. I no talk with him in long time, thought he was dead and buried in da ground. Hey, thanks for showing me where he still lives."

"Why don't you work on a duet with him, Kimo? Pick up your guitar again and let Tutu Kane sing through you. Maybe your kids would listen to him. Maybe it would take one heavy load off this heart of yours. Some people diet to lose weight. Maybe you need to sing to lose burdens."

"Hey, you one good *haole* guy. You must be *hapa*, 'cause you talk like you got Hawaiian blood in your own heart. Maybe you come out our place sometime for talk story some more. I like have you as one guest. You come see our land, we play music, maybe I even teach you a little slack-key. Den we have luau; my wife and daughters make *ono-kine kau-kau*, you know. So good, it broke your mout!"

"Thanks, Kimo, I will. I'm planning a couple days off on your side of the island next month, I'll stop in. Meanwhile, that's it for now, your exam is done, you can put your shirt on and *halé on*, head home. Your doctor will give you his "official" medical opinion, but I think you're in pretty good shape."

The ocean breeze was blowing gently off the turquoise water while rainbows sparkled in the light mountain showers as Steve drove along the coast a month later. A rusty gate, hanging cock-eyed on its hinges, marked the long driveway down to Kimo's *hale*. The sweet musky scent of mangoes, guava, and passion fruit mixed with the fresh salt air around the little white plantation house where a picture-perfect Polynesian couple were serenading the dogs and chickens that adorned the lanai. Kimo quickly handed his old guitar to his smiling wife as he burst off the steps with an ear-to-ear grin. He grabbed Steve in a big Hawaiian hug and squeezed tight.

"Good to see you, my friend. Hey, other doc tell me heart is getting better. I no need no medicine, or nuthin'. I got one big heart 'cause I'm one big guy, with lots for giving. Come, come, I gonna show you why." He led Steve down a path through a banana grove along the beach. Kimo pointed ahead to a large hut being built. "See, dis just beginning."

"Are you building a new house?" Steve asked.

"Yes, but not for me. New house for boats, for music, and for da *keiki*."

"I don't understand."

"Tutu Kane, he show me. Dis da place where Tutu Kane and Tutu Wahine buried. I no tell you before, 'cause it's illegal, but I feel I can trust you now. We never put dem in cemetery, just got gravestones there for show. I bring dem here and bury in dis cave, jus' like traditional Hawaiian grave. I always keep dis place sacred, never like nothing built here, nevah even tell my *keiki* about da graves. Dat's why dey no understand why I couldn't let go of dis land. But I think of da place in my heart, just like when you tell me, den I ask Tutu Kane. He say he want dis site for foundation place for *keiki* — for enjoy da land and da sea, for learn da music. Dey buried up dere on da cliffs so dey can look down and see dis good ting. Tutu also tell me my son not useless, he know lawyer friends. He also tell me no yell at dem no more either, sing to dem like you tell me.

"David, my son, talk to lawyer and find out we no going sell da land or lose it either. We find one way for give land for da Hawaiian people — we have one cultural school here. It's in trust now, so we get donations for paying taxes. Now all

kids can come here and learn how for speak and sing Hawaiian, build Hawaiian canoe, learn how for farm and fish in da old ways. Dey learn for take care of da land too, pick bananas, mangoes, all kind fruit for pay da expenses. Now dis land can pay for itself, no need get condos built, no need get taken by da government.

"And, I make my *keiki*, son, daughters, all of dem, directors on trust board, so dey got responsibility for all people even long after I and my wife gone. But you know what, Steve? I going be around for one long time now. Tutu Kane show me dat kids really not so bad, dey jus' nevah like da land go for nothing. When we found dat we can work together, keep da land, and, dey nevah have to get dey hands dirty, everything okay. I find out dey pretty good at dat kine legal and business stuff. Still stay work, just different kine." He beamed a smile. "I guess even da old kings and queens had bean counters too," Kimo chuckled. "Now I can laugh again, be happy like Tutu Kane, not one grump Papa, like mines one was. I going live for see grandson Kawika be one teacher at dis school."

Kimo stepped in close, putting his big hands on Steve's shoulders. Steve looked at this mountain of a man, gazing up into his eyes and graying hair as though he was surveying Mauna Kea, the now dormant and peaceful volcano, with a dusting of fresh snow. "I gotta say *mahalo*, thank you, Steve, for showing me one good picture in my heart."

"You're welcome, Kimo." Steve blushed. "The picture was always there, though. It's just like rainbows are always there. The rain just uncovers them. All I did was uncover what you already had."

"Yeah," Kimo beamed again. "Now I'm using music for get into my family's hearts. And when I die, I know I going live in da heart of each of my *keiki.* Eh, Steve, maybe one day you look at their hearts with your machine too, and you can see me there. You'll know it's me, Steve, 'cause I'll be smiling and you'll hear echoes of my songs. You can take my picture and show them. Maybe dey build one foundation near my grave too, so Hawaiian ways always grow and not stay buried in da ground.

"Come." He took Steve by the arm. "Now I teach you for play slack-key like you play dat machine." 🐚

Share stories, pass it on:
Woman's health promotion through storytelling

ALLISON M. COX

WHEN MY CO-WORKER AT THE health department asked me to share some stories with women that would highlight breast and cervical cancer education, I eagerly agreed. My grandmother died from breast cancer, and my mother survived her own bout with breast cancer. When my sister had several lumps removed from her breast, all benign, and the family breathed a collective sigh of relief. My oldest daughter and I have both had repeated cryosurgery to prevent the cervical cancer that threatened when our tests showed that dysplasia, a pre-cancerous condition, was evident. So I have more than a passing interest in breast and cervical cancer education.

My co-worker, a public health nurse, planned to follow my stories with education about available screening methods that women can use to detect these cancers and prevent deaths. Washington was one of ten states working with the federal Centers for Disease Control and Prevention (CDC) at this time on a national Breast and Cervical Health Program. We wanted to reach women identified by the CDC as high risk because they had not received annual screenings. In our district, minority and low-income women, especially elders, were our intended audience.

So I went to visit my local librarians for ideas. When they saw me approach the library desk, they laughed, "What is it this time — rats, cockroaches, head lice ...?" These wonderfully resourceful women had helped me through multiple story searches related to health topics in the past.

"I'm looking for stories I can tell about breast and cervical cancer. Any suggestions?"

Their smiles faded a bit, but, undaunted, they dutifully began searching the computer terminals and bookshelves. They brought me a pile of autobiographies of women who had fought their own battles with these cancers. I read several books and learned so much more about the challenges these women faced physically, emotionally, and spiritually when diagnosed with life-threatening disease, but I felt that I could not tell the personal stories of others.

So, I called a friend who headed the state's Breast and Cervical Health Program and asked her for some ideas. She was so excited about the concept of educating others through storytelling that she immediatly asked me if I would tell these same stories at the State Conference on Breast and Cervical Health. I said, "Yes — I'd love to!" But I hung up the phone none the wiser as to what stories I was going to tell in any of these venues. So I called her back and asked, "What important points do you want the audience to walk out of that conference knowing? What do you hope they will feel/think/remember as a result of hearing stories on this subject?"

She responded immediately. "I think it would be important for them to hear stories about taking responsibility for your health, not letting a problem go till it gets too big to handle, and facing your fears."

Well, there I had it! And after reading all those autobiographies on the challenges that women experienced when diagnosed with cervical or breast cancer, I decided to add "offering support to each other" to that list. With these simple pointers, I could pare down the subject from overwhelmingly big issues to topics with achievable components.

I was able to find folktales, legends, and literary stories on each of these subjects. For examples of "taking responsibility for your health" and "not letting the problem go till it gets too big to handle" I adapted "Not Our Problem" from Margaret Read MacDonald's book *Peace Tales*. In MacDonald's version, the king accidentally drips some honey, which triggers a series of escalating events. As each event occurs, the king tells his advisor it is "not our problem," until finally war breaks out and the palace burns to the ground. I found variations of this tale featuring a female main character, so I changed the story to focus on the queen and her companion, and the rest of the story followed naturally. I had the queen drop that "lump of honey" on her chest initially, before she flicked the honey to the balcony wall, where it oozed down and plopped to the ground, only to have a fly land on it, which was eaten by a lizard, which was chased by a cat ....

When I ended the story with the queen surveying the ruins of the palace, saying, "Perhaps that lump of honey *was* my problem," I paused and looked at the audience and added, "One out of every eight women in North America will contract breast cancer in her lifetime. Cervical cancer is 100 percent preventable if caught in time. If this doesn't affect you, it will be your sisters, mothers, daughters, wives, aunts, neighbors, or friends. Encourage them all to go to their doctor for yearly exams. Tell them to be sure to ask their medical providers about screening procedures for these cancers. Offer to drive them, watch their kids, hold their hands — whatever it takes. Urge them not to wait. Help prevent unnecessary deaths through early detection. Breast and cervical cancer is *our* problem!"

With each additional story I told at Elder Meal Sites and Community Centers, the audiences asked more questions, and many women shared their own experiences. We distributed information about free mammograms and pap smears (the common screening tools for these cancers), affordable insurance, and additional referral resources. We were excited by the response — people were hearing our message and becoming actively engaged in discussing their concerns.

When the public health nurse contacted the interpreters we work with at a center for Asian elders, she sensed that the translators had some trepidation about our plans to present this topic. "This is a subject that is not often talked about — the privacy of a woman's body," they told us hesitantly and paused before adding, "But also, in our culture, the teaching should come from an elder or a person in authority."

We talked to the translators about the importance of our message and how it could save some of the seniors' lives. We wanted to use story, we explained, because this method had worked well in the past with the elders. The seniors felt comfortable listening to stories — storytelling was familiar to them. Then I had an idea. Sometimes I have to consider if a story needs to come from someone other than myself. I was easily 20 to 40 years younger than these elders, but I could ask my mother to tell these seniors our family stories. My mother had been active in cancer support groups for years before moving west to live with me, so she readily agreed.

Just before we left our house to go to the Asian center, my mother asked me, "Do you think I should bring my cane?"

"Yes, please! Some of these people are using walkers!"

At the center, Mom told personal stories about losing her mother, being afraid for her own life, and the experiences of her daughters and granddaughter. Her words were translated simultaneously into Cambodian, Vietnamese, and Laotian. At the end of her story, my mother urged the women to go to their doctors and get breast and cervical exams. She told them, "If you don't want to do this for yourself, then do it for your children and your grandchildren — they will need you here in the years to come. Tell your daughters and granddaughters to go, too." I watched as each translator repeated her words and the elders began nodding their heads and commenting to each other throughout the crowd. The translators were smiling. I knew then that this message had gotten through and would be taken home to the younger women in their families as well. I caught Mom's eye from across the room and silently mouthed, "Thank you!"

My mother accompanied me to the State Conference on Breast and Cervical Health and was one of the welcoming speakers at the opening session. I followed my mother's personal stories with my telling of "Not Our Problem." I also taught a workshop at the conference encouraging health professionals to incorporate stories in their educational presentations on these cancers.

At the workshop, one of the stories I told was "The Buried Moon." This English folktale tells of the moon coming down to earth as a shining heavenly woman to protect her people from the evil swamp creatures that wander the lands, harming any they encounter during the dark of the moon. In the story, even the moon was afraid, but she persevered, determined to safeguard the people. The hood of the moon's cloak becomes caught and she cannot release her protective light when the swamp creatures overcome her, push her down under the swamp waters, and roll a great stone over her to keep her buried. As the dark nights continue, the people are worried that the moon will never return and they seek the help of the wise woman to recover the moon. The wise woman tells them to place a stone in each person's mouth so as not to cry out, to link arms, and to search for the moon together in the swamp. As frightening as this is for the villagers, the thought of losing the moon forever seems even worse — so they follow the wise woman's directions and find a glow emanating from beneath a great rock in the middle of the swamp. When the villagers overturn this rock, the moon rushes back up into the sky, sending all the malicious goblins scurrying away from her shining light. The moon, to this day, has never forgotten what these people have done and still shines more brightly in this place than anywhere else in the world.

I asked audience members if they would share what the story brought to mind in the context of the conference. We talked about how the villagers were not able to cry out and how often people feel that the subject of cancer, especially breast and cervical cancer, is not to be discussed publicly. Seeking the advice of a wise woman echoed what many had heard during the conference: that it is important for women diagnosed with cancer to be able to turn to other women who have had similar experiences and can offer guidance. I asked my listeners their reactions to the idea of the moon protecting others from evil, but not being able to keep herself safe. We discussed the pattern of so many women who will look after the health of their families but neglect their own well-being. I shared that the autobiographies I had read mentioned repeatedly that women grew weary of being poked and prodded by medical professionals — just as the moon was tormented by the creatures in the swamp — and how important it was to them to be treated respectfully or even with humor. "After all" one woman in a previous presentation had told me, "I wasn't dead yet and I had no intention of dying — but some people acted like it was only a matter of time and cut themselves off from me emotionally."

Most importantly, we all heard that it took the entire village to discover the needed advice, find the moon, overturn the stone, and bring these issues out into the light again. "If we are going to urge women to seek testing," I suggested, "then we must be ready to offer support to those who will come back and tell us that they do indeed have cancer. And like the moon — these women will never forget that you offered your help."

For more information on these topics, contact the following organizations:

- Centers for Disease Control and Prevention — http://www.cdc.gov/od/owh/whbc.htm
- The American Cancer Society — http://www.cancer.org/ or phone 1-800-ACS-2345
- National Cancer Institute, Cancer Information Service — http://www.nci/nih.gov or phone 1-800-4-CANCER
- Susan G. Komen Breast Cancer Foundation — http://www.komen.org/
- The Mothers' Living Stories Project — www.MothersLivingStories.org or phone 510-531-1571 (This San Francisco Bay Area pilot project brings compassion, support in parenting, and dignity to mothers with breast cancer by helping them record their life stories and personal legacies. These living legacies foster communication within the family and help mothers and their children hold each other in life and after death.)

Losing and Getting

NANCY DUNCAN*

IN JULY 2000, I told 12 minutes' worth of this story in a workshop, "We Cried So Hard We Laughed," conducted by my daughter Lucy Duncan, Roslyn Bresnick Perry, and myself at the National Storytelling Conference in Kingsport, Tennessee.

The focus of the workshop was using humor to crack the trauma of our experience so it can be shared in story. I wasn't feeling all that well the day of the workshop; I was between chemo treatments, fairly stable, but ravaged by shivers from my medications and the persistent air-conditioning. Chemotherapy manages to reduce a person's IQ by at least 30 points. There were brilliant storytellers in the audience. I didn't think they'd miss 30 points, but I knew I did! I also feared I might forget the whole story in the middle. That's exactly what happened. Roslyn and Lucy tried to prompt me, but I just hung loose there, worried,

and the story came back. So the telling became a lecture/demo. Every day something happens, and I note it, and the story extends. Eventually, I suppose, it will be a small chapbook, or a performance piece. Who knows? Many with breast cancer, I've realized, just want to do the treatments, get it over with, and go back to their normal lives as quickly as possible. Some don't even want anyone to know they've had it. I respect these responses. Employed women have been demoted or fired because they took sick leave for treatment. But once cancer drew me into its dance, once I realized I had been thoroughly initiated, I knew I could never be the person I was before. My toes are bruised and numb because my dancing partner is sometimes very heavy-footed, but this is a dance of essence, and I'm just learning the beat.

> *When I was in the fifth grade, I was in love with a tall blonde boy by the name of Clinton. I brought hard candies to school and slipped them into his desk when Miss Fugit had her back turned.*

One day he looked at me with this sort of sweet/sad expression and I thought, uh, oh, here it comes. "Nancy, you are very nice, but I'm in love with Lethe Hunter because she has mountains on her chest."

In the seventh grade I was waiting in line with the rest of the girls in my class while our gym teacher pinned tucks in the bodices of our May

Day costumes. When it was my turn I said, "Miss Ligon, you didn't pin any tucks." She replied, "You don't need any tucks."

In the eighth grade I was obsessed by French and typing. I practiced both in bed, typing out the French words with my toes. One night my grandmother shook me awake. "Nancy, I don't mind your talking in your sleep, but you have to

If retelling this personal story, please tell it in the third person.

speak English."

"What was I saying?"

"Sounded like 'the grand tutton'."

"Oh, it's a joke, Les Grands Tetons — those mountains in Wyoming, the Big Tits!"

"Ah," my grandmother scooped me into her arms and I nestled against the huge shelf of her bosom. It was perfectly clear to me that tucks are essential, and breasts are flesh, not rock.

I did experiment with falsies for a while. I had to whittle them down a little. These could not possibly have sprouted over a weekend. But they were a nuisance because they migrated around inside my clothes. One day in the cafeteria line I reached up over the counter to get my plate and, looking down, saw two breasts, like a stoplight, right in the middle of my chest.

I finally just gave them up; they were too much trouble. And at my women's college I got to play all the men's parts, sometimes even in a full beard, in what were known in Atlanta as the best drag shows in town. Who needed breasts?

But eventually, with a lot of encouragement, affection, and practical assistance from Harry Duncan, along came our children, Barnaby, Lucy, and Guy, and breasts that waxed and waned, and waned. But this was the 60s! Everyone I knew, except my mother, burned their bras — and the world was filled with breasts of all sizes, jiggling and bouncing in liberation!

Finally I bought a bra in celebration of the fact that I'd graduated from an A to a B cup! Well, I had to buy a bra just to figure that out.

In March of 2000, on a Tuesday night, I discovered a lump in my right breast. An inch and a half long, big around as my finger, hard as a rock. I knew it was cancer, but scheduled a mammogram for Wednesday to be assured by my doctor from the dimpling on the surface and the size, shape, etc., that I was probably right. There was a biopsy on Friday, and then waiting over a long, long weekend for the official confirmation.

I rented a bunch of sad movies, bought a murder mystery by Josephine Tey, and made a nest for myself in the sofa bed in the library, with all the green tea I could possibly want, pillows, a notepad and paper, and a big box of Jordan almonds. For the first time since I can remember, I turned off the telephone.

Most of Saturday was soggy. I was regretting all the things I wouldn't get to do if I died. I progressed from this to planning my funeral. The final version of it included six 7½-foot by 10-foot rear projection screens, 12 projectors, and all 986 slides from my recent major theatrical production, with personalized listening stations and prerecorded audio messages for everyone. On Sunday I was bored by the sad movies, relished the murder mystery and the almonds, and began to think of action as a possibility. Ye gods, is there a war in my own body? How can I handle this — I'm a pacifist! What I need now is a cancer-threatening LIFE.

Then I planned the funerals of about six people who need to die before I do.

By Monday, I was ready for the news. A Grade 3 aggressive tumor. Mastectomy scheduled for March 21. Then I told my family and my friends.

Their responses extend along a sort of ... continuum of condolence. At the left is something like "It makes me sad to see you in so much pain. I'm leaving soup on your front porch. Give me something to do." In the middle, "Nancy, you are a survivor, a fighter through and through, a Nebraskan in your soul, go big RED!" And at the far end, "Thank you for being a part of my life. I

just want you to know I'll never forget you."
Many said, "Nancy, cancer is going to teach you
many lessons. The most important is for you to
learn how to allow us to love you, to let us help
you." One friend didn't say anything. I sank into
wonderful deep hugs — the magnificent comfort
of Les Grand Tetons!

I had trouble sleeping because my breasts
whispered to each other in the night:

R: *You were the one the doctor was watching — why
isn't it you?*
L: *Try to imagine how I'm going to suffer — carrying
the burden of suspicion all by myself.*
R: *It's her fault — she never really valued either of us.*
L: *She ate a lot of crunchy vegetables — didn't they like
her?*
R: *I'm frightened. I was too small to even be a memory.*
L: *I'm ... I'm going to miss you.*
R: *If there is any chance I can come back as a ghost, you
are the one I'm going to haunt!*

I immediately drafted two friends to help
make a rubber mold of my right breast so it could
be a memory. When I told my 13-year-old British
grandson, Matthew, that I was going to send him
a chocolate breast for Christmas, he said, "You're
weird, Nancy." And a week later he called to say,
"Uh, Nancy, you know that chocolate breast?
Well, you don't need to send it, because it would,
it's well, you know, it might, uh, it would melt!"

"I get it, Matthew, a chocolate breast could be
too much for a 13-year-old. I'll send it to you
when you're 18."

He must have thought he'd hurt my feelings,
rejecting something so intimate, because a week
later he phoned back. "Nancy, you know that
chocolate breast? Well, could I have it in toffee
apple flavor?"

I began serious bargaining with my surgeon.

"Look," I said, "I'm not going to have all that
reconstruction business, taking skin and fat from
my belly and moving it up to my chest, tattooing
on a nipple to make it look like a real breast that
won't ever FEEL anything because it hasn't any
nerves — I don't want any of that, BUT the
insurance company doesn't know. So could you
just take four little tucks, two each on the sides of
my face, right here by the hairline, and sort of lift
everything up and put it on the insurance papers
as RECONSTRUCTION?" He laughed, but
said he wasn't the guy to do it. When I first saw
the scar he left on my chest, I was shocked and
thought he was probably right. I wouldn't want
something like that on my FACE! But now that
I've seen a variety of other scars, I realize how
skillful he is and think I could have been happy
with whatever he'd managed to come up with.

My friends began to call with stories of their own
cancers, prepping me for what was to come.
Thelma said her first chemo treatment was ghast-
ly, but about twelve days later her husband, John,
took her to Kansas City to celebrate. They
planned to visit the museums, shop, eat in wonderful restaurants. As they walked across the
bridge into the Plaza, a gust of wind lifted
Thelma's hair and took a large hank of it off in
front of her over the water. "My gosh, by the time
I get to the restaurant, I'll be bald." Another gust
of wind, more hair, this time rising in front of
them as they came off the bridge. "Oh," said
Thelma, "I know what a tree feels like in the fall."
A bird flew in, grabbed a wad in its mouth. "Look,
Thelma, you're going to be part of someone's nest."

Germelina called from Kearney, Nebraska.
"Nancy, about a month after my mastectomy my
whole family signed up for a golf tournament,

and I decided to go along just to save my marriage. I didn't have my prosthesis yet. The Cancer Society gave me this cotton substitute to stuff into my old bra, and even though I had large breasts, I thought I could make it work. But I'm a terrible golfer — I decided the one thing I could do well on this trip is to look good. So I bought $500 worth of new outfits. We went to the tournament and I met another friend there — also a bad golfer, so we played together. About the third day, we were between the fourth and fifth holes, when I said, 'Oh, my goodness, I've lost my breast.' I had to tell the whole story to my friend, and then we started to look for it. There it was, a white tent of cotton, lying in the middle of the fairway behind us. My friend said, 'Germelina, that has nothing to do with you. It never had anything to do with you. Absolve yourself of that breast.' So we ignored it and played through.

"At the end of the tournament, everyone in my family, even the eight-year-old, won some kind of trophy for their excellent playing. After all the trophies were given out, the MC said they were giving a very special new trophy this year and called me up to the podium. I was so embarrassed. He said, 'Germelina, we are giving you this trophy because you are the best dressed golfer.' I said, 'You shouldn't give me this. I don't deserve it. Right in the middle of the tournament, I lost my shoulder pad.'"

Twelve days after my first chemo, all my gray hair began to come out in the brush, so I shaved it to a half-inch. One morning a week later, all the dark hair hit the floor of the shower stall. Wow, I thought, a photo opportunity. I rearranged the hairs into words. "HELP. Leaving." And I saved all the hairs themselves to use in a little voodoo doll, just in case one of the people who *should* die ....

Chemotherapy. I suppose there are some people out there who have it easy, but for me there is only one world to describe it: HELL. I survived my first three months of a mix including Adriamycin and Cytoxan pretty well. The anti-nausea medications really work — at $50 a pill! I'd be sick for three days and then gradually regain my energy over the next three weeks until I was zonked again. But when the regime changed to Taxol for three months, all I can say is ARRRGG! Taking the drug wasn't the problem, just four hours in a recliner, reading or listening to tapes. But four days later — WHAM. Horrible deep bone pain from my knees to my toes, and ZAP, a fleet of nettlefish began to swim through my nerves, shooting poisonous darts every 40 seconds. The darts hit one at a time, wherever, my neck, my groin, my armpit, intense stinging for ten seconds fading into a "whacked my funny bone" sort of tingle. This assault of side effects lasted a full week the first round (I can live through HELL if it only lasts a week), two weeks the second (I can live through HELL if it only lasts two weeks), and three the third (I'm not really sure I can live through HELL if it never stops). The pain and darts were masked by painkillers, but they, too, had their side effects, and I languished in a lala-land of wobbly dreaming, stretched out on my bed, restricted from everything but the walk-abouts in my mind to all the places I had been and loved. As my anxiety built for the fourth and last dose, I gave up. "I just can't do this again," I told my oncologist, and her response was: "Well, all the studies are on eight treatments. We don't have any on seven. It's your choice: seven-eighths of a cup should be as good as a full one. See you in January."

Most of my friends and family supported my choice. (They know me well enough to know they'd better.) One friend said it made him anxious to think I hadn't done all I could do to stay alive because he wanted me to stay alive. I said, "Thanks, you're welcome to take that last dose for me."

One doctor friend who had just finished his chemo for leukemia said he was afraid, should my cancer (God forbid) recur, that I would blame myself for not taking that last treatment. Hmmm, yes, perhaps, and yet if that should happen, I'll have so many more potent rages to occupy my mind. There's that major, ongoing rage: Why is nothing being done to find the cause? Billions of dollars are being made on the CURE, but if we take the cause into our minds, do we discover that we are all culpable, all afraid to change our lives?

This story isn't over ... many of the meanings of my journey are still a mystery. I miss my right breast. No one designs clothes for one-breasted women. My granddaughter Weezie assured me that I SHOULD get a prosthesis. When I protested — "They're hot, they'd fall out, the dog might chew it up" — she nodded and said, "I really NEED you to get one so I can take it to show-and-tell."

I've realized it's not possible to lose something without getting something back. Not the same thing, certainly, not what you've lost, but something else. My hair could come in RED. It is rather luxurious to scrub my bald scalp with a washrag. (This is a secret men have been closely guarding.) One day I looked down and thought, "Whoa, look at this." Anything that happens to miss my mouth has a straight shot to the floor. All those years I wondered why there were more crumbs under Harry's chair than mine. Now I think I know.

Perhaps I'll never be a grandmother with a grand teton of bosom to offer to my grandchildren, but I suspect it was never a possibility. There are other shelves to nestle on — like this one, the shelf of story. And always, every day, toffee apple! 🍎

I Don't Want ✎ to Talk About It! ✎

TOM FARLEY*

FOR CHILDREN AGE SIX and up, sleepwetting is a common and embarrassing issue. It affects about seven million school-age kids and teens in the U.S. and Canada.

Estimates are that about 12 percent of school-age children and teens experience sleepwetting more than once a week. Affecting over a third of all five-year-olds, the incidence gradually declines to around 3 percent at age 18. Out of every seven children who sleepwet most nights, only one will "grow out of it" in the next year without help. Six will not.

Most children try to keep it a secret, even from relatives. Many families let sleepwetting go on for years with little support or treatment. Some children receive harmful responses. This can range from blaming and shaming to punishment and emotional and physical abuse. Behavior, learning, and health problems are possible side effects of untreated or badly treated sleepwetting. Criticism or punishment for sleep-

wetting can often have the reverse of its intended effect.

Sleepwetting is not just an issue for those who never have a dry night. Many go through a period of mixed wet and dry nights with little certainty as to which it will be on any given night. This stage reflects growth and progress. But wet/dry uncertainty can increase frustration for both child and family, particularly if the child is moving into preteen or teen years, or if any family members believe it means the child is lazy or not trying hard enough. Resolving sleepwetting conditions is not a simple task as there may be one or more developmental causes as well as contributing environmental factors. Some children find it easier or safer to pretend they don't care than admit trying and failing again and again at something society expects them to be able to do. It should be no surprise that many of these children don't want to talk about it.

> *"Please, Larry!"* His dad frowns at him. *"It's too early on a Monday morning for yelling. We're all right here in the kitchen."*

"I'M NOT YELL — Sorry." Larry lowers his voice. "But you promised, both of you! That was the deal we made when school started. I have to clean up every morning, take a bath before break-

fast, run my stuff in the washer. You said you'd always have the washer empty for me. And you promised not to say anything unless I forgot. In two months, I only forgot once! I had a good excuse. I cleaned up soon as we got back from my soccer game!"

"Larry," his mom says. "I know that wasn't your fault, but I thought you'd —"

"Mom, please!" Larry interrupts her. "No thoughts! No reminders! No hints or questions. Not even 'looks.' If I want to talk about it, I'll tell you."

Larry's mom opens her mouth, closes it again, and nods. His dad just nods.

Outside their classroom that morning, Larry's friend Karl hands him a folded piece of green paper. "I can only have ten boys at my birthday party," Karl whispers. "Same as the age I'll be. So make sure your mom calls mine. Bring your soccer shoes and uniform. Our teams play each other Saturday afternoon."

Larry unfolds the invitation. At the top, Karl has drawn a soccer ball with ten candles on it. Below is the usual party stuff, including the time: 5 p.m. Friday to noon on Saturday. Larry crumples the invitation and stuffs it into his pocket.

Larry's soccer team doesn't practice on Mondays and Fridays. On those days, now that he's in Grade 5, Larry walks home from school alone and lets himself in. This Monday afternoon, he runs his wash, tosses it in the dryer, and has the fresh warm sheets back on his bed before his parents get home.

"Here, Mom." Larry hands her the wrinkled invitation. "Please call Karl's house and say I can't come Friday night. What's our excuse?"

"The real one," his mom tells him. "Grandpa Henry's birthday dinner. We'll pick you up from school just after two o'clock. Be sure to pack your soccer stuff. We may have to drop you off at your game on the way back Saturday afternoon."

"I need better shin guards by then," Larry reminds her. "Can't we come back Friday night? It's only a couple hours away."

"Three," his mom corrects him. "And Henry insists we stay over. Remember to set up your sleeping bag before you leave for school Friday morning."

"You don't have to remind me!"

Larry does not stay to listen while his mom calls Karl's house.

Tuesday, Larry's parents stop for groceries and laundry supplies before they pick him up from soccer practice. While his parents put things away, Larry moves his wash to the dryer. In a shopping bag in his room he finds a new pair of shin guards. Under them is a package a bit bigger and heavier than a new roll of paper towels. Blue letters on soft green plastic say "Waterproof Absorbent Underpants."

"NO!" Larry frowns. "I got too big to sleep in training pants in first grade. How can they think these would fit me now?" He throws the package down on his plastic mattress cover and notices the size: Large, 65 to 85 pounds. These could fit him.

"Mom!" Larry finds her reading the newspaper. "I don't want them. Take them back. Why did you get them?"

"You said you need a new pair for your game Saturday."

"Not the shin guards!" Larry holds his hands in the shape of the package. "The other things."

"Ahhh, those." Larry's mom looks up from her newspaper. "Another mom mentioned to me how well they worked for her family, especially for trips."

"Oh," Larry says. "You mean —"

"Friday night at Grandpa Henry's?" Larry's mom finishes his thought. "If you feel like it. But I thought you didn't want to talk about it."

Larry opens his mouth, closes it again, and nods.

Larry puts the package back into the shopping bag and shoves it under his bed. He doesn't think about it again until he wakes up Wednesday morning. Wearing those pants could save him from doing a lot of laundry.

At bedtime that night, Larry opens one end of the plastic package. He pulls out one of the pants and unfolds it. It's all white with stretchy sides and a padded waterproof middle. At Grandpa Henry's house, one of these would be a lot easier to hide than the big trash bag and bath towel he'd put inside his sleeping bag there before. Larry tries to fold up the pants and stuff them back into the plastic package. It doesn't want to fit. He throws the package and the pants back under his bed.

All day Thursday, Larry wonders how well those pants really work. That night he decides he better try one out before his trip to Grandpa Henry's.

Friday morning Larry wakes up with dry bedding and a different problem. He hops out of bed and stops his dad in the hallway.

"How do I get rid of it?" Larry whispers.

"Rid of what?" his dad asks before he notices Larry's dry pajamas. "Oh, wait." He finds a plastic bag newspapers come in. "Put it in here. Tie a knot in the bag. Be sure you empty the bathroom trash before you leave for school."

"I won't forget!" Larry is just glad his dad didn't ask if it was wet.

The pants work great at Grandpa Henry's house. Larry gets back Saturday in time to help his soccer team beat Karl's team 3 to 2.

After the game, Karl says, "Sorry you missed my party, Larry. Can you come tonight? My big brother went on a Scout campout, so I've got two beds."

"No!" Larry tries to think of an excuse.

"Did you have a good time at your grandfather's birthday?" Karl asks. "Did you try out those pants my mom suggested?"

"Your mom?" Larry stares at his friend. "How did she …? Do you …?"

"Not since the end of summer," Karl says. "Until then I wore them every night. Please come tonight. Bring whatever you want to sleep in. I won't tell anyone."

Larry opens his mouth, closes it again, and nods.

For going to bed at Karl's house, Larry puts on a pair of the pants under his pajamas. Karl notices that and takes pants like them from a box under his bed.

"I thought you didn't need those anymore," Larry says.

"Got four left," Karl answers. "Thought you'd feel better if I wore one if you did. They're just pants. Wearing them is lots better than waking up in a wet bed, right?"

Larry opens his mouth, closes it again, and nods.

Karl takes a book from the box. "But here's what I really want to show you."

"*Dry All Night.*" Larry reads the title aloud.

"There's a story in it about a boy like us," Karl says. "Last summer I read this every night and practiced what it said. It took a month before things started to change much, and three months before I'd be sure to sleep dry. You've got five months until our class goes to Outdoor Education Camp for a week next spring."

The two boys sit together on the floor to read the story. Then Karl gets out the folder of charts he kept all summer. On them, Karl had marked if he woke up wet or dry or almost dry, and when he'd done his exercises.

"Exercises?" Larry asks.

"To make my bladder bigger and stronger," Karl says. "Mom had this tutor come and tell us how to do them and why they work. He made it lots easier for us to talk about it. He gave me the blank charts and checked back each week to see how I was doing. If you want to get a tutor for learning to sleep dry, I think my mom could do that now. It's free, but one of your parents has to call her to set it up."

Larry opens his mouth, closes it again, and shakes his head.

"Well at least let me loan you the book," Karl insists. He puts *Dry All Night* into Larry's backpack along with some unused charts. And here's copies of those two exercises, just in case you feel like trying them."

At home the next day, Larry takes his backpack to his room and gets out the book. He rereads the story. Then he reads all the other parts of the book for kids and most of the parts for parents.

Just before Sunday dinner, Larry walks into the kitchen holding the book and charts and exercise pages behind his back.

"Mom, Dad? I — I — I'm ready to talk about it." 🍂

TELLING THIS STORY

When I use this story, I make it clear that the characters are fictional, but the situations are drawn from real life, including use of the book Dry All Night and having a tutor work with someone who sleepwets. Friends from several Quaker Meetings in Northern California have encouraged my vision of a family-to-family support network to offer such tutoring. This concept of volunteer tutoring is based on the model developed in effective community literacy programs such as Project Read. Tutors can help families understand causes, agree on a management plan, identify reasonable goals, and work toward them together.

For several years now I've served on the staff of a one-week Quaker residential summer camp for nearly 30 kids entering Grades 5, 6, and 7. I get to drive a van, tell stories, and be a sort of honorary grandfather, especially to campers who have some difficulty being at camp. I usually share this story on the first night as part of our support for campers with disabilities, medical conditions, dietary needs, etc. About all we can do in a one-week

program is encourage acceptance, responsible management, and mutual support. I sometimes follow the story with a discussion using the first seven questions below. I then close with the last two questions for kids to think about on their own.

1. What is the "it" Larry doesn't want to talk about and why?
2. How is that revealed in the story?
3. What do you like about Larry's family?
4. How do you feel about the deal Larry has at home to start with?
5. What helps Larry decide to talk about it?
6. What do you think will happen then?
7. What are some other issues kids might not want to talk about?
8. Do you have or could you be a friend like Karl?
9. Do you know someone who needs that kind of friend?

Each year the camp directors try to be aware of any new campers likely to sleepwet. One year I shared this story with such a camper ahead of time. I helped find roommates who could be trusted to support that camper's privacy and security. The camper agreed to bring GoodNites™ waterproof absorbent underpants, wear one each night, and — if wet — dispose of it properly in the morning. Besides the two of us, only the directors, counselors, and the three roommates knew of this plan. That camper had no problems and has used plans like this for wilderness camps, sports team trips, and other overnight stays. The next summer, that camper returned along with three others who needed sleepwetting support. One had a hard time admitting this and talking about it. I used a longer story about kids with similar issues to help that camper accept support from staff and talk about sleepwetting with the returning camper. They ended up sharing a tent at another week-long event. Their experience has led me to develop more stories of kids sharing important issues with each other.

Using stories to help school-age children end sleepwetting is also part of the process in the book *Dry All Night* by Alison Mack. She uses the term sleepwetting rather than bedwetting for loss of bladder control when asleep because she feels it brings up fewer negative emotional responses and describes the condition more accurately. The children's section of *Dry All Night* contains two stories, one for boys and one for girls. The stories show children using imaging or visualizations similar to those used by many individual performance athletes. Both stories are written at about Grade 3 readability level, but could be adapted for teens or read aloud with children as young as six. Because this process can take some time and includes rereading the stories almost every night, a child may need a personal copy of the book.

To order *Dry All Night* or learn more about understanding, managing, and ending sleepwetting, visit the Sleepwetting Forum website at <http://www.spont.com/sleepwetting.html>.

CHILDREN
WITH
MEDICAL
PROBLEMS
RECLAIM
THEIR LIVES

Digital storytelling with band-aides and blackboards: When chronic illness — or some other medical problem — goes to school

JOAN FLEITAS

BAND-AIDES AND BLACKBOARDS (www.faculty.fairfield.edu/fleitas/contents.html) is a website created to sensitize people to what it is like to grow up with medical problems. Children around the world who are doing just that have written and posted more than 100 stories that are poignant and varied and speak of the stigma that so many of them experience. In addition to the narratives, the site contains fantasies; hints from the children to health care providers, parents, and teachers; and a hospital tour in which children in the hospital orient their healthy classmates to the ins and outs of hospital life. Through the tour, children with medical problems are able to move from the role of victim to the more empowered role of expert. The title of the site — Band-Aides and Blackboards — suggests the link between hospital and school, and is a response to many teachers who tend to treat the medical issues of their students as if they are invisible.

On the website, children with serious medical problems have spoken about a wide range of dilemmas. For some children, the dilemma is the ambivalence of enjoying extra privileges, yet hating the reason that they are offered. For others, it is the shame associated with medical diagnoses, and a need that grows from that shame to keep hidden what is not directly observable. For many,

it is the ache to be popular and the belief that popularity is purchased with the coins of conformity. When that conformity forces children to ignore their need for medication and treatment, and when it demands of them a secrecy that consumes energy as it isolates, the price is very high.

The children who share their stories are bothered to some degree by the social dimensions of their medical conditions. Many prefer not to talk about, or even acknowledge, their differences. Acknowledging them seems to tattoo the reality of the disease, condition, illness, or medical problem on their identity. What they call it, then, becomes extremely important, with certain words having more power to isolate than others. As one child wrote, "I have this condition called diabetes. It's not a disease, because you can't catch it." And from another, recalling his early school experiences with muscular dystrophy, "What I have is neither a chronic illness nor a disease. It's just a condition that seemed to affect others more than it did me, though I was teased unmercifully for my differences."

The following remarks, from a page titled "Tips for Teachers from the Band-Aide Experts," are a challenge to all of us:

I wish you would treat me like a student instead of like a patient. I'm not sick, so when you ask me if I feel okay all the time, this heart problem that I have feels like a heavy weight.

Remember the bag of hospital supplies that I brought to class? Thanks for letting me show the stuff to everyone. I felt really cool, since I knew what everything was, and most of the other kids didn't.

I really want to be just like everybody else, so please don't expect me to give lessons about my leukemia to the class. Then I stand out like a sore thumb.

I have to drink a lot of water to stay healthy, and it was so nice of you to let everyone in the class keep water bottles on their desks. It didn't make me feel weird.

When you asked me privately if I'd like to tell the class about my arthritis, it made me feel special, like I was in charge. Thanks!

When I'm not paying attention in class, it's often because my heart isn't sending out enough oxygen, not because I'm being bad. I wish that you would know those signs, so that I wouldn't always be getting in trouble.

Since none of my classmates have problems like that, I really appreciated it when my teacher read a book about taking epilepsy to school. The neurologist sent it to my mom, and she gave it to the teacher. The good thing is that now the teachers know about seizures in case I have one at school. It also felt pretty cool to have the teacher read a book about me!

What a surprise to get a videotape from the class when I was in the hospital. All the other kids were so impressed. My roommate said, "Boy, you must really be popular."

Please be aware of how much of an impact you have on little ones. I was diagnosed with diabetes when I was in second grade. My teacher sat the entire class down and told them that I had "a disease." From second grade on through high school, friends were few and far between; not many people wanted to be friends with "that girl with the disease."

When kids were making fun of me for being clumsy, you had a class meeting about all of our differences. I never thought of my muscular dystrophy that way before, and it really helped me.

The website provides a peek at the incredible resilience of children in the face of serious illness. As such, it reminds us to cherish the children we care for and to better appreciate our lives.

This kid called me the human bowling ball when I came back to school without hair. I just told her that I sold my hair for a million dollars. I told her that I was going to buy a kangaroo with the money, and of course a zoo to keep it in.

Sally Goes to School

JOAN FLEITAS AND CHILDREN FROM AROUND THE WORLD*

THIS IS A STORY WITH many authors. Children from around the world participated in its development, children growing up with some type of medical problem — with some type of wrinkle in the fabric of their childhood. They wrote to me of their lives, and I have tried to incorporate much of what they shared in this story. Their notes to me provided snapshots of their humor and courage, childishness and wisdom. I hope that I have done them justice and have conveyed with accuracy the reality that children with health concerns are first of all children.

The story takes place in an elementary school Grade 3 classroom. I chose eight-year-olds because teasing seems to peak in Grade 4, and I thought that some of it might be nipped in the bud if children learned to be more tolerant of differences before that time. I've tried to write the story for an audience of children in Grades 2 through 5, with the hopes that other children and adults will not feel excluded by the characters or language.

> *"Welcome, Sally, come on in — I've saved a seat for you."*
> *The teacher pointed to a desk right in front in the very first row.*
> *As I closed the big door and walked across the room, I started to blush.*

I could feel my face turning bright pink, and I was sure that everybody was looking at me. Why couldn't I make myself invisible, like in the movies? It just wasn't fair. But I did as I was told, and as I slid down into that seat, on this fourth day of school, in Mrs. Edward's Grade 3 classroom, I tried hard to disappear.

The room was big with lots of windows and lots of desks (the kind that open up), and an old-fashioned blackboard with everybody's names written in script. The windows had little blinds in front of them, but you could still see outside if you looked hard, and outside, right across the street and behind some bushes, was the children's hospital.

I didn't go to school on opening day because I was in that hospital, on the fourth floor, in the green room with the television set and the two magic beds. I thought that the beds were magic because I could make mine go up and down, just by pushing a button. And when I pushed another button, a nurse would talk to me, right through the wall. I guess that button was part of a walkie-talkie, sort of like the one I got for Christmas last year. There were so many new things to learn about in that place.

And at first I was afraid. There was a lot to be scared about, too. All those doctors, and all that medicine, and my mom and dad looking like they were going to cry. And there were the strange feelings in my body, and the strange things that I saw in that hospital. It was so much for an eight-year-old to get used to. But I did, finally, and I even found some things about the hospital that were funny! Not funny enough to make me want to stay there, though. I was very happy on the day that I left that place, on the day that I got dressed up in my 101 Dalmatians overalls and said good-bye to all the hospital people. So much had happened to me since I left my cabin at the camp. It was hard to believe.

But that's not what I was thinking about right now. How could I, when I was absolutely sure that every kid in the room was staring at me? I'm just like everybody else, I kept thinking. Just like everybody else! It *is* true that I like pizza and jump rope and going to the movies like Amy and Margaret and Fred and even Joshua (though he was terrible at jump rope). And it *is* true that I love animals, especially wolves, and so does Stephanie. But it is also true that I, Sally Kathleen Preston, got sick and they didn't — at least not like I did. They didn't get the kind of sickness that just doesn't go away, the kind that I'll have to live with from now on. From now on! At least that's what they told me. And it made me so sad.

Here's how it all began. I was eight years old on August 30, and it was the last day of sleepover camp. Everybody came to my cabin in the morning to sing happy birthday and to bring me a big stack of pancakes. The pancakes were spectacular! "Sally" was written on the very top in purple frosting, exactly the color of my old Barney doll. And there were nine candles, too, one for each of my eight years, and an extra one for good luck. I was so excited and so surprised that I really didn't notice the weird feeling in my body! And after the cakes and the song, when I did pay attention to it, I tried my best not to think about how strange I felt.

I had never been eight before, after all, and I figured that maybe getting older was supposed to be like this. I decided to think about Mom and Dad coming to pick me up instead. They would want to know about all my amazing camp adventures. You see, this was my very first time away from home, and I had been at camp for six whole nights. I had so much to tell them that I tucked my body feelings away and concentrated on everything else. There's always a lot to do in a cabin the day that camp's over.

And that's what I was doing, concentrating hard, using all of my energy to pack my clothes. When I had stuffed half of them into my giant striped bag, this sickness pounced into my life like a mean tiger from a nightmare. That's how scary it seemed. All of a sudden I felt very tired and very thirsty and very hot and so dizzy that the cabin began to spin around. And then my eyes slammed shut.

When I woke up, I was so confused — I didn't know where I was. I thought that I should still be in my cabin, but Mom and Dad were both right there with me, holding my hand and smiling, telling me that I was in the hospital and that I was okay. Okay? I was scared to death! This was the second time I had ever been in a hospital, and the first time was terrible. That's the time I was visiting Dad's grandpa. He was very sick and he died the day after I went to see him. So when my mom said that I was in the hospital, I figured that I was stuck in the middle of a bad dream. I wondered if I would die too.

The next thing I did was open my eyes really wide and look around. There were people with blue and green clothes on like pajamas, and the room I was in was big and noisy with beds everywhere, and mystery sounds all around, and television screens hanging from the ceiling. If it weren't for Mom and Dad, I know that I would have screamed. Just then Dad reached over to give me a big hug. That's when I felt the tube attached to my arm, and that's when I saw it, and that's when I began to cry.

That's what I felt like doing right now, too, right in front of Mrs. Edward and all the students in that Grade 3 classroom. Even though I saw some of them smiling at me when I sat down, I could see that Peter was not. In fact, he was sticking his tongue out at me and scrunching up his face in the ugliest way. I didn't want to cry, but that's what was beginning to happen. Crying is a babyish thing to do, I kept telling myself. So although everyone knows that it's hard to squeeze tears back in when they make up their minds to swim out, I tried to do just that.

And it worked, too, until I heard Nina whisper to the new boy sitting next to her, "Look at that baby. I bet she's going to start crying any minute!" Well, that's exactly what happened next. I was horrified! As the tears wiggled down my cheeks, I covered my face with my hands and pretended that I was invisible. That used to work when I was a little girl — If I couldn't see anyone, then I thought that no one could see me. Presto! Magic! But no such luck today.

Abby was sitting in the desk next to me, and when she saw what was happening she raised her hand and asked Mrs. Edward if the two of us could be excused to go to the bathroom. Abby was such a nice friend, and she knew just what would make me feel better. She gave me a big hug when we got into the hall and told me that Nina was a meanie. Then we held hands all the way to the girl's bathroom. When we got there, Abby turned the cold water on and rolled out some paper towel. I made a cup out of my hands, filled it with water, and took a giant drink. Lots of the water escaped onto my face, and some of it stayed on my eyelashes, but it sure made me feel better!

"I was so scared that everyone would tease me because of this stupid sickness, Abby. I hate it!" I was about to cry again because I was feeling so sorry for myself, but instead I swallowed hard and turned my mouth rightside-up, into a smile instead. "Thank you for being my friend," I said. "If you can keep a secret, I'll tell you all about what happened, but you have to promise not to tell anybody, not even your sister."

When Mrs. Edward came in to see what was going on, she found us sitting on the floor of the bathroom, giggling. I had told Abby everything about the hospital and about my medical problem and the medicine that I'd have to take forever. And Abby didn't make fun of me. Not at all. So next I told her about the funny clothes that everyone wore and about the trick that I played on my nurse and about the magic bed and the walkie-talkie. Everything seemed so much better now.

Mrs. Edward took one look at the two of us and she started to smile. "Sally," she said, "it looks like you had a tough time in the classroom. I'm happy that you're feeling better now. This year we will be doing a new activity in the third grade. I think that it will be a lot of fun and will help us to learn about one another. I call it 'This is My Life.' Every Friday, one of the children will get to be the star for the day. Everyone who wants to will have a turn. The stars will get to decorate the bulletin board with photographs of their life and with anything else that they'd like to tell the class about .... Would either of you like to go first?"

Well, I looked at Abby, whose eyes were big and sparkly and whose smile told me that she thought it was the greatest idea.

I wasn't so sure. "I just came out of the hospital, Mrs. Edward, and I don't think I want anyone but Abby to know. What if the kids laugh at me or treat me like I'm special? I'd hate that! I want to be like everyone else."

"Special? I think that each one of the children in Grade 3 is special," Mrs. Edward said. "And as for laughing, well, I think that kids laugh mostly when they don't understand, and when they're afraid." I thought of the way I had giggled when I first saw Heather in the hospital, and I knew that what Mrs. Edward said was true.

Heather was a girl I met in the hospital who didn't have any hair. What she did have was a baseball cap, so without any hair she looked a little bit like a boy. That was certainly confusing to me. I thought that I might catch whatever it was that made all the hair fall out. People would think that I was a boy too. Yuck! So here's what I did. I pretended not to look at Heather, even though we were both in the playroom. Maybe, I hoped, if I don't look at her, she'll go away.

Just when I was about to sneak a glance to see if the trick worked, a nurse appeared and said, "Oh, here you are, Sally. Have you two met one another?" I just giggled (that's what I always do when I'm nervous), and I started to leave the room when Heather said, "Nope, I just came in today." Before I could escape to my own room, the nurse, whose name was Tanya, introduced the two of us to one another, and Heather reached out to shake my hand. That's right, to shake my hand! I was so scared, thinking that I would turn bald any minute, but what could I do? Well, I did what I learned to do when I was younger. I went ahead and shook Heather's hand, and when Heather said, "Nice to meet you," I stopped giggling long enough to say, "Nice to meet you, too."

That's how our friendship started, and for the rest of my time in the hospital, the two of us were always together, like ketchup and French fries. My hair didn't disappear either! When I learned that Heather had a different kind of medical problem, and that her hair fell out because of the strong medicines she needed to take, and that she

was still nine-year-old Heather — funny, friendly Heather — then I relaxed, and I wasn't afraid of her anymore.

Because of Heather, I got to meet other kids who were sick. I'm shy, so there's no way that I would have met anybody by myself. With her, it was easy and it was fun. She'd just knock on a door, say, "Hi, how come you're in the hospital?" and the next thing I'd know, we'd all be watching a video together. Everybody had a story to tell, and I learned about all of the kids and a little about the diseases they had to put up with. What I learned most was that the diseases and the kids were not the same thing. Just like me. I've got something called diabetes. It's a problem that I'll just have to get used to. But it's not who I am. And believe me, there's a big difference! I met so many children and made so many friends while I was in the hospital.

I was still thinking about Heather and the hospital and this diabetes thing, and I was still sitting on the floor of the bathroom with Abby. Mrs. Edward was standing next to us, real nice, waiting to see if one of us would like to be star for the day. I just couldn't decide what to do. Mom said I didn't need to tell anybody about what happened if I didn't want to. She said that it might make me feel better if I told my favorite friends, though, because then they would understand if I had to leave the class to go to the nurse. Dad said that talking about things that bothered him always helped him to feel better, and that it might help me, too. I didn't have to worry about what to do right away because Abby beat me to it and said that she'd like to be the star this Friday. She wanted to tell everybody about the new bike she got for her birthday, and about her baby brother who fell down and cut his lip last week.

The three of us walked back to the classroom, and the rest of the morning was much better. I knew that I'd have to go to the nurse to test my blood every day at lunchtime. That's what you have to do if you have this type of problem. The test checks how much sugar is in the blood. If there's too much sugar, then I need to get a shot of some medicine called insulin. I hate the blood test with the needle poking my finger, and I hate the insulin too, even though it made me feel better in the hospital. I certainly do NOT want to get sick like that again, so I guess I'll just have to put up with the finger pokes and the insulin. The neat thing is that I'm learning to do the test, and the insulin all by myself. That does make me feel sort of important. Eight-year-olds aren't babies anymore, you know! In the hospital, Tanya told me that if I eat healthy foods and check my blood when I'm supposed to, I'll feel great. She said that I can still jump rope and camp out and play video games and paint wolf pictures. So that's good. I'll still be Sally Kathleen Preston, just like before this whole thing started!

Ms. Hall was the school nurse, and when I went to the health office, there she was. She was new this year, and she looked like a grandmother. She had orange curly hair, and her dress was the same color of lavender that was in a box of crayons. She had a voice that purred a little bit when she talked, and a way about her that was so comfortable. She made me feel happy, and she made me feel calm. I told her how Peter and Tina made fun of me.

"Sometimes," Ms. Hall told me, "people get so busy worrying about themselves that they don't stop to think what life might be like for others, and they can't imagine what it's like to feel different. That goes for all people — big ones, little ones, and in-between ones," she continued. "I have an idea that might be good for everybody in the class," she said as she helped me get ready to poke my finger and test my blood. When I asked her

to tell me about it, she looked as if she might, then she turned her face up to look at the ceiling, as if she were deciding. Then she told me, "I'll tell Mrs. Edward about it, and you will learn about it soon enough." I love surprises, but I hoped that I would learn about this one soon.

The next day when I went into the classroom, I was with Abby. It was easier to start the day with my friend. I still noticed Peter and Nina. First, Peter made a face at me, and when I looked at Nina, she just turned hers away. I wish they had diabetes. I wish they could be me so that they would know what it feels like to be the only one to have this stupid problem.

Mrs. Edward told us that we would all get to wear stars today. She asked us to line up at the front of the room so we could choose our stars. The stars were in a covered box. On the top of the box there was a hole just big enough for a hand to reach inside. When we took the stars from the box, we were supposed to write our names in big letters so that we would soon get to know one another. You see, there were a lot of new children in Grade 3 this year.

We noticed that some of the stars were red and others were blue. Once we wrote our names on them, Mrs. Edward helped us pin them to the front of our shirts. We all looked very pleased. The blue star that I chose made me feel important. Everybody started to return to their seats, but Mrs. Edward stopped us and said, "Not so fast. We will be switching seats. The students with the blue stars will sit in the last three rows in the room, and those with the red stars will sit in the first three rows. Red stars, you go first. You may choose your seats."

This was fun, I thought, like some kind of a game, except that Abby had picked a red star and wouldn't be able to sit near me. She was sitting down in my old seat instead, in the very first row.

It took me a few minutes to gather up my school supplies because my arithmetic book slid off the desk. The pages got discombobulated (I think that means all messed up), so I had to straighten them out first. By the time I reached the back of the room, there were only two seats left — one next to Nina, and the other next to Peter. Yikes. I wondered why we needed to change seats, anyway. It wasn't so much fun after all, I decided. I sat down in the desk next to Peter and made sure not to look at him. I was looking instead at Marcus, the tallest boy in the class. He had still not reached the only seat left — the one next to Nina. I think that he was confused about this star thing.

Mrs. Edward started tapping her foot, and she said in a very stern voice, "It seems like the blue stars are slowpokes. Just look at them all." Well, all the kids in the front of the room turned around, and they started to giggle. Mrs. Edward giggled too. I couldn't believe it. She wrote these words on the board, "Obey quickly," and then she told all of us with blue stars to copy them down ten times. We grumbled about having to do such a stupid thing, and she then wrote some more words, "The teacher is in charge," and told us that we now had to write that sentence ten times too. We decided that we'd better not say anything else.

While we were busy with all of this writing, I could see the kids with the red stars gather in a circle around her desk. She passed out some colored clay for them to work with and then suggested that they make animals for a project about Africa. The lucky ducks. I wished I had chosen a red star.

After we were finished with our work, we started to talk to one another. Peter turned to me and said, "This isn't fair, is it?" and I had to agree. Mrs. Edward looked up from her own sculpture and said, "It's very difficult for us to work up here with all that noise in the back. When you're finished writing, fold your hands and be quiet." And that's not all she did. For the rest of the hour (though it seemed like at least five hours), she told the red stars that they were the artistic ones. Now that was just plain silly, because Fredrika Evans was the best artist in the world, and she had a blue star pinned right on the middle of her shirt.

Then she read a story to the whole class, and when she asked questions about it, she only called on the kids with the red stars. Even when their answers were wrong, she thanked them for trying and told them that their answers were "good guesses." Mrs. Edward let her "teacher's pets," the kids with the red stars, go out and get water from the fountain, but when we asked to go too, she told us that we couldn't. She said she just knew that we'd create a disturbance in the hall.

While they were out getting water, Mrs. Edward did something very interesting. She came to the back of the room and asked us how we were feeling. At first nobody answered. I know that I was scared to say anything, and I guess that everybody else was too. Then Peter said that he was mad, and sad too. I looked at him and nodded my head, telling him that I knew just what he meant. Oliver said that he felt left out of all the good stuff. Clarise agreed and wished out loud that she were back in Grade 2. Mrs. Edward told us to remember those feelings. She said that they were important and that we would be talking about them after lunch.

When the kids with the red stars returned to the room, Mrs. Edward was still in the back, talking to us. We were laughing now, just imagining the sight of a blade of grass running away from its yard. That's the story she was telling us when the other kids walked into the class. She looked annoyed when Abby and a new boy, Harold, came to the back to see what was so funny. Mrs. Edward told them to sit down in the front and to take out their spelling books. Then she told them all to turn to page 23 and to memorize all of the words. Words like stomach and potato. Hard words that we hadn't even looked at before. That's what she said to them. And she told them that they would have a test on those words in 30 minutes. Leaping lizards — that sounded just plain awful! She whispered to us, "You don't need to take the test because I know that you already know those words." Of course we didn't — at least I didn't, but I sure wasn't going to tell her!

So there we were, in the back of the room but feeling like we were on top of the world because Mrs. Edward was being so nice to us. I wasn't even thinking about my medical problem anymore; I was just thinking about how much fun I was having. While the red stars were doing another assignment (this time writing the names of each state), we were taking turns telling everyone about our summer vacations. When I told about going to the hospital, Peter looked at me differently. I think that he was amazed about all that had happened to me. He wasn't looking mean at all, just sort of impressed, if you know what I mean. All of a sudden I heard the school-bell ring, and I knew that it was time to go to lunch.

Lunch was a little strange, too, because all of us who had been sitting in the back stayed together. I know that I didn't want to sit with Abby because I figured that she would be mad at me for having a good time while she was doing work. I knew that I was a little mad at her for being in the favorite group earlier. At least Peter wasn't being mean to me anymore, and even Nina didn't do anything at lunch that made me sad. In fact, Nina was talking about how confused the whole morning had been, and I could sure agree with that. We ate our chicken nuggets and peas and macaroni salad, and when everyone was drinking milk with their ice cream, I just took out some special cookies to eat instead. Now I have to admit that I was embarrassed about that, but I didn't want to get sick again, that's for sure! And the cookies that Mom had baked actually tasted good. Maybe diabetes wasn't the end of the world after all.

When we walked back into the classroom after lunch, Mrs. Edward had arranged all of the desks in a circle, and she asked us to sit down wherever we wanted. Then she pulled up a chair between Ramona and Joseph, and, boy, did they ever look uncomfortable. Soon they calmed down, as we all did, because she was being so nice to everyone. She said that Ms. Hall had told her about an interesting experiment, an idea that she had to help us understand something special. Mrs. Edward said that she decided to try it out this morning.

"And that's exactly what I did," she explained. "Can you figure out what the experiment was all about? What the special something was that Ms. Hall hoped you would learn?"

Abby told Mrs. Edward, "I learned that I didn't like it when you were telling stories to the blue stars and we had to do work." Peter added that he felt the same way when he had to write "The teacher is in charge" ten times over while the red stars got to make clay animals. "It seemed like they were treated special and we weren't," added Nina.

"How about when I was nice to your group — how did you feel then?" Mrs. Edward asked us. Kids started answering around the circle: "It was fun." "I felt good." "I felt like you thought we were smart." "I wanted it to be that way all the time."

"So, then," Mrs. Edward said, looking around the circle, "what do you think the special something to be learned was all about?"

(Ask your audience the same question: "What do you think the special something to be learned was all about?" listening to what the children in your audience suggest, continue the story with:)

Joseph pointed at the clock on the wall over the desks and we saw that it was almost time for our gym class. I wondered if we would ever find out what the secret was. And then, here's what Mrs. Edward said to us: "Did you think that I wanted you to learn what it feels like to be left out? Did you think that I wanted you to experience how awful it feels to be treated unfairly? Did you learn that the world would be a better place if everyone cared about everyone else? Did you learn that differences on the outside cover up special treasures on the inside, and that to hunt for the treasure you have to understand about the difference? If you thought about these sorts of things, I think that you are one very special person, and the world is a better place because you're in it!"

That was Ms. Hall's plan that made my life in school so much happier. Now I know that it is not so bad to be Sally Kathleen Preston at eight years old. In fact — I think I'm going to like it a lot! 🕭

QUESTIONS ABOUT THE STORY FOR STUDENTS TO DISCUSS

1. Most kids are nervous and excited at the same time when they start school. What goes on in your head the very first day of school each year?

2. What if you learned that you had a medical problem over the summer? What would you be feeling? How would you behave when you came into the classroom?

3. After you have heard the story "Sally Goes to School," write a paragraph explaining what the nurse's great idea was all about.

4. If you were the principal of your school, what would you do to make the school a kinder place for kids with any type of difference? How would you suggest Sally behave if she gets teased anymore?

AN IDEA FOR SCHOOL OR HOME

Everybody dreams of being popular. Discover what's special about each of your classmates, friends, or family. Remember what's special about you too! Share with each of them what you think their gift is that makes them someone special to you.

Kinka:
A Story About the Birth of a Very Special Tortoise

DEBORAH ROBINS*

AUSTRALIAN TEACHER-LIBRARIAN Deborah Robins is the mother of a 14-year-old son with a common (and catastrophic) genetic disorder — Duchenne Muscular Dystrophy. There is no known cure. For years, Deb and her e-pal Pat Furlong (founder of Parent Project Muscular Dystrophy and mother of Christopher and Patrick, who both succumbed to Duchenne in their mid-teens) have been "howling our grief into our computer screens, like she-wolves howling across a lake — only the Pacific Ocean is a big lake!"

Kinka was originally conceived as the first in a series of picture books designed to explain catastrophic disease to children. Deborah writes,

"My aim was to illustrate the basic question one asks in the face of suffering, which is pretty universal — Why? Why was I born? Sometimes it isn't about us — it's about the effect we have on others and how that might snowball years later. Also, I wanted to show that by a twist of fate, sometimes a handicap can be an advantage, the old 'one door shuts, and another opens' proverb."

Deborah adds, "To distance the child sufficiently from her/his symbolic self, the anthropomorphism was necessary. But although the animals talk, the life cycle of the western swamp tortoise is accurate … the predators, too!"

— *David H. Albert*

All day the hot sun burned into the hard dirt by the waterhole.
But that evening the sky grew gray and then purple and then black.
Hard drops of water pelted into the cracked ground until the dirt melted into a thick,
oozy mud and loosened the sandy bank where I was sleeping in my egg.

That's what Mama said happened just before I hatched. She and Papa had left their own burrows and were waiting in the waterhole. Neither had seen each other nor any other tortoises since the water dried up. They had burrowed down deep into the moist earth to escape the hot sun and to sleep through the summer. The rain must have woken them. Mama watched the nests along the creek bank. She had laid five eggs there last spring.

She saw the first of my brothers and sisters and cousins break out of the mounds two days after the wet season began. They were only as long as young gum leaves, but they were clever. They knew which way to the creek, and they headed off straightaway.

Mama said that by the next daybreak, 10 or 20 more baby tortoises had dug their way out of the nests. The rain had set in and was making the waterhole bigger and bigger. Soon, if the weather held, the waterholes would join up and Mama and Papa would see all their friends again.

Sometimes Mama and her sisters remember the babies that didn't make it to the river. Some of the little ones were taken in the beaks of the swooping shadows and some by the big land lizard, old goanna. They never saw them again.

Now and then, the grownups will look at me and say that I am *palari* — different. They tell Mama that it would have been better if old goanna or one of the black sky shadows had taken me instead. Mama doesn't answer; she just tells them the story of my hatching.

The last batch of babies had hatched and they were scurrying for their lives to the river. Mama looked toward her nest one last time and saw me poke my head out of the sand. Mama knew there was something different about me. I wasn't like the other babies. My shell was not a perfect oval shape. One side of my back was large and gnarled, and the misshapen shell made me slow and awkward. She wondered how I would carry my heavy burden down to the river.

I don't remember this, but Mama said that I was clever, too. I sniffed the air once and headed straight for the river.

Mama's heart was in her throat as she watched me crawl down the muddy bank. The black shadows crossed over me again and again. They didn't seem to think I was a tortoise.

Maybe I was the wrong shape!

I made it to the river. There were baby tortoises up ahead.

In the river was a new danger. The river lizard waited. Mama had seen him snapping at the babies and scooping them up in his long jaws.

I reached the cool water and waded straight in. I could swim much better than I could crawl! I wasn't far behind the other babies anymore. I felt free and flimsy in the water. Mama was far away in the mangroves on the far bank, but she saw what happened next.

Death sliced through the murky water. Croc was closing in. Like an arrow, he was cruising just behind us. He opened his mouth wide and snapped.

I swam hard. The two rows of teeth smashed together. Lucky for me, I had changed course.

Mama's eyes twinkled with amusement. She said that I never did swim straight. My shell was crooked and it made me swim crooked. It is true. Sometimes I swim around in circles if I don't concentrate!

When I got to Mama and Papa, there were only two other babies left in our little family. Up close, Mama could see that I was not like any baby she had ever seen before. My strange shell didn't matter to Mama, though. She said that I was meant to live, that I had struggled hard to live.

She called me Kinka. It is what the black people do when they are happy. They make a call like the kookaburra. It is the happiest sound Mama ever heard.

I heard her tell all the other nosy old tortoises that I am special. Mama says that I have a big heart, just like my big, lopsided shell. I love Mama. And I don't think my crooked shell is so bad either. It got me to the river and it got me past Croc to Mama! 🐢

Binding the unraveled sleeve:
Story and music come to oncology camp

TOM MCDERMOT

FOR THE PAST SEVEN YEARS I have had the privilege of sharing stories and songs with kids of all ages in oncology camps and pediatric hospitals across the United States. The opportunity came to me through my work with Celebration Shop, Inc., an award-winning, non-profit company dedicated to providing healing resources and performances to chronically ill children and adults. The company is headed by singer-songwriter Jim Newton, who, along with co-lyricist Noel Paul Stookey (of Peter, Paul and Mary), tours hundreds of hospitals and dozens of camps each year. I initially joined the company as a musician and singer to accompany others on hospital tours. Eventually I was invited to lead group singing and facilitate healing drum circles at the camps, as well.

As a storyteller, I was interested in bringing stories, as well as music, to the hospital and camp setting. At first, nursing staff and Celebration Shop members thought stories might be too long for children's attention spans in a hospital setting, and too difficult for children on medication to follow. While these turned out to be valid concerns, along with such issues as the noise level in the hospital setting and the various "beeps" and "bleeps" of monitoring equipment, carefully chosen and crafted stories proved to be powerful tools for conveying messages of hope and strength. In addition, stories had a resiliency effect, which songs often did not. Images from stories, along with their therapeutic metaphoric qualities, seemed to stick with kids long after they heard the story.

Of course, I am foremost a storyteller and singer, not a therapist, so learning what stories work in such settings, and why, has been a process of experimentation, feedback, and awareness. I often run material and ideas for songs and stories past pediatric oncology nurses and other health care professionals. And the kids themselves have taught me much about the power of stories to encourage, empower, and heal. Being honest with myself, open and vulnerable to what I might learn from others, and appreciative of the opportunity to be in the children's presence has allowed for the greatest learning.

What I have learned most from my experiences as a song leader, storyteller, and drum circle facilitator with special needs camps is that kids just want to be kids. They crave fun and, more than many of their adult counterparts, have discovered what it means to live life fully and in the moment. They want more control in the choices that affect their living, in what they get to do and what they choose to experience. Obviously, many of these choices are stripped from them when they experience a life-threatening illness and enter into the high-tech medical side of institutional health care. So while I feel the messages of the songs and stories I offer are important tools, I am even more concerned with the kids' opportunities to choose what they will do, to increase their feeling of being in control.

My song leadership and storytelling in camps is largely group-based. The large-group song sessions, incorporating participation and relevant themes, enhance group identity and cohesion. The same seems to be true for the camp-wide storytelling experience. Because the camp-wide storytelling sessions often involve campers aged 5 to 18, I carefully select stories that contain opportunities for participation and varying levels of humor (both subtle and obvious) and of meaning. Many of these children are not nearly as aware as their peers in schools, perhaps because of their medication or the nature of their illness. The use of music, rhythm and percussion, drums and songs in stories can ensure that I keep all the campers connected to the tale, as well as its message. I often accompany my stories with guitar, ukulele, trashcans, hurdy-gurdy, and any assortment of instruments and sound-making devices that create an experience as kinetic as it is aural.

Many people have asked me what stories should be told in the special needs camp setting. First and foremost, I tell the stories that speak to me and from me in an honest way. I have found that kids in these camps love to hear stories of all types. Stories that present humorous twists and characters (trickster tales and tall tales), as well as tales connecting the listener with the environment (animal and Native American tales), seem to work very well in the camp setting. Stories that emphasize adventure and heroic quests work well, especially in more intimate settings with fewer kids, where the material can be made age-specific.

Because much of the experience of a chronic or life-threatening illness involves losing control over one's living and choices, I particularly like stories that involve quest themes. Quest narratives place the listener vicariously in the position of being in control of how one chooses to respond to life's journey. They provide an excellent medium for adapting relevant metaphors and parallel images to the listener's experience. Since they often describe an uncertain journey, quest narratives readily lend themselves to embellishment. A teller can add metaphors and images that parallel the chronically ill child's experience, thereby providing potentially helpful, healing messages. For example, in the following story, "Nobody's Good for Nothin'" I took the familiar Jack tale from Ireland and embellished the theme of friendship with the experience of uncertainty, self-questioning, and the animals' fears. But then I added humor to counter experiences of chaos and anxiety. The message of hope in the midst of uncertainty is reinforced with the song and refrain.

Through conversations with health care professionals and pediatric nurses, I have discovered certain story images (as well as songs) may trigger discomfort in, or frighten, special needs kids more than others because of their special condition. For younger campers, snakes were often perceived negatively and reminded kids of needles and IVs. At the same time, a story I wrote features a child heroine using water hoses to dissolve mud creatures terrorizing a village. The hoses seem to provide a positive parallel image to the IVs and IV pole necessary to treat a child's illness. Similarly, a long, dark, and unfamiliar corridor or labyrinth can seem terrifying to a child when described in an evil, nightmarish context. But the same image used with splashes of humor and participation can provide the listener with a non-threatening and healing parallel to the experience of being in a hospital for the first time, or provide one with clues for navigating the unfamiliar territory of a chronic illness.

I have found the addition of percussion to stories can augment and intensify the emotional experience of a tale. Drumming reaches kids at a variety of levels. For one thing, kids (and adults) love to bang on things, whether or not they actually hit the beat. It provides yet another avenue of control. When used with storytelling, drumming seems to connect listeners at a deeper physical level, as well as providing one further means of holding their attention.

A number of researchers have shown that the drumming experience as a whole has very powerful physiological healing effects on people, even to the point of increasing levels of serotonin, reducing heart rate and stress, reinforcing pain management, and decreasing levels of T-cell growth in cancer patients. Through community drumming, individuals not only begin to gain a sense of playfulness and mastery of their environment, but they also enter into a level of entertainment that enhances their story listening at a more visceral, as well as unconscious, level.

Nobody's
⮜ Good for Nothin' ⮞

AN IRISH FOLKTALE RETOLD BY TOM McDERMOT

One morning, young Jack ran up to his mother and exclaimed,
"Momma, I'm feelin' restless, bored, and frustrated today.
I have decided to go out into the big, wide world and make my way."

"Well, Jack, that's great," she said. "What way are you gonna make and just where are you gonna go?"

Jack's wide smile suddenly turned into a frown. "Well," he sighed, "I don't know. But I know my way is out there; and as soon as I find it, I'm gonna make it!"

"Okay, Jack," his mother smiled. "You make your way in the world, and don't go too far. Then," she added quickly, "you make your way back home before it gets too dark."

Jack quickly loaded a small backpack with important items for making his way in the world. He threw in some grapes and a peanut butter sandwich, a notebook for his important ideas and drawings, a canteen with water, and an extra pair of underwear (in case there was an accident).

He started out the door and down the road, singing a traveling song.

I'm moving along, making my way,
Step by step and day by day.

I don't know where I'll be when I reach the end,
But I'll find some adventure and make some
friends.
Then Jack shouted, "Hoodeedoo!"

He headed to the edge of his neighborhood as the morning sun was making its early rise into the sky. He wasn't too far down the sidewalk when he heard a terrible and sad whimper of a cry.

"Bow-wow-a-rull-a-boo-hoo-a-ruff!" Sitting off to the side of the road was Mr. Dog, crying and kicking up dirt and stuff.

Jack saw it was Mr. Dog and asked, "What's the matter with you?"

"Oh, Jack," he cried, "my life is through. I'm just a tiny, helpless, scared toy terrier. I run from my own shadow and at the sound of the postal carrier. I guess it's true, there's no use fussin'. My owner said I am good for nothin'!"

But Jack said, "Nobody's good for nothin'. Everybody's good for somethin'. If you'd be good enough to join with me, we'll go where we'll go and see what we'll see."

Mr. Dog jumped up and shouted, "That sounds good to me! Bow-wow!"

So the two of them continued down the road, singing their song.

We're movin' along, making our way,
Step by step and day by day.
Don't know where we'll be when we reach the
end,
But we'll find some adventure and make some
friends.
Jack said, "Hoodeedoo!" And Mr. Dog barked,
"Bow-wow!"

They had walked just out past the edge of town when they saw the sun was halfway across the sky. So they stopped to share some lunch when they heard another sad but muddled cry. "EEhh-a-haw-haw-haw!"

Ms. Donkey was standing to the side of the road. So Jack asked her, "Ms. Donkey, what's the matter with you?"

She looked down at the ground shyly and said, "EEhh ... well!"

Jack paused and then asked, "Well ...? What?"

Again Ms. Donkey looked away and whined, "EEhh ... well!"

"Well, is there anything else?" he added, a little more impatient now.

She said, "EEhh ... well! I guess I'm a little shy. I guess I'm a little slow. The farmer said I was so lazy that I had to go. I guess it's true. There's no use fussin'. He said I was good for nothin.'"

But Jack quickly replied, "Nobody's good for nothin'. Everybody's good for somethin'. If you'd be good enough to join Mr. Dog and me, we'll go where we'll go and see what we'll see."

Ms. Donkey jumped in behind Mr. Dog and brayed, "Sounds good to me!"

We're movin' along and makin' our way,
Step by step and day by day.
Don't know where we'll be when we reach the
end,
But we'll have some adventure and make some
friends!
And Jack said, "Hoodeedoo!" Mr. Dog barked,
"Bow-wow!" And Ms. Donkey brayed, "Hee-
haw, hee-haw!"

They continued to make their way into the country. By now the sun was on the other side of the sky. That's when Jack and his friends heard one more sad and pitiful cry. "Cock-a-doodle ... a-boo-hoo-hoo!"

Jack saw Mr. Rooster over by a run-down fence and asked, "What's the matter with you?"

Mr. Rooster cried, "Oh, Jack, my sense of timing is wrong and my life is through. The farmer said I sleep when I am supposed to 'cock-a-doodle-doo.' I guess it's true. There's no use fussin'. He said that I was good for nothin'."

But Jack said, "Nobody's good for nothin'. Everybody's good for somethin'. If you'd be good enough to join Ms. Donkey, Mr. Dog, and me, we'll go where we'll go and we'll see what we see."

Mr. Rooster crowed, "Sounds good to me. Cock-a-doodlee-doodlee-doo!"

Jack and his three new friends continued out into the country as they sang their traveling song.

We're movin' along and makin' our way,
Step by step and day by day.
Don't know where we'll be when we reach the
end,
But we'll have some adventure and make some
friends!
And Jack said, "Hoodeedoo!" Mr. Dog barked,
"Bow-wow!" Ms. Donkey brayed, "Hee-haw,
hee-haw!" And Mr. Rooster crowed, "Cock-a-
doodlee-doodlee-doo!"

They would have kept singing, too, if they had not noticed an old cabin sitting in the woods just off the road. Jack got excited and said, "Here's some adventure. Let's go see what we can see!" So they followed him up to the cabin just as the sun begun to set. Jack very carefully crept beneath the front window. Then, taking a firm hold of the windowsill, he slowly lifted his head to peer through the window pane. When he dropped back down, a broad smile crossed his face as he looked at his friends and shouted, "Nobody's here. But there is a leather bag on the table and it looks like it is filled with ... video-game tokens! I have adventure and have found my way. I can play video games for the rest of my life and I will never have to pay!"

Jack went inside to look around and started counting those video-game tokens. His friends were sitting outside in the dark when they heard a strange sound coming up behind them. They quickly ran inside, closed the door, turned out the light, and looked out the window.

Coming toward the cabin were five of the meanest-looking bullies they had ever seen. Some of them were big and some of them were small. But one of them was a whole lot meaner and uglier looking than the rest of them all. Jack could hear the big, mean-looking one arguing with the others. Then Jack heard him brag, "Just don't forget, I am the one who stole the tokens in that bag!"

Jack whispered to his friends, "Those fellas are robbers and they are coming back inside. There's nowhere to run so we had better find someplace to hide!"

Mr. Dog was so scared that he quickly dodged under the table. Mr. Rooster was so confused that he flew up the chimney and held onto the bricks as best he was able. Jack wasn't so sure about this new adventure he had found, so he hid in the kitchen closet and didn't make a sound. Ms. Donkey was so slow, she hardly had a second more. So she just stood stiff and still behind the front door.

(Jack and the animals whispered their song to themselves to gather their courage.)

Jack peeped out of the closet and saw the biggest, meanest-looking robber slowly open the door. He slowly stumbled into the dark cabin and across the floor, making his way to the table and lamp. When he got there, he started to reach for the lamp. But that's when he felt something under his shoe, as though he were standing on a long rubber hose. He bent down to see he was standing on a tail. Mr. Dog barked, "Bow-ow-wow!" Then he bravely bit the robber on the nose.

Well, the robber ran to grab the charcoal poker, over by the fireplace. With perfect timing, Mr. Rooster dropped down from the chimney, "Cock-a-doodle-ssppittt!" and blew ashes in his face.

The blinded robber stumbled around to the first door that was close. It was the closet, where Jack was on the other side of the door moaning, "Ohhhhhhh!" And the robber yelled, "It's a ghost!"

By now the robber was so scared, he wanted out of that place and quick. So Ms. Donkey slowly opened the cabin door and, with all her strength, gave him a helpful kick. "Eehhh ... well!"

The other robbers caught up with their screaming friend and asked him why he was running. Jack heard the man shout back to his friends, "There's a sharp-toothed creature under the table, and a fire-breathing dragon up the chimney. There's a ghost in the closet and a big man at the door ready to hit you with a stick!"

Of course, that is all that had to be said. Those robbers ran out of the woods and they never looked back. Jack turned on the table lamp and smiled. "Look here, Ms. Donkey. They forgot the leather sack. I have found my way. I can play video games for the rest of my life and I'm never gonna have to pay!"

Ms. Donkey frowned back and brayed, "Eehh ... weeel."

And that is all she really had to say. Because Jack and his friends knew what she meant and they knew just what to do. "If I keep these video-game tokens," he confessed, "I guess it would be like I was stealing them, too." So they all got on Ms. Donkey's back and she quickly carried them into town.

When they got to the video-game store, the owner of the store saw Jack with the leather bag and heard their story. He smiled and said, "Well, Jack, you did the right thing by bringing those tokens back to me. So, as a reward, you come on over any afternoon you like, as long as you have your homework done, and you can play these games for free."

So Jack's adventure turned out pretty well. His momma was happy to have him back home, safe and sound. She was also happy with the new friends he had found. They had helped him make the kind of choices that could help him make his way.

And those friends are still hanging around to this day. People who pass by their home can sometimes hear them say:

We're movin' along, makin' our way,
Step by step and day by day.
We don't know where we'll be when we reach
the end,
But we'll find some adventure and we'll make
some friends.
Jack will say, "Hoodeedoo!" Mr. Dog will bark,
"Bow-wow!" Ms. Donkey will bray, "Hee-haw,
hee-haw!" And Mr. Rooster will crow, "Cock-a-
doodlee-doodlee-doo!" 🐾

STORIES
IN THE
HOSPITAL
AND
BEYOND

I Want to Tell *You* a Story

MICHALE GABRIEL

I FIRST HEARD MICHALE GABRIEL tell Alex's story as the introduction to an evening of storytelling held as a fundraiser for the Tell It All for Children program at Children's Hospital in Seattle. By the time Michale had finished, there wasn't a dry eye in the house.

— *David H. Albert*

"Willie! Wait for me!" cried five-year-old Alex,
busily maneuvering his bicycle across a busy street in Anchorage.
He was trying to keep up with his older brother.

He never saw the car until it was too late. The impact sent his bicycle flying. Moments later, Alex was being raced to the hospital in an ambulance.

For the next 30 days, his family hovered at his bedside while doctors assessed the extent of the damage. The prognosis was not good. Alex would be permanently paralyzed from the neck down. It was called a C2 fracture — the same fracture that actor Christopher Reeves would suffer just a few months later.

Alex would need around-the-clock care the rest of his life. He would need complicated surgeries and would have to learn how to breathe using a ventilator. And he needed to be in a hospital that specialized in pediatric trauma cases. The decision was made to move him to Children's Hospital in Seattle.

He had been at Children's Hospital for ten days, undergoing a series of tests and procedures, when Jacki, one of the child life specialists, asked if I would work with him. As founder and director of the Storytelling Residency Program at

Children's, I often had patients referred to me by hospital staff.

Jacki told me that although Alex could nod his head "yes" or "no," he showed no expression in his face — only in his eyes. A breathing tube was inserted into his trachea. She cautioned me to have no expectations.

Before the accident, Alex was an effusive, talkative child, ready to comment on everything both in English and his native Spanish. He was one of seven siblings and the youngest of two boys. Now he was frightened, confused, and hesitant to speak with the newly implanted tube. His Latino parents tried unsuccessfully to coax phrases and sentences out of him. He would only speak when spoken to and used only single words to express his thoughts and feelings. No complete sentences.

Jacki added that a singer's visit to his room earlier in the day had produced no response, even though, according to his mother, he was familiar with the songs.

When I entered the room, Alex's mother led me to the bedside of her son. Staring up at me was a beautiful child with raven black hair and penetrating black eyes, framed by thick, dark lashes. He was hurting and afraid. The only sound in the room was the bellowing rhythm of the ventilator, which filled Alex's lungs on command with life-giving air through the tube in his trachea.

"Alex," I said softly. "Would you like me to tell you a story?"

He said nothing. He just nodded his head, which was the only part of his body he could now move.

"This is an old, old story about a man who sold caps. It's called 'Caps for Sale.' And it goes something like this …."

I told him the folktale about a peddler who fell asleep under a tree with his hats on his head. When he woke up, his hats were gone. He found them on the heads of monkeys seated in the branches above him. The story is filled with the sounds of monkeys and repetitive dialogue such as "You monkeys you! Give me back my hats!" To illustrate the story I used actions ranging from the peddler stacking the hats on his head to shaking his fists and stamping his feet at the mischievous monkeys.

I watched Alex's eyes follow my fingers when I pointed into space at the imaginary tree. Twice during the story I saw his mouth move to form a word during a refrain. Good, I thought, he is making a connection.

After the story was over, I asked Alex if he would like to hear another. He nodded his head.

My intuition said to choose something that would be very familiar and that could actively engage him.

"Alex, I think you might know this one. It's called 'The Three Bears.' Do you know it?"

He nodded.

"Good! Once upon a time there were three bears …."

I came to the line "One day the mama bear was making some …" I stopped. I watched Alex's mouth open. He whispered, almost inaudibly, "Soup."

Taking my cue from him I answered, "Yes, that's right Alex. Soup. But that soup was too …" and I waited. Sure enough, he whispered, "Hot!" I continued, "And so the papa bear and the mama bear …" But I went no further. The story had already wrapped itself around him and Alex was ready to take control. Using the tube in his trachea, he exhaled and then on the inhaling breath, which is just the opposite of how we normally speak, he began to slowly and painstakingly form the words he wanted to say. "The Paapa Bear (exhale) and the Maaama Bear (exhale) and the Baaaby Bear (exhale) went for waaalk (exhale) in the woods." We witnessed the miracle. The first full sentence he had spoken since the accident. And it was a story that had brought him back. He continued telling "The Three Bears" as the tears flowed freely down his grateful mother's face.

I went into Alex's room every day after that and told him folk, fairy, and literary tales. He retold those stories to everyone else, much to their delight. He did not allow hospital staff to poke, prod, or change a dressing without hearing a story first. I noticed the staff never complained about this process. They became like little children as he enchanted them with his gift of telling. Afterward, he would insist that they retell the stories he had told them to someone else.

One of those stories was "The Little Old Lady Who Wasn't Afraid of Anything."* Alex changed the heroine's words to "I ain't afraid of nothing." He repeated those words every time his healing process offered him new challenges.

*My retelling of this story is based on Joanna Cole's *Best-Loved Folktales of the World* (New York: Doubleday, 1992) and Heather Forest's *Wonder Tales from Around the World* (Little Rock: August House, 1995).

One day, just before Christmas, I was rushing out of the hospital to attend a Celtic music concert. I was feeling stressed and in search of the holiday spirit. A friend was waiting at the performance hall with tickets. As I was making my way along the corridor toward the waiting elevator, Alex's sister flagged me down and said, "Oh, Michale, Alex has had such a bad day. Can you tell him a story?" I looked at my watch and made some quick calculations. If I could keep my story to five minutes, I would arrive one minute before curtain. So I went into Alex's room, told him a quick story, and was heading out the door when he said excitedly, "Michale, I want to tell *you* a story!"

"You do?" I answered.

"Yes," he said beaming. "From inside of my head."

I looked at his radiant face. In it I saw a gift, waiting to be given. I realized there would always be another concert. But there would never be another moment like this one. I released the concert, trusting my friend would understand. I sat down next to Alex, took a deep breath, and opened my heart to the moment.

He started his story in a time-honored tradition. "Once upon a time," he began. Suddenly I heard the words *Write this story down.* I stopped Alex mid-sentence, slipped out of the room, and grabbed a notepad off the nurse's station. I saw several nurses, a doctor, and a physical therapist standing nearby. I heard the words *Invite them.* I did, and they invited others. Within minutes (good news travels fast at Children's Hospital) nine people — doctors, nurses, therapists, aides, and orderlies — surrounded Alex's bed, gently calling forth his story through their enthusiastic listening. I wrote down every word. The more we responded to Alex, the more richly detailed the story became. As I looked around the room, I could see that he had successfully transported all of us to that place where time stands still and miracles are created. I didn't have to travel to a concert hall to be filled with the holiday spirit. It had come to me in the form of a five-year-old boy expressing his gift.

When Alex finished, we broke out in thunderous applause. He rolled his eyes as a way of deflecting our unabashed adoration, but he clearly loved the attention.

I turned the notepad toward him and began flipping the pages. "Alex, look at this. These are your words. You are a writer."

"I am?" he replied, his expressive face turning into a question mark.

"Yes, Alex, look at this. You are a storyteller."

"I am?" A huge grin was making its way across his face

"Yes, you are. Alex, I'm going to put your story on the computer. We'll print it out and it will be your first book. We will now call you Alex Guerreo — author and storyteller."

"Really?" he asked incredulously. He had to repeat the words "author" and "storyteller" so that they could sink in.

"Alex," I added, leaning forward so that it looked like I was peering into the top of his head.

"What, Michale?"

"Alex," I replied, leaning even closer.

"What?" he asked quizzically.

"Alex," I sang a third time because we always did things in cycles of threes.

"What, Michale?" he demanded.

"Alex, I see hundreds more stories inside your head."

He immediately rolled his eyes skyward, attempting to see what I saw. "Michale, are you sure?" he replied.

"I'm sure, sweetheart, I'm sure."

After that, whenever anyone walked into

Alex's room he would say, "I'm going to tell you a story from inside of my head. Write it down." Soon his original stories lined the walls of his room.

Alex would often ask me to act out his stories as he directed my every move. "More expression! More expression, Michale!" he shouted as I galloped about his room, whinnying like a horse or snorting like a pig. He loved being in control of another person in this antiseptic setting where so much was beyond his control.

It was through the power of storytelling that he also began to create meaning out of his accident. One day he said to his mother, "Mommy, a long time ago, when I was inside of your tummy, I was happy. Why was I born?" The answers to that question reside deep inside. As he is ready, he will communicate them through metaphors and stories.

Alex left Children's Hospital two months later, using his head to expertly maneuver his electric wheelchair decorated with Alaska husky-puppet armrests. Dozens of cheering medical staff and volunteers lined the halls, giving voice to their love for him and their commitment to his healing.

Alex had discovered something very important during his rehabilitation. He was not bound by the body that held him captive. Through his imagination, love, and the power of story, he could travel anywhere in the universe and back again. And so, I discovered, can we. ✿

The Search for the
∼ Magic Lake ∼

A FOLKTALE FROM ECUADOR RETOLD BY
CRISTY WEST*

AS PART OF MY WORK as a teller in the pediatric wing of a hospital, I first told this Ecuadorian folktale to a 10-year-old boy, just admitted for a two-week stay. I can still remember how strongly he identified with the sick son and the concerned father. When I came to the part where the helpful birds step in with their gift of feathers, I produced three brightly colored feathers (from cheap supermarket dustbrushes), which I then wrapped with a pipe cleaner. I left behind this "fan" as a sort of healing talisman for the ordeal that lay ahead.

The motif of life-giving waters is widespread throughout folk literature — it is a true archetype, as Jungian psychologists would say. In a version collected by the brothers Grimm, "The Waters of Life," the opening conflict focuses on an ailing monarch. But in this telling, an Incan emperor's only son is the one who is sick, and a golden flask appears that must be filled with waters from a particular Magic Lake. It is a young girl who finally succeeds in accomplishing the task. In my tellings I often strike a small chime when the flask appears, a dramatic embellishment children seem to enjoy.

Long ago, the land that today we call Ecuador was part of a rich and prosperous Inca kingdom. But the ruling emperor was sad because his only son had fallen ill. None of the doctors could help this boy, and his father was worried that he might die. He went to the temple and prayed to the Gods.

"Oh, Great Ones. I pray to you, please make my son strong and healthy so that one day he can rule my people when I am gone."

Suddenly a voice came out of the fire burning before the altar. And it said,

*The young prince must drink water
from the Magic Lake,
The lake at the end of the world,
Where the sky touches the water.
The prince can be cured only with
water from the Magic Lake.*

The fire flamed up brightly and then it sputtered out. And there in the ashes lay a golden flask.

The old emperor was too old to journey to the end of the world. And his son was too sick. So the emperor sent forth a proclamation throughout the land, offering a rich reward to any person who could fill that golden flask with water from the Magic Lake.

It happened that in a valley, some distance from the emperor's palace, there lived a poor farmer, his wife, two sons, and a young daughter. And when they heard the emperor's announcement, the two sons said, "Father, let us go in search of the Magic Lake. We will help the prince and bring back the reward."

The father agreed to let them go, but made them promise to return before the next new moon, in time to help with the harvest.

So the two sons set off together. They journeyed from one beautiful lake to another. But nowhere could they find the Magic Lake, where the sky touches the water. And they kept watching the moon. When they saw that it was almost new again, they knew it was time to return to their father as they had promised. So they sat down and they thought what they would do.

And the younger brother said to the older, "I know what we can do. We can fill our jars with this water right here! They'll never know the difference. Surely the emperor will reward us for our trouble."

So the two boys went to the emperor, and they said they had water from the Magic Lake, even though this was a lie. When the sick prince was given a sip of it, he became no better.

Then one of the doctors said, "The water must be put into the golden flask." But when they brought the flask, a very strange thing happened. When the water was poured into the golden flask, POUF! it vanished. The doctor said, "The flask is telling us that the brothers have lied. For it will accept only water from the Magic Lake, the lake at the end of the world, where the sky touches the water."

The emperor was so angry, he ordered that the boys be thrown into prison. Once again the message went forth through the land, calling for someone to bring the precious water.

When the father of the two boys heard what had happened to his sons, he was ashamed that his boys had lied. But then his little daughter, whose name was Sumac, stepped forward.

"Father, please let me go. I will find the Magic Lake. And perhaps I can save my brothers."

And the father said, "No, my little Sumac, you are too young." But she begged and pleaded, and finally her mother interceded on her behalf. At last the father gave his permission. "After all," he said, "we must think of our emperor, and the sick prince."

Sumac was excited to be setting out on this journey. Her mother gave her a woven bag filled with toasted kernels of corn to eat along the way. And she had for company her pet llama, who also carried her provisions.

She'd gone only a little way when she saw a flock of birds pecking in a stony field. She felt sorry for them because they looked so hungry. So she threw them a handful of her corn.

That first night she curled up next to her llama under the overhang of a great rock. But all through the night she heard the hungry cry of the puma cat. She became afraid it would creep up and attack her llama. So she sent the llama home, and the next night she slept alone, hidden high up in the branches of a tree where the puma cat could not find her.

The following morning, she woke up to ... the sound of voices? When she opened her eyes, she found that she was surrounded by birds. Amazingly, she could understand all they were saying.

One bird said, "This is the same girl who gave us corn when we were so hungry."

And another said, "Poor child, she will never find the Magic Lake she is seeking."

And another said, "But of course we could help her."

Hearing this, Sumac sat up and said, "Oh, please help me! My brothers are in prison and the emperor's son is sick. Someone must go to the Magic Lake!"

The birds agreed. Each one reached under a wing and brought forth a special feather and gave this to Sumac. They told her to take the feathers and make a magic fan, and they said that this would protect her in times of danger, taking her wherever she wished to go.

One bird also warned her that she would have to face many dangers at the Magic Lake. He said, "Be brave. And the fan will help you."

Sumac thanked the birds for all their help. Then she held up the fan and said, "I wish I were at the Magic Lake!" In an instant, a soft breeze lifted her gently out of the tree, up, up into the sky, out over the mountain peaks. And it set her down on the shore of a beautiful lake.

She realized that this must be the Magic Lake because here the sky touched the water. But what could she use for a container? Then she had an idea. She held up her magic fan and said, "I wish I had a jar." Then, "Ping!" The golden flask itself appeared at her feet.

Sumac went to the water's edge and began filling the flask when suddenly a strange voice ordered, "Leave the water alone!" She turned, and to her horror she saw an enormous hairy-legged crab, nearly the size of a pig, coming after her. Quickly she held up her fan. And the crab fell asleep.

No sooner had she quelled one danger when another appeared, this time a huge toothy alligator that emerged from the water and was coming straight for her, warning, "Leave the water alone!" But once again, when she held up the fan, the alligator also toppled over and sank out of sight.

Then there was a shrill screech from above and Sumac looked up to see a winged serpent descending from the sky, fire spitting from its eyes, shrieking, "Sssstay away, stay away, leave the water alone!" For a third time she raised her fan, and the serpent fell to the shore, stunned and powerless.

Now, finally she could fill the flask without difficulty. As soon as this was done, she held up her fan and wished herself back at the emperor's palace. In a blink, there she was, in the very room where the prince lay spread out on the bed, pale and lifeless, the doctors standing beside him.

Sumac went to his side and poured a sip of the water into his mouth. At once the prince opened his eyes, and the color came back into his cheeks. He sat up in his bed and drank some more.

The emperor was overjoyed by his son's recovery. He offered Sumac any reward she could name.

Sumac said, "I desire only three things. First, I want my brothers to be set free. When they lied about the water, it was only because they wanted so much to succeed. They meant no harm."

The emperor agreed.

"Next," said Sumac, "I want my parents to be given a farm all their own, with herds of llamas and vicunas and alpacas to graze there. That way they will never be poor again."

The emperor agreed to this as well. "And what is your third wish?" he asked.

"My third wish is for the feathers of my fan to be returned to the birds who gave them to me." As soon as she said this, the feathers floated out of her hand, out the window.

"But won't you stay here and live with us at the palace?" said the emperor.

"Oh, no," said Sumac. "You are very kind. But my place is with my parents and my brothers. They will be missing me."

So Sumac said good-bye to the emperor and his son. And when she reached home she found that the royal workers had already arrived and were beginning construction of a fine new house and barn. That night, she and her brothers celebrated with their parents, rejoicing that the family was together again. She was also happy to be with her llama again. They all stayed up late into the night, hearing of Sumac's journey to the Magic Lake and how she had brought back the healing waters to cure the emperor's son. ❧

Some successful stories and story interactions

CRISTY WEST

PEDIATRIC HEALTH CARE IS ONLY one of the many therapeutic settings in which storytellers can be effective. Yet there is a frustrating lack of instruction for those wishing to learn how to do this kind of work. I hope that, in time, structured training programs will become available to help storytellers build up a knowledge base and allow them to share their understanding of effective practice. Storytelling has, through the ages, provided healing and solace. There exists still today

ample opportunities for the old traditions to mend, transform, and heal.

If I were to offer advice to a newcomer doing this work, I would emphasize, "Find stories you like and tell them your own way. The following is a small collection of specific stories that I have found to be effective in pediatric settings:

- "Let's Go On A Bear Hunt" appears in many collections, including my principal source, *The Parent's Guide to Storytelling: How to Make Up New Stories and Retell Old Favorites* by Margaret Read MacDonald (Little Rock, AR: August House, 2001). One morning when the group was as chaotic as it could be, I thanked my lucky stars that I had just prepared this tale. It has a call-and-response structure, with the audience echoing everything I say and copying my gestures. The hunt goes over a bridge (fists thumped on chest), through a swamp (sucking noises, with hands imitating feet in yucky mud), across a lake (swimming motions), etc. Finally, when the bear is discovered in a cave, I usually pull out my teddy bear and throw it up in the air, much to everyone's delight. Then we all "run home," repeating the words and gestures in reverse order. With its strong rhythms and active participation, this story draws in the most withdrawn of children. It also offers a great outlet for hyperactive children, and infants get a generous dose of sensory stimulation. This story has become a staple and can be varied to add more obstacles along the way according to suggestions from the audience.

- "Mr. Wiggle and Mr. Waggle." I learned this silly fingerplay from British storyteller/schoolteacher Tony Aylwin. A version titled "Mr. Brown and Mr. Black" appears in *Stories to Play With: Kids' Tales Told with Puppets, Paper, Toys and Imagination* by Hiroko Fujita (Little Rock, AR: August House, 1996). Mr. Wiggle is the thumb on my right hand, and Mr. Waggle is the one on the left. (While telling, first hold thumbs up, with hands out to either side, then fold all fingers around each thumb as the tale begins). One morning Mr. Wiggle wakes up, opens the door (fingers of clasped hand springing out), looks around (thumb popping straight out), and decides to go see his friend Mr. Waggle. He goes up the hill and down the hill and up the hill and down the hill and up the hill (extravagant arm motions, voice sliding up and down) until he comes to the house of Mr. Waggle (left fist with thumb hidden inside). He knocks three times, but when no one answers he goes home — up the hill and etc. The next day, Mr. Waggle gets up and goes through the same process. On the third day, they both wake up, have the idea of a visit, meet in the middle, and play together (here I invite audience suggestions — Ring-around-a-rosy? Wrestling? Hide-and-seek? No, sorry, they didn't bring along a football, can't do that). After tiring they go home, open their "doors," go inside, close their doors, and go to sleep (hands becoming fists with thumbs back inside). The end. It's easy to see how young children can be hooked by this story. I tell it as much for the parents and nursing staff, to give them a simple tale to use themselves. Older children, too, will have fun learning the story so they can pass it along.

- "Who's In Rabbit's House?" This story is available as a children's book by Verna Aardema, *Who's in Rabbit's House? A Masai Tale* (New York: Dial, 1990). Rabbit comes home one day and cannot get into her house because the door is locked. A voice cries from the inside, "I am the long one. I eat trees and trample on elephants. Go away or I will trample on you!" A little frog tries to help, but Rabbit shoos him away because he is too little. Well-meaning animals come along and offer one bad idea after another (burn down the house, trample it, tear the house apart). Finally, Rabbit accepts the help of Frog, who takes a leaf for a megaphone and delivers a loud counterthreat to the Long One, who is just a caterpillar, playing a trick. The story builds suspense and delivers a great message: Fears can be insignificant when you talk back to them.

- "Bear and Chipmunk." This tale is available on the tape *The Boy Who Lived with the Bears and Other Iroquois Stories* by Joseph Bruchac (Parabola Storytime audiotape series, Caedmon, 1991). Bear boasts that he is the strongest and most important of the animals; he can do anything. Chipmunk challenges him — if he is so important, can he, Bear, tell the sun not to come up? "Harumph, certainly!" says Bear. The two animals chant through the night "Sun will not come up" (Bear) and "The sun will rise again" (Chipmunk) with the help of audience participation. When the sun rises, Chipmunk laughs and taunts Bear. An angered Bear clamps a big paw down on top of Chipmunk, who changes his tune and flatters Bear until he manages to get away, down into his hole. But Chipmunk has scars left on his back that become the stripes we see to this very day. The moral Bruchac offers is:

"Be careful who you make fun of." I add: Don't let anyone tell you the sun will not come up, because sooner or later it always does.

- "Little Burnt Face," often known as "The Indian Cinderella," is a Micmac tale that appears in many collections under various titles. My telling is based on a version found in *Ready-To-Tell Tales: Sure-Fire Stories from America's Favorite Storytellers* edited by David Holt and Bill Mooney (Little Rock, AR: August House, 1994). The story tells of a mighty warrior, Strong Wind, who can make himself invisible. All the village girls want to be his wife and lie that they can see him, knowing he will marry only the one who does. Little Burnt Face, who ultimately succeeds, is the youngest of three sisters. Her jealous sisters have burned her face and singed her hair, but "she is beautiful and has a gentle heart." In a test given by Strong Wind's sister, Burnt Face sees that a rainbow draws his sled and that his bowstring is made of the Milky Way. When his sister bathes the girl's face and combs her hair, the scars are healed and the girl's hair grows back "dark and sleek as a raven's wing." Cancer patients in particular will respond strongly to the image of the heroine's disfigurement and cure. Her transformation offers hope and consolation, healing on both a physical and spiritual plane.

The medicine of the heart

LAURA SIMMS

Our holy space

ONE OF MY FIRST DAYS working at Beth Israel Hospital, I told stories to four patients in an airless room at the end of a hallway. Nurses sat with the patients. I watched everyone as the story began. "There were once three men who ..." Eyes that had been glazed over moments before, now turned outward from a preoccupation with self toward my voice. By the middle of the story they were listening. Through my speaking and my presence they were able to project themselves into the story and then backwards to themselves, imagining the unfolding narrative. Afterwards, I asked, "How did you feel about that story?" Since there was no right answer, each person's response took its own place in the room. Not only did they get to know a bit about each other and express their voices, but the small airless room seemed to expand through the inner space created by their involvement. An old man whispered to me, as he left, "It felt like our holy space."

Just as a mother sings a baby to sleep, the voice of the storyteller, when it resonates from the heart of one's personal understanding of the potency of the story and the listener's engagement, soothes by the lullaby of authentic presence. This lullaby does not put one to sleep, but numbs the power of the habit of negative or limiting ideas. The way of the storyteller is not about informing someone of possibilities or of giving yet another explanation. It is about creating the space in which one feels alive and participating. One is meeting one's own truth, which is the natural state of listening and hearing. Hafiz, a Persian poet, once wrote, "If the light of the love of truth falls on your heart and soul, you will become lovelier than the sun in heaven."

The room of women

Another day in a four-person room: An elderly woman was too panicked to listen to a tale, so I sat down next to her bed. She told anyone and everyone her dilemma. I listened to what she was saying and how she was saying it. Her voice was filled with frustration, pain, terror, and anger. Had I not made the decision to be simply interested, it would have propelled me away like a bad smell. She had heard that she would not walk on her legs again. She had no family or anyone else to assist her. She was frightened and uncertain about her future. She began to weep. Her blue eyes were bright. I was as attracted to her eyes as I was dismayed by her voice.

After her complaint, I said, "You have beautiful eyes."

She angrily replied, "I have always needed glasses. My eyes are ugly. My sister never needed glasses. The kids in my class made fun of me." From what place did this anger arise? How far back was the origin of her sense of injustice and ugliness, abandonment, and unfair treatment. I mirrored her dismay and began a story about a little girl who had beautiful eyes that were stolen by a bird. I made up the story. She listened. When I had no idea where to go with the story, I asked for her assistance — "And then what happened?" Caught up with the story, she gave me an answer — "The bird flew away with her eyes." We made a story, incident by incident, on the energy of her dissatisfaction. The girl had lost what was most precious. The bird swallowed the eyes. We went on for 20 minutes until the story ended with the girl regaining the eyes when she was an old woman.

"So what is the meaning of that story?" the woman demanded, hurling her question at me.

I answered, "I don't know. It's just a story."

She said, "But it isn't true."

"But it was a good story," I replied.

Then she looked at me and said, "You have beautiful eyes." I thanked her and told her that when I was little, an Austrian man, a survivor of the Holocaust, who always wore a three-piece wool suit even in the heat of August, said to me, "Remember those eyes of yours were given by God. Don't become proud." Then for some reason she and I burst out laughing. The whole illogic of the story, the energy of her complaint, the directness of our communication — in which I did not respond to her actual problem — seemed to break through her preoccupation and suddenly we were talking to one another.

The doctor arrived just at that moment. I was able to ask him to describe slowly, in my presence, the diagnosis he had given her the day before. With her mind more at ease, and with the doctor being asked a question without accusation, the answer could be heard. The prognosis was not as dire as she had assumed. That was the grace of the moment. He apologized for his rushing

through it the day before. He admitted guilelessly that he was too busy and tired. She was able to appreciate his apology and dilemma. It was a stunning moment.

When the doctor left, another woman demanded, "Couldn't you tell me a story as well?" She wanted to participate. Another woman called out in a commanding voice from across the room, "If you speak a little louder, I can hear too."

The woman beside the blue-eyed lady was a small, black-haired Spanish woman who had accidentally been poisoned during a blood transfusion. The blood was being removed and replenished. Her body was undergoing an unforeseen transformation through this frightening mistake. She had to lie in bed for days while new blood circulated from without to within. She had the look of a traumatized person. I told her we were making up stories. She said, "I like true stories."

I asked her if she had any memories from her own childhood. She pulled herself up to a sitting position and told us, "I grew up in Florida beside a train track. My sister and I used to walk along the track to a circus where there were carnival games, animals, and magicians. We loved to watch the magician. My sister always wanted to go behind the scenes and find out how the magic really worked. I never wanted to know. I loved the mystery."

This extraordinary memory arose naturally, it seemed. Intuitively, she had signaled her own healing strength through the realization that she was undergoing an inexplicable mystery. Everyone loved the story.

I said, "Let me tell you a story." I told the Moroccan tale of the boy who sees a magician in the marketplace who can turn ordinary things to gold with the touch of his magic finger. No matter how much the magician offers to turn to gold, the boy says, "I want more." Finally, the magician asks, "What do you want?" And the boy answers, "I want the magic finger."

Another woman, who had been silent until that moment, spoke up in a British accent. She was wearing an elegant pink silk nightgown. "We all want to be mistresses of our destiny." The room of women asked me to come back the next day.

I returned and told a Turkish tale of a young prince's journey to three worlds beneath ours. In each world there is a demon or monster to overcome, until he arrives at the lowest world, where he confronts an eagle mother and is finally taken on her back up to his own world. As I told the tale, I realized that one way of looking at that story was as a symbolic journey of uncovering the root causes of one's illness. Each quest into another world led us back to a particular emotional event that occurred long before the obvious problem in the uppermost, surface world. But even when he touched the root of the problem, the prince's journey was not completed.

The prince's compassion was tested. As the eagle mother carried him, she lost her strength and feared that she and the young man would fall to their deaths. He took pity on her and cut flesh from his own leg to feed her. She did not swallow the meat. And his selfless kindness gave her strength. She took him all the way home, reminiscent of the shamanic stories of journey and return. It emotionally took us out of our present fixation on illness and outer events, and urged us within to the world of visceral imagination, where image is body and we live out the story that is being told within ourselves.

The African storyteller and healer Malidoma Some writes, "Primitive cultures normally deal with the physical world at the last stage. What goes wrong in the visible world is only the tip of the iceberg. So to correct a dysfunctional state of affairs effectively, one must first locate its hidden area, its symbolic dimension, work with it first, and then assist in the restoration of the physical (visible) extension of it. Visible wrongs have their roots in the world of the spirit."

Just as the Spanish woman described her fear in the language of the soul and empowered herself with her own courage and sense of mystery restored, I told the Turkish tale not knowing why when I began. I listened to what was called for within the situation, and from within myself. The challenge of the storyteller is to know the right story to tell at the right moment and to whom. Or to know when not to tell a story, but to listen.

Befriending death

One day I walked onto the Planetree Ward at the hospital. No one wanted to hear stories. However, a man attached to an IV, dragging one leg and looking very weak and distracted, was leaning against a wall. I asked if he would like to hear a story. He turned and said, "I am in a lot of pain."

I said gently, "Perhaps I can distract you for a little while. If you would like to come and listen, I could arrange for you to be brought down the hallway." I think it was his desperation that made him agree.

He said, "I will come on my own." It took him 15 minutes to drag his leg and the IV down the hall. When he sat down he was exhausted. I was very moved by his pain and the effort he had made. My mind went blank. Suddenly I thought of a story that not only seemed bizarre, given the situation, but was also one that I hardly knew. I said, "I read a story the other day that interested me a lot, although I didn't understand it." He nodded, giving me permission to go ahead.

I began the story, tentatively at first. It was a Pawnee story about a girl who is abandoned by her tribe and ends up being captured by a skull in a forest. She attempts to escape, aided by a spirit being, and is pursued again and again by the skull. She cannot get away. Finally, she takes refuge with five young men who go out to destroy the skull. The skull cannot be destroyed, but rolls back to the forest.

The young men feed her and she teaches them agriculture. She finds and plants seeds. Eventually, the young men turn out to be stars and go up to the sky. She follows. They are the Pleiades. She is there with them. And the seeds that she plants become the first corn.

The story took a long time. The man half listened, his eyes opening and closing. I hoped that he was able to get at least a little relief in the listening. When I was done, he said, "I liked that story." I was surprised. He added, " I understand that story. It is my story. I am also pursued by death and cannot get away from it. But it has a happy ending. She becomes a star. I always think that death cannot be final. And the seeds bring new life to the earth. I like that story." He left as laboriously as he had arrived. Later, in the hallway, he caught my arm and said, "Thank you. I needed to hear that. It gave me a chance to think about my death."

The power of story

There are so many incidents from my three years in Beth Israel. Each one was further proof of the possibilities of storytelling. Listening to stories took people out of themselves and then returned them to themselves. Listening promoted an instantaneous joining of mind and body and heart, without which there can be no peace of mind, nor any energy for actual healing. As listeners imagined the story, they enacted it psychologically within themselves. Even if there were a thousand people, each person would listen uniquely and feel as if the story were being told just for him or her. The very process of being in the story has its own satisfaction, for there is satisfaction of something that has a definite form: a beginning, middle, and an end. This form helps to give some meaning to an unfamiliar and scary situation.

For many in the era of managed health care, a hospital stay is a stressful or fearful event. It is exacerbated by the fact that how long one stays is determined not by the need of the illness or healing, but by how many days the insurance company is willing to pay. Some people need a long time for their healing, but can only stay for three days. The satisfaction of the story, which defies time and logic, and has form, becomes a stabilizing event.

A HOW-TO GUIDE FOR RETELLING STORIES

The process outlined below will help tellers learn stories quickly and heartfully, without memorization. The memorized story can stand between yourself and the listener, making the words of the story and the performance more important than your relationship to the listeners and their inner experience of the tale.

A. Read the story aloud to yourself as if you were telling the tale to your own mind.

Listen, feel, imagine.

B. Ask yourself what moved you the most: a certain image or event? Write it down and then, as if it were a dream, free associate on that particular event. You are beginning to find your relationship to the story.

C. Make an outline of the events of the narrative (without writing the text) so you can follow the thread of the sequence of events. The outline releases you from the written rhythm of the story.

D. See the landscape of the story, either by walking through it as if it were an invisible pop-up map or by literally drawing a map of the places of the story to see where it takes place and what happens in each setting.

E. Retell the story as you remember it to a friend, almost as if it were casual gossip. How does your friend feel about the story? What did you remember and what did you forget? Begin to find your individual rhythm and language.

F. List the characters, the symbols, the objects, the animals. List the numbers that occur and repeat.

G. What questions do you have about the cultural background of the story? Research these.

H. Make a chart of the emotional roadmap of the unfolding story from start to end. Concentrate on the emotional changes each character undergoes.

Now, you are ready to begin telling the story. Remember that the most important story is the one that the listener hears — and *each person hears his or her own story*. So tell the story from the heart. Be present: don't disappear or melt into the narrative. In this way you can pay attention to both the listener and your telling. Try first with-out any voices and special effects. Let the story inform your telling, and when you try voices, become familiar with the characters and the role they play in the tale rather than choosing carica-tured sound effects. The story is not a cartoon, but a living reciprocal event that demands your willingness to bring it to life with dignity, feeling, and communication. Play and pay attention.

True-life stories can be approached in a simi-lar manner. Our own life events can be a source of inspiration and comfort to others. Begin the tale in a specific place and time to make certain that your listener can easily create an instant setting.

Further suggestions for retelling sessions in health-related situations

- Ask people what the story reminded them of in their own lives, or if it reminded them of another story they might know from their own childhood repertory.

- Ask how they might want to change the story. Would they change the ending if they could? Enjoy the exploration with people without judgment and the atmos-phere will be filled with trust and sharing.

- Engage someone in telling his or her own experiences simply and directly. This helps to relieve people from the loop of concern for the often baffling facts of their illness and situation. Since you will now be the listener, listen openly and you might dis-cover a significant idea or feeling that can-not be verbalized, or the teller's own intu-itive signals about what road to follow toward healing and/or self-acceptance.

- Listening is the most profound talent you can develop. Listening without bias or the need to do anything to change the story helps the teller to hear his or her own story more clearly and make his or her own assessments. Questions about details can help the teller make more visceral and logical sense of the story and encourage the teller to be communicative.

- Retell the story back to teller in the third person, if you feel confident doing so. For example, "There was once a girl who ..." Listening to one's own tale is a luxury that is fun and affirming. It also allows people to hear what they might not have known about their own experience.

- Slow down the engine. When someone tells you the same litany of facts about a personal problem over and over, ask him or her to retell it to you slowly, almost in a monotone. This makes it less stressful and allows the teller to hear it also. You can ask questions: What would you change if you could make anything happen? Bringing their voice back into their bodies, without the panic of repetition, can release creative energy much needed for rest and healing.

- If you are in a situation that allows it, write down someone's story or the tale you told that they liked, and make a collage about it with photos, drawings, and pictures in magazines. Then place the words of the story in a little box or in an area in that picture where they think it belongs or is safe.

COPING
WITH
GRIEF

Storytelling and bereavement

GAIL ROSEN

My friend Jackie's father died. He was nearly 80. He'd been sick for a few years. When he died, Jackie's daughter, Debbie, explained to her son Kevin, who was four years old, "We've lost Pop Pop, but we'll always remember him in our hearts." Some months later, the family was on an outing. Jackie's husband was driving. He and Jackie were in the front seat. In the back seat was grandson Kevin. Following them in another car was Kevin's Uncle Howard and assorted cousins. They got onto the beltway and traffic was heavy. Suddenly Jackie's husband looked into the rearview mirror and said, "Darn! We've lost Howard!" And in the back seat, four-year-old Kevin knew just what to say. "But we'll always remember him in our hearts."

FROM THE TIME I FIRST identified myself as a storyteller and began to look for stories I wanted to tell, I found myself drawn to stories about life and death, suffering, and the search for meaning. There were people who loved me who said, "Tell the funny ones! Nobody wants to hear those sad stories." But I wanted to hear them, and to tell them. I would "sneak" them into other programs, but I found that my repertoire of "difficult" stories was outnumbering the "entertaining" ones. Then I was asked to tell for a hospice volunteers' appreciation day event. Epiphany! I realized that I didn't have to learn a single new story. This was where people would want to hear these stories I love, where they needed to hear them, and where they served people.

I now tell stories and present workshops to caregivers who work with the dying and bereaved — social workers, hospice volunteers, health professionals, clergy, bereavement groups, and storytellers. Stories are perfectly suited to bereavement work and are wonderful for people of all ages, adults as well as children. Stories paradoxically allow us to keep a safe distance from feelings and events that may be difficult or painful, while at the same time drawing us in to identify with characters and, through them, to experience catharsis and insight.

Some of the stories I have found for this work are funny, some moving. Some are personal, some are folktales from various cultures. I love knowing and sharing how people around the world and throughout time have wrestled with the same problems of loss and healing. We are all trying to make sense out of what we can perceive of life and death.

I am aware these days of our aloneness. Each of us is in our own skin, no matter how surrounded by friends, family, partners, lovers, children, colleagues. And most of us are reaching for contact, connection — in intellect, in spirit, in skin-to-skin contact, in affection or in antagonism, in partnership or enmity, always seeking a common experience of some shared perspective, some moment of respite from that eternal aloneness. When I am hurting, if I'm not in the curl-up-in-a-ball-in-the-corner stage, if I am seeking out a healer or a friend, what is it I am seeking? What medicine or magic do I need? When I offer myself to someone who is in pain, what am I offering?

I think that what I seek and also what I offer is a sense of recognition, of being known and knowing another. When I look for someone to receive my pain so that I can be relieved of the fullness of its weight for a moment, I watch for a certain stillness in the other, an emptiness ready to receive me without expectation or judgment. When I am with a friend or a client who is in pain, my intention is to offer the emptiness in myself, the quiet part. I want to make room to see and hear the other, to recognize what we share and how we are different, to form a bridge of knowing that reaches across the boundaries between us.

Stories can take us to a place of quiet where we can truly see ourselves and each other. I tell a Buddhist story about someone who finds a cocoon and takes it home to watch the moth emerge. A hole appears in the cocoon and the moth can be seen inside, struggling, but the hole gets no larger. Finally the watcher takes a sharp blade and opens the cocoon, releasing the moth. But the moth's head is swollen and its wings are frail, its body shriveled. It will never fly because it is the struggle through the hole in the cocoon that pushes the fluid from the head into the body and the wings, giving the moth the strength to fly. When I tell this story, I relate its impact and meaning to me. I was raised, you see, to be a "Jewish mother." If you are in pain, my first impulse is to feed you, then to hold you or do my best to distract you. It is counterintuitive to me to allow you to have your pain. What I have learned

from those who have allowed me the privilege of accompanying them on part of their journey in grieving is that often the most generous and effective thing I can do is allow people to have their struggle. Telling that story, and talking about how I hear it, lets people know that my intention is to honor their story and their struggle, not to talk them out of it or push them through it, but to allow them to find their own strength.

Through the stories I tell, I reveal myself and I invite people to then reveal themselves in response to the stories. In that way, we can see and recognize each other. It feels like a blessing: to be seen. It validates us, makes us real and right.

The benefits of story as a tool for healing are now acknowledged by storytellers, therapists, clergy, and health care practitioners of all kinds as well as by people who work in other service professions. "Cure," in my dictionary, means "a method of remedial treatment for disease; a remedy." To "heal" means "to become whole or sound." They seem quite similar, but I think of them as distinct. I think of cures as interventions: surgery, drugs, radiation, things to do in order to stop or reverse the course of disease. By healing, on the other hand, I mean an inner process, the natural growth of an organism becoming whole, physically, mentally, emotionally, and/or spiritually. No cure can take place unless there are inner resources for healing.

So where does story fit into this? I know first-hand the power of stories. I have experienced that energy, that connection, that insight through a particular story, and as a result I have decided to tell stories in the context of healing. Any story I choose to tell must speak to me in some personal way, must inform or nourish me, adding to my own resources for health and growth. Stories can transmit information and offer possibilities for growth and change. Stories can provide some of the nourishment and resources needed for the healing that comes from within each individual.

When I offer a story to others, they may hear in it some of the same qualities that I do, or they will hear it differently, depending on their experience, their strengths, and their needs. If the story speaks to them at all, if there is something in it that catches their attention, then that something will add to their resources, will contribute to their health and growth. I may not see what strength they draw from it. Indeed, they may not even be consciously aware of how they can make use of the story, but I must believe nevertheless in the efficacy of the telling based on my own understanding of the story and on the many "testimonials" that people have offered in the past in response to story.

Storytelling is an art form. I don't believe that it can be prescriptive: "Tell this particular story to a person with this illness or 'problem' and all will be cured." But like other art forms, we can learn to use story more consciously and effectively in a way that serves our listeners. We can increase our knowledge of stories and our knowledge of the human response to them. We can improve our performance skills and add to our teaching and facilitation abilities to offer workshops, residencies, retreats, and other ways for people to "work the stories," to find within the stories that which speaks to them, informs, inspires, nurtures, and heals.

"Outwitting Death" is one story. And it is two stories. There is a traditional folktale and a very personal remembrance. As I tell them together, I am reminded of the meanings we can find in the metaphors that stories offer. I have used these stories in bereavement groups. Telling stories in this setting helps relax everyone and brings them present to the group. It helps put people in "listening mode" and, I think, enables them to be better listeners to each other. The story provides a focal point for discussion in a way that allows people to make their own connections and to talk about them as they feel comfortable. After everyone "checks in" and says how their week has been, I tell a story. I may pose questions to the group that relate to the story, but often group members will take up the story and relate it to their lives and their losses without additional direction. Some of the issues that arise in this particular story include the denial or acceptance of death, how we retain our feeling of connection with people who have died, how memories can often surprise us when they are stimulated by seemingly mundane objects or events, what comfort exists or does not exist in the act of remembering, and how we can find meaning in our grief through memory. People who have heard this story have sometimes been moved to tell or write down memories of their own connection with the person they are grieving.

⪻ Outwitting Death ⪼

A HUNGARIAN FOLKTALE RETOLD BY GAIL ROSEN*

*Maybe it's true and maybe it isn't, but once there was an old woman.
She was very, very old. Older even than the gardener who planted the
first tree in the world. But she was full of life and never dreamt of dying.*

She was always busy in her house, baking bread or sewing new curtains. Or in her garden, planting flowers or weeding the vegetables. Or in her yard, building a shed for the goats or helping to birth a new baby lamb.

But one day, Death remembered the old woman. He came and knocked on her cottage door. "Old Woman, I have come to fetch you."

The old woman was kneading dough for bread. She looked up, brushing the flour from her hands. She saw a dark, cloaked figure.

"Death? Oh, Death. I'm afraid I'm much too busy. I have to finish kneading this dough. Then I have to wait for it to rise. Then I have to knead it again and form it into loaves, then wait for it to rise again, and then bake it .... If it must be, Death, could you come back tomorrow?"

There was a long pause before Death spoke again. "Very well," said Death. "I shall return for you tomorrow." And with his bony finger he chalked on her door the word "Tomorrow." And he went away.

The next day, Death returned. "Old Woman, I have come to fetch you."

The old woman was tending her rose bushes. She looked a little startled, but unconcerned. "Oh. Death. Death, I'm afraid you've made a little

mistake. You see, you said you'd come tomorrow. *Tomorrow.* See for yourself what you wrote on the door."

And Death looked. And there on the door was the word "tomorrow." "Very well, Old Woman," said Death. "I shall come for you tomorrow." And he went away.

The next day, Death returned. "Old Woman, I have come to fetch you." The old woman was sewing a new party dress. She looked Death squarely in the eye and burst out laughing. "Death? Oh, Death, I'm afraid once again you are mistaken. You see, you said you would come tomorrow. Tomorrow, not today. See for yourself what you wrote on the door."

And Death looked. And there on the door was the word "tomorrow." "Very well, Old Woman," said Death. "I shall come for you tomorrow." And he went away.

Well this went on every day for a month and at the end of that time, Death was getting annoyed. "Old Woman, you have been cheating me. I shall come for you one last time." And with his sleeve he erased the word on the door.

Now the old woman wasn't laughing anymore. She was frightened. She tried and tried to think of a way to outwit Death. She was up all night thinking. In the morning she hadn't thought of anything, so she looked around her cottage for a place to hide.

In the corner was a large barrel. It was filled with honey. She climbed inside it and crouched down low, with just her nose sticking out. But then she thought, "Oh dear. Death is clever. He's sure to find me here."

So she climbed out of the barrel of honey. Across the room there was a large chest. She opened the chest and climbed inside. It was filled with goose feathers. But then she thought, "Oh dear. Death is clever. He's sure to find me here." And she climbed out of the chest.

Just as she did, Death burst through the door. He looked around and he couldn't see the old woman anywhere. In her place he saw a strange creature. It was huge, covered with white feathers, and something thick was dripping from it. Death was so startled he cried out, "Aaagh!" And the thing screamed back, "Aaaaaagh!" And Death was so frightened that he ran away. And he never returned.

On the day before Death came for my grandmother, my father's mother, my Bubby ... On the day before Death came for my Bubby, I was sitting next to her bed in the nursing home. The bars on the side of the bed were up. She was lying on her back with her eyes closed tight. "Bubby. I'm here, Bubby. Bubby, open your eyes. Bubby, look at me." But she didn't.

I don't remember the color of my Bubby's eyes. I do remember her hands. When she sewed, she didn't put the needle in and draw it through, put it in and draw it through. She would put it in, and in, and in, and then pull. In, and in, and in ... Everything she did had that economy of motion. When she knit, she didn't put the needle through and then wrap the yarn around it. She would hold the yarn in back so she could put the needle in and pull it through in one continuous motion. In and through, in and through.

I remember her hands — and the top of her head. When I was a little girl, I would stand on the kitchen table and she would measure my skirts to hem them. I would have to stand very straight and turn very slowly. The pins prickled my legs. I hated it. But I didn't dare slouch. My Bubby was not a patient woman.

I remember her hands kneading dough for baking, all her movements were fast, strong, hard edged, angry in a way. Bubby was angry about a lot of things. She was angry that she couldn't read and write better than she did, but she'd been taken out of school after third grade. Her mamma needed her at home to help with seven younger brothers and sisters.

She was angry about her marriage. Bubby only ever told me one nice thing about my grandfather. I have a pin he gave her as an engagement gift. Silver, with her initials in marcasite. Y.D.B. Yetta Davidson Burgan. I never saw her wear it. I never even saw a picture of her wearing it. We found it in a box of old costume jewelry and broken beads after she died.

I never knew my grandfather — he died when I was an infant — but from everything I hear from other relatives, he was a lovely man; quiet, gentle, he loved opera, knew all the plots of Shakespeare's plays, and was a hard worker. But Bubby told me he wasn't ambitious. He didn't have common sense. She told me about a job offer he had had in Philadelphia. She thought it sounded wonderful, but he wouldn't risk the move. Bubby's sister, my great-aunt Alice, said, "Yetta should have been the man."

Bubby was angry that after she married, she couldn't continue to work. Bubby first went to work when she was 14, in the factory where her father worked. Her father worked in a garment factory. He cut the pieces for men's suits. Only men could be cutters. Bubby was a seamstress. She sewed the pieces together. In those factories back then, like now, they paid by the piece, and she was so fast that within a year she was bringing home more money than her father.

But after she married, well, it was a "shonda," a shameful thing, for a married woman to work outside the home. And then her husband's factory went on strike and he didn't have work, so they had to give up their little apartment that she loved and move back in with her mother. Bubby told me that when she married, she was building "castles in the air and they all came falling down." "Castles in the air" — and I had never thought of Bubby as a poetic woman.

Oh — the one nice thing Bubby told me about my grandfather ... She told me that on their wedding night, she was 19 and she was frightened. She told me that on that night, he was a gentleman. That first night, they slept. She told me things like that over the phone. I would call her from college. Over the phone. I still couldn't see her eyes.

She told me about another day, the day she ceased to be a girl and became a young woman. She went to her mother because she was scared. She didn't understand about the bleeding. Her mother slapped her across the face. And I don't think Bubby knew why. But my great-aunt Alice told me that they thought if you slapped a young woman on that day, she would have a nice complexion. And Yetta, she said, always did have beautiful skin.

So different! When it happened to me, I knew, because they'd shown me a movie in Girl Scouts. Our lives are so different, my Bubby's and mine. And yet, some things — the same. You see, Bubby figured out a way to work, to pursue her own ambition. It was terrible for a married woman to work outside the home, but it was respectable if it was a family business. So Bubby bought a grocery store and moved her family in on the second floor. And she worked there for ten years — every day.

One day her daughter said, "Mamma, let me take you to a movie. You got to get out of the store sometime." But she wouldn't go. She said with that quarter she could buy a whole case of soda. After the grocery store, there was a luncheonette. And after that she did mending and alterations at home.

So some things seem the same. I have my own business. I sew. I bake. But I think of Bubby most in the spring, at Passover time. I always have a big crowd for Seder, the ritual dinner. I race around, juggling my business and my family and my guests, and there's matzoh ball soup on the stove, a turkey and brisket and tzimmes in the oven, a sponge cake on the counter, and in the refrigerator, gefilte fish — made from scratch, I don't mind telling you. When I'm moving at top speed, I look at my hands. And I see my Bubby's hands. I still don't remember the color of my Bubby's eyes, but I think that while I'm here, doing and remembering, in some way, my Bubby outwitted death. ❧

Here are a few other traditional stories that I have told in bereavement groups:

- "The Mustard Seed" (Buddhist) and "Blessings and Disasters" (Chinese) from *Soul Food: Stories to Nourish the Spirit & the*

Heart, edited by Christina Feldman and Jack Kornfield (San Francisco: Harper, 1996).

- The title story in *The Cow Tail Switch and Other West African Stories*, by Harold Courlander and George Herzog (New York: Henry Holt and Company, 1986).

- "Elijah's Mysterious Ways" by Peninnah Schram from *Jewish Stories One Generation Tells Another* (Northvale, NJ: Jacob Aaronson, Inc, 1987).

Infinite Resource and Sagacity

DIANE ROOKS

AS WE SHARE STORIES of survival and resilience with others, we offer encouragement that they too can survive. Perhaps stories help us hold on until we find the significance and wisdom we need. Trying to make sense of the death of my son, David, helped me know who I am and what is important in my life. This sorting-out process revealed to me that I could find inner truths and strengths that I did not know existed. Stories nourished my spirit during this long dry spell and made me realize that I could find healing even in situations that could not be cured. This experience revealed to me that life and joy are available on the other side of loss. I am now convinced that we all need to hear stories of hope — again and again.

When David was a little boy, he was the most precocious child you'd ever meet. Of course all mothers think their children are the cutest, the sweetest, the smartest — but he really was. He asked more questions.

In fact, I spent half my life looking up or making up the answers to his questions because "I don't know" never satisfied him. He loved books and stories and words. Perhaps it started when he was only two months old and I returned to school to study English literature. Every day for two semesters I read to him from Beowulf, Chaucer, Shakespeare, Wordsworth, and Elizabeth Barrett Browning. The words and the sound of my voice charmed him.

As he got older, he continued to love looking at books and being read to. One of his favorite stories was Kipling's "How the Whale Got His Throat." This story talked of a man of infinite resource and sagacity, and David loved the sound of those words. He went around talking about this man of infinite resource and sagacity. The funny thing about it, he was only two years old. Imagine a little guy with blond hair, blue eyes, a big smile, and few teeth talking about a man of infinite resource and sagacity. People were amazed when they heard him. One day someone asked if he knew what all of that meant. David answered, "Yes, it means the man is really smart."

As he got older, he loved challenges — puzzles, surprises, riddles, tricks. My brother, who wasn't married, enjoyed spending time with my children. David loved Uncle Tom's ability to perform magic. One day while Uncle Tom was visiting us, David begged, "Do some magic, do some magic." Uncle Tom agreed and started with simple things like making a quarter disappear and then suddenly plucking it from behind David's ear. After a few more tricks he said, "David, how would you like me to make you disappear?"

You could see the wheels turning in that little head. He wasn't so sure about this at first, but after thinking for a minute, he said, "Okay, that would be great."

So Uncle Tom called out, "Everybody gather around — I'm going to make David disappear. This is going to be tough because I've never done anything quite like this before." He began to rub his hands together and say his magic words, then, "Poof — I did it! He's gone. I made David disappear."

David looked around, looked at his hands and clothes, touched himself, and seemed a little concerned. We all started talking as if he weren't there. After a while Uncle Tom asked if we were ready to bring David back. I said, "No, not yet. It's really nice and peaceful around here now. Maybe I'll finally get some rest."

David's eyes got bigger and bigger as he looked around the room from one person to the next, seeking some sign of recognition. He started jumping around, making a little more noise, stomping his feet and waving his hands. Then he began yelling, "Hey, it's me, David. I'm here — I'm still here."

Finally I said, "You know, even though it is quieter, I really love that little guy and I'm beginning to miss him. Maybe you'd better bring him back."

Uncle Tom nodded in agreement and said, "Okay, but this is really going to require some concentration. I've never done this before either, and it may be harder than making him disappear."

Everyone, including David, got really quiet. His eyes were so big, they were about to pop out of his head. He hardly breathed. Uncle Tom rubbed his hands and said his magic words again. As he rubbed and mumbled, our eyes were glued to his hands until he shouted, "Poof! He's back. David, you're back. It's so good to see you. Where have you been?" We all cheered and rushed to hug David and Uncle Tom.

Magic fascinated David for a long time. Uncle Tom gave him tricks every year for Christmas and his birthday and taught him how to perform them. We bought black material and made him a big cape; he got an old briefcase from his grandfather to carry his tricks in; he had a tall black hat and a wand. But he never allowed Uncle Tom to make him disappear again.

As he grew up he continued to seek things a little out of the ordinary. While in high school, one year at the state Latin convention he wrote and gave a speech — in Latin! In college, he and his roommate wrote a computer program for *Dungeons and Dragons*™, long before computer games were on the market. They installed it on the Vanderbilt University computer system and it worked! He went to work for Kodak as a systems engineer and got married. He loved riding his mountain bike, playing the piano, brewing beer, and baking bread — always looking for new and curious things to experience and learn.

Then one day, when he was 29, he had an allergic reaction to an insect bite and was gone. A parent's worst nightmare! My whole life turned upside down, taking with it so many hopes and dreams for the future. His young wife was two months pregnant with their first child. This unborn child of theirs would never experience the joy of knowing David.

Struggling with all of this, I realized one day that he *was* the man of infinite resource and sagacity, for now he had all the answers and I had the questions. As I continued to try to make sense of something that made no sense, I did a lot of reading, writing, screaming, grasping, questioning, thinking, searching — none of the traditional answers fit anymore. As time passed, gradually the thought emerged that death is not the end, but rather a transition to another state or dimension that we don't fully understand. And the frustrating part is that we're left not knowing how to communicate. I am convinced that he heard me and knew my feelings. I expressed them often enough. But I didn't know how to understand him, until I noticed he was using my thoughts, my memories, my dreams, and my stories.

One day while jogging, I allowed my mind to be clear and free and open. Suddenly that incident when David was four years old — when Uncle Tom made him disappear — popped into my head. I hadn't thought of it in at least 20 years, and the memory comforted me. Later that day in my kitchen, I ran across a small metal box that I hadn't seen for a long time. Wondering what was inside, I opened it and found a stack of David's business cards. Because he worked for Kodak, his picture was on the cards. As I looked at his face, I suddenly knew he was telling me, loud and clear, "Hey, it's me, David. I'm here — I'm still here."

Then I saw his gift hanging on my dining-room wall. About a year before his death, David was on a business trip and picked up a copy of Robert Fulghum's book *All I Ever Needed to Know I Learned in Kindergarten*. When he returned home he called and said, "Mom, you really need to read this book. I think you'd like it because it's full of great stories."

I read it and I did like it, and I noticed in the front of the book Fulghum's "Storyteller's Creed." When I returned the book to David, I told him that I wanted to get a copy of that creed. Using a fancy font on his computer, he printed it on rice paper and framed it for me for Christmas. It touched my heart at the time, but now the message from the man of infinite resource and sagacity leaves no doubt:

> *I believe that imagination is stronger than*
> *   knowledge,*
> *That myth is more potent than history,*
> *That dreams are more powerful than facts,*
> *That hope always triumphs over experience,*
> *That laughter is the only cure for grief*
> *And I believe that love is stronger than death.* 🐚

Writing David's Story

DIANE ROOKS

I WROTE THIS STORY AFTER struggling with my son's death for two and a half years. I could not have written it sooner, although it seemed a very natural part of my healing process.

At a workshop on developing personal stories with storyteller Donald Davis, I began thinking of the events in this story as connected. Donald asked us to tell a story about someone that would "cause the listener to know us better." The story seemed only for me at first because I found so much healing in it. But as I struggled with it at the workshop that weekend, others encouraged me to tell it.

A friend at the workshop called several weeks later and said she had not been able to stop thinking about the story. She had told someone about it, and that person also had been touched. She closed by saying, "You have to tell that story. It gives me and others hope that we could survive, whatever our loss might be."

Part of my concern about telling the story was not wanting sadness to be the dominant feeling listeners were left with. I have heard stories of personal events and tragedies and felt the teller should be relating them to a therapist, not to an audience. I resent being told stories that are so heavy that I end up feeling depressed. I believe a story should not make listeners deal with grief that has not been fully explored and dealt with by the teller.

This is not to say that there should be no emotion in a story. I love stories that make me laugh and cry and feel all sorts of emotions, but I just don't want to be left hanging with a feeling of unresolved sadness or hopelessness. Good stories should elicit feelings, but not more than the audience can handle.

That was my concern. I didn't want my story to leave people sad. The story was really about my relationship with David, and I wanted listeners to feel the love and joy in that and not be overwhelmed with the sadness. In addition, I did not want to dissolve into tears when I told it in front of an audience. But because I felt David's life and the story were gifts, I didn't want to keep them to myself if they could be helpful to others. I began telling it in small family settings. We all cried, but each time I told it I got a little stronger. Then I told it to Compassionate Friends, a support group for parents who have lost children. Tears are always appropriate there, but I got through without crying, although my voice quivered at one point. The group members encouraged me to keep working on it. They obviously sensed the sadness but had felt hope — for me and also for their situations. That was exactly what I wanted to hear.

The following week I attended the Florida Storytelling Association camp and signed up to tell it Sunday morning during a session called

Stories from the Heart. Even though I have found storytellers to be supportive and helpful, I almost took my name off the list several times. When Sunday morning came, I told the story to an audience of about 150 tellers.

The response was extraordinary. One woman said she had a situation in her life that she wanted to tell a story about, but she had never been able to do so. She told me a beautiful story about her husband planting some tulips not long before he died. She said her daughter needed to hear the story and I had shown her how she could tell it. Another woman told me she had recently lost her mother, with whom she was very close, and my story had given her so much to think about in dealing with her loss. One woman pointed out that we all suffer losses in life, and my story revealed how loss could be dealt with in creative ways to make us better people.

I have told the story many times since then. I am mindful to tell it in situations that are appropriate and not just for the effect it has. Many times when I arrive at a performance, I feel led to share it. Every time that happens, at least one person comes up afterward and tells me that I must have told the story for them because it was exactly what they needed to hear. So I try to be open to telling it when I get that feeling.

The magic continues

At times during this process I have asked myself: Am I kidding myself thinking in this way? Do I have delusions of grandeur? But then I wonder why I doubt the power of the universe and the power of stories to work in the world and on me. I have seen so much evidence of that power working in me and through me as I tell stories to others — as long as I am open to receive it. I have felt healing power in the stories of others. All of the 27 writers and storytellers I inter-

viewed for my book about dealing with loss through story confirmed my belief as they talked about the part stories played in their healing processes.

John Ward, a writer and consultant, said, "Often times you never know until later when a story has proved healing for another. For a story to heal, I believe one must be open to the possibility. There are stories I read or tell again and again because I still need their therapeutic value. For example, my youngest daughter was a 'preemie.' The doctor said she would not survive. I refused to accept his words, and through the intensive care glass partition I pleaded, 'Be a fighter, be a fighter.' She was, and she survived. She still loves to hear that story, as do I ... as it continues to work its magic."

When John Ward told me about that incident, neither of us knew how important it would later become to my own family. Many months later my daughter, Wendy, was expecting her first child and had a difficult pregnancy. She developed severe toxemia and had to deliver her baby six weeks early to protect her health. The baby boy weighed five pounds three ounces, but he had breathing problems and had to be taken immediately to the neonatal intensive care unit (NICU). The little guy was put on a respirator and had tubes running in and out of every possible spot.

That evening Wendy insisted upon seeing him, even though she was still having blood pressure problems. She and her husband went inside the NICU, scrubbed down, and put on hospital robes. My husband and I watched through the window as they looked down at their tiny baby without being able to hold him. Tears streamed down their faces. This was not the moment of their hopes and plans. In their eyes I saw pain, fear, disappointment, disbelief, and yet thankfulness that he was alive. I wanted to hold all of them and promise everything would be fine, but I knew that would bring little comfort.

All of a sudden I thought about John's story and started to say through my tears, "Be a fighter, be a fighter." When we returned to Wendy's room, I told her the story and we all started saying "Be a fighter" to baby Davis every chance we got. He, too, was a fighter and went home after ten days in intensive care. I'd like to believe our thoughts and positive energy helped his rapid progress, but I *know* telling the story that first night lessened our fears and helped us all to hang on to our dreams. And that is what the power of story is all about.

Readers may contact Compassionate Friends at P.O. Box 3696, Oak Brook, IL 60522; by phone at 630-990-0010; or through the website (www.compassionatefriends.org).

Honoring a Life Through Sharing Stories

ALLISON M. COX

WHILE I WAS WORKING on this book, my mother, Madonna Jean O'Brien Sturmer, suffered a series of strokes over a month's period and then died. Time stopped its day-to-day dance and I stepped outside of the music — lost in a deep silence. My parents had lived with me in Washington State for the last five years, but before that they had migrated like gypsies across the nation, leaving Chicago at middle age to follow their hearts' desires. Mom had told us she wanted a simple goodbye — no casket, just cremation. Dad wanted us to stay in Washington for any type of funeral services, rather than return to Chicago where all of us grew up and most of our relatives reside. Dad also insisted, "I don't want any priest or minister that didn't know your mother talking about her at her memorial," and the rest of the immediate family agreed with him. But we needed to acknowledge the passing of our mother, companion, lover of life, chef to our feasts, dear to our hearts.

How could we include all the many people across the U.S. and beyond that my mother had befriended in somehow saying goodbye? Friends and family were calling me throughout the day and into the night, asking "What can we do?" I took to wandering in the woods behind our house, cell phone to my ear and soothed by the trees, ferns, moss. As we talked, my mind went back to all the times spent together with these people — in their living rooms, kitchens, and backyards. Each voice brought back memories of everyone sitting together, usually laughing, often eating some of Mom's good cooking, and *always* telling stories. And so through these conversations I realized exactly what was needed to be able to say goodbye to Madonna — these stories needed to be told, the same stories that people would be telling if we could all be transported back to Chicago to hold a grand Irish wake. "Send me your favorite stories about Mom along with a blessing, poem, or prayer for her," I told them, "and we will share them at her memorial."

The outpouring of kindness and support that flowed into this house sustained us. Stories arrived from across the United States and overseas. Storytellers on the internet storytelling list-serv who didn't even know me sent their favorite tales. Over 60 e-mails of stories, songs, blessings, and prayers arrived in three days. More came through the mail. The night before the memorial, my family covered two large pieces of plywood with Mom's linen tablecloths, and we pinned our favorite pictures chronicling the 68 years of Madonna Jean's life to these displays to place in our yard. We also discussed all the many accomplishments of my mother's life and compiled them into a story. This was no small task since it became obvious that my mother's life had already reached legendary proportions, with details about which none of us could agree. We had to keep asking my father to tell us which parts were true! We reread all the stories we received from others, chose portions to share, and decided who could best read them. Giant baskets of flowers and plants filled our backyard. A local church and the Eagles' Club lent us some folding chairs. The billboard for community events on the main street of our island read "We'll miss you Madonna" and posted the time and place for the memorial.

On that early August evening, torches lit the yard as over 100 people walked across my neighbor's field, where they had parked, and filled our backyard. They came from all ends of the island and beyond. Islanders shared music, too — there was a bagpiper, a fiddler, and Mom's friends had even formed a choir to sing their favorite songs from her water aerobics class. Many brought foods in memory of Madonna Jean's gourmet cooking. The family and gathered friends each took turns sharing segments of stories that others had sent or that we each remembered. At the beginning of the service an owl landed on the roof of the house, watched over the proceedings, and flew off to the last strain of the bagpipe playing "Amazing Grace."

Here are just a few of the stories shared:

Renny from India: I had come to live with the Sturmers as an exchange student. I was to receive free room and board in exchange for helping care for the children and do some housekeeping since both Donna and Allan worked. Even though it was my job to watch the children when they went out, sometimes Donna would hire a babysitter when they went to the movies so that I could go with them. Donna said she wanted me to experience America while I was here.

Shelly from Illinois: I remember that your dad and mom joked a lot. I always thought that they had a passionate relationship, even before I knew what one was. Your mom looked like and acted like a schoolgirl when your dad would tease her, and sometimes she would get downright mad and her face would almost match the color of her hair ... when it was red that is! The first time I ever went camping was with your family in the Winnebago. Your mother made us the best meals and kept us fed the whole time with her great organizational skills. It didn't seem to shake her the least bit with kids running through the tiny kitchen, and she sang too while she was cooking — she really enjoyed whatever she was doing even if it was just cooking a meal. I loved camping after that!

Virginia from Florida: For the first half of 1987, while undergoing chemotherapy, I lived alone and found myself ordering in a lot of junk food, too weak to go shopping myself. When Donna discovered this, she started making big pots of different flavors of vegetable soup — sometimes chicken, or beef. She would put them in individual-serving-size containers, froze some, and kept me supplied for most of the six months of my treatment. This lovely lady also invited me for dinner so often I began to feel like family. She was such a "good cooker" — a familiar expression — that she kept me on the road to recovery much healthier than I would have ever been without her. I'm happy that I knew her and can remember all the good times together.

Patty from Illinois: I was just remembering that high-school dance when we doubled for junior year. I was invited at the last minute and there was a crisis about what to wear. And your mother made me a dress! I remember there was a last-minute late-night sewing session, but she beat the clock. And this wasn't for her daughter, but her daughter's friend!

Nan from Vancouver, British Columbia: She was the most immediately friendly, open, and unaffected person I've ever met. Whenever I visited you, she always popped out to say hello, purely, it seemed, impelled by a spirit of gracious warmth. She was lively and enthusiastic and she shared her enthusiasms generously. After hearing about my arthritis, it took her about three seconds flat to get me on the phone ordering a catalogue from her discount vitamin store. I think of her every morning now when I take my supplement. I have been searching for something of hers to keep alive in myself, and I have decided on this: her unselfconscious friendliness. If I can emulate that in some small way, then perhaps the world will not be so sorely at a loss for her having left it.

Bob and Yvonne from Wisconsin: Just before Donna and Al were first married, I was visiting one night at Donna's parents, Jeanette and Basil, where Donna and Al planned to live. Al and Basil were wallpapering a bedroom upstairs. After finishing the job, Donna and her mother went up to inspect the work done by their two men. I recall hearing gales of laughter, especially Donna's laughter, coming from the upstairs. When Donna and Jeanette came downstairs, they explained, wiping their tears and still laughing because "the boys applied the wallpaper upside down!" At the time I really thought that was a funny story, but much later in my life I came to understand what a wonderful person Donna was. She could have been angry and could have berated both her husband and father, but she was able to see the bright side of what happened, accept the upside-down wallpaper, and get on with her life. What a beautiful way to live. I was to see that side of her many times over the years.

We then turned to the photo displays and pointed out the upside-down wallpaper in the background of the photo with Madonna donning her wedding veil.

We shared Mom's favorite Irish blessing at the closing of the memorial:

May the road rise to meet you
May the wind be always at your back
May the sun shine warm upon your face
May the rains fall softly upon your fields
And until we meet again
May the Lord hold you safely
In the hollow of his hand.

Story by story, we each took a step back into the world, less frozen and immobilized by grief and now warmed, drawn closer by this sharing of the life stories of the woman we had all loved. What was most rewarding to me was that my daughter's friends were awe-struck at the power of that night. They said that they had never experienced anything like it — celebrating a person's life by sharing stories — and thanked me for asking for their help. People came up to me for weeks afterwards to comment on the beauty of that evening.

We compiled all the contributed stories, poems, blessings, and prayers in a scrapbook. I dried the petals of the flowers sent to us from around the country and, assisted by my daughters, made a potpourri with these flower petals for each person who sent flowers and stories. Dad then traveled around the country visiting family and friends, distributing the dried flowers, sharing the photos we had chosen to display and, of course, the stories — and heard so many more healing stories along the way.

We took a photo of Madonna Jean, surrounded it with her pressed flowers, and scanned it, then printed the following poem over the images to create a gift to offer to all who shared their memories:

Do not stand at my grave and weep.
I am not there. I do not sleep.
I am a thousand winds that blow.
I am the diamond glints on snow.
I am the sunlight on ripened grain.
I am the gentle autumn rain.
When you awaken in the morning's hush,
I am the swift uplifting rush
Of quiet birds in circling flight.
I am the soft star that shines at night.
Do not stand at my grave and cry.
I am not there. I did not die.
Life is eternal and love is immortal and death is only a horizon
And a horizon is nothing more save the limit of our sight.

— *Anonymous*

SPIRITUAL HEALING

Buried Treasure: Sacred tales and healing

Elisa Pearmain

As a storyteller and counselor, I have worked with stories in the process of healing myself and others. I have also come to rely on stories to guide me on the spiritual path. Although Western culture would keep them apart, healing and spiritual growth are inseparable. Stories offer support for both and help us to make that bridge.

Spiritual and cultural traditions the world round have long provided teaching tales describing how others have danced and stumbled along life's path. I have found these short wisdom tales or sacred tales to be especially powerful and have learned over time how to work with them to cre-ate new possibilities for living well. Sacred tales speak to the innermost yearnings of our souls, lead us to a connection with the divine, and teach us to live gently on this earth. You need not, however, consider yourself to be in search of the divine to benefit from these tales. They lead us joyfully toward personal growth and connection to others as well.

I was inspired in my search for story by the late author and Jesuit priest Anthony de Mello, who put it well when he said, "The shortest distance between truth and the human being is a story." So let us begin with a story from the Sufi tradition.

There once was an aging farmer who lay upon his deathbed, worrying about the fate of his lazy sons. Near his final hour, an inspiration came to him. He called his sons around his bedside and bade them draw in close. "I am soon to leave this world, my sons," he whispered. "I want you to know that I have left a treasure of gold for you. I have hidden it in my field. Dig carefully and well and you shall find it. I ask only that you share it amongst yourselves evenly."

The sons begged him to tell them exactly where he had buried it, but the father breathed his last breath and spoke no more.

As soon as he was gone, the sons took up their pitchforks and shovels and began to turn over the soil in their father's field. They dug and dug until they had turned over the whole field twice. They found no treasure, but they decided that since the field was so well dug up they might as well plant some grain as their father had done. The crop grew well for them. After the harvest they decided to dig again in hopes of finding their buried treasure. Again they found not a treasure, but a field prepared for sowing. This year's crop was better than the one before.

This went on for a number of years until the sons had grown accustomed to the cycles of the seasons and the rewards of daily labor. By that time their farming earned them each enough to live a happy life. It was then that they realized the treasure their father had left for them. 🍂

This story describes well the true path to healing and spiritual development: the slow daily incorporation of awareness, practices, and presence that reward us with treasures more precious than gold. It also offers us an example of how to work with stories in order to deepen our connection to the sacred and to healing. Just as the sons found their treasure through patience and work, if we wish to allow stories to serve as our teachers we must plant their wisdom in a fertile soil that we create in daily practice.

In thinking about the story, we can probably all relate to the sons who wanted a quick miracle to make their lives easier. What kinds of miracles are you holding out for? What daily actions could you take towards the outcomes you desire? Could these daily steps not transform your life more quickly than a miracle?

What is this treasure that we are seeking in healing and spiritual growth? This story from India can help us gain a stronger feeling for what we are after.

Once on the outskirts of a village, a holy man slept against a gnarled tree. As the sun rose over the forest, a man from the village ran to the sleeping man and shook him awake.

"The gem, the gem, where is the gem? I had a dream in which Lord Shiva told me to find a holy man at the edge of the forest who had a gem that would keep me wealthy for the rest of my days."

The holy man reached into his bag and produced a diamond the size of a coconut. "I suppose you mean this?" he said. "I found this on the path."

The villager took the diamond and ran back to his home. There he paced and paced through the day and all that night. Early the next morning the villager was back at the gnarled tree.

"Please," he asked the holy man, placing the gem at his feet, "share with me the wealth that allows you to give away this gem so easily." &

I feel excitement as I am reminded of what I truly desire and the different paths that I can take in this life. Stories do that for us. They remind us of what is most important and what will quickly pass away. We need these stories for inspiration on a daily basis as much as food. I think it is fair to say that in our own way we are all searching for the wealth described in the tale above: that connection to, and experience of, what is sacred, timeless, mysterious, and love-filled.

Here is an example of a story that connected me to the sacred in daily life, providing greater awareness and humility and sustained healing.

Once upon a time in India there was a king who had a wise and loyal advisor. But this advisor had a strange habit. No matter what news he was given, good or bad, he would always respond in the same manner. He would smile, stick his finger in the air, and say, "All is as it should be."

You could tell him that the crop had failed for the third year in a row, or that enemy soldiers were approaching. He would always respond by saying, "All is as it should be." His habit was strange, but the king put up with him. Until one day. The king and many of his advisors and servants had gone out on the hunt. They were deep in the thick of the jungle, the buzz of insects and the sounds of animals all around them. Suddenly from out of nowhere a large snake dropped from the trees into the path of the king. The king's horse reared up and the king fell off. He kept hold of the reins but was dragged through the forest until his foot caught between two trees and he let go. When his followers gathered round him, they saw that his boot was gone and his big toe had been severed from his foot. As the servants and advisors began to offer their condolences, the advisor turned to the king.

"All is as it should be," he said.

"As it should be!" screamed the king. "How can you say it is as it should be when the king loses his toe? You are fired from your post. Go from my sight."

The advisor turned to go, but as he did, the king distinctly heard him say, "All is as it should be."

Eventually the king learned to walk without his toe and again went out into the forest, this time to survey the boundaries of his property lines. All of a sudden his party was ambushed by a group of tribesmen from just over the border. Seeing the king in his finery, they grabbed him as the others escaped into the forest. The king was taken back to their village, where he was stripped and prepared for sacrifice. The king was tied to a pole in the center of the village and the chief walked around him, surveying him from every angle. Suddenly he began to wave his hands and to yell, "This one is no good. He has already been cut. We cannot sacrifice one to our god who has already been cut." With one swipe of his knife, he cut the king free. The king hobbled back to his palace. He had his old advisor brought to him.

"You were right," he said. "Because I lost my toe I was not sacrificed in a ceremony today. But tell me, why did you say 'all was as it should be' when I sacked you from your job?"

The advisor bowed. "I am no magician, sir. I cannot see the future, but I have learned that from each experience comes something beneficial, or at least something valuable to be learned. Today I see what it was. As you recall, I was a faithful advisor, always by your side. If you had not sacked me, I would have been by your side today, and seeing how I am in possession of all my fingers and toes, I would have been next in line for the sacrifice." 🐾

How would our lives change if we could stop at each occurrence and say "All is as it should be," or at least "What could be good about this situation?" It opens us to the mystery of life, adding faith and reverence for the order of things.

This Indian tale has served as my teacher and healer. A number of years ago I did a storytelling performance in my hometown library. To make a long story short, there were some unruly older kids there without parents. I tried an audience participation story that got out of hand. I had to stop the story and ask the kids to sit down. I felt embarrassed, beyond what I usually would have felt, because many of the adults in the audience were people that I saw on a regular basis. As I drove away that day I found myself feeling shame and anger toward myself.

Luckily my little advisor came to the rescue. "Remember the story 'All is as it should be'?"

I asked, "What could possibly be as it should be in this situation?"

"Good question," it continued. "What could be good about it?" It stopped me in my mental tracks. Well, I asked myself, how would I be feeling right now if things had gone perfectly? I would be on top of the world, thinking about how great everyone thought I was. Was that really any better? Either way I was ruled by ego. The seesaw nature of ego would never let me have simple peace and acceptance of myself. I decided to get off the seesaw and to simply accept myself for the perfectly imperfect person that I am. Since then I have been better able to focus on giving my gifts to the world, and less focused on how well they are received. The "as it should be" turned out to be an invaluable lesson.

Self-awareness is the first step in the process of healing and of spiritual development. Here is another example of a story that can help us to be aware of ourselves in the present moment and thus to live more consciously. I use this story frequently in my work with individuals addicted to drugs and alcohol, and persons suffering from depression.

There is the story of Nasrudin the Hodja (teacher), who was seen out in front of his home one night, searching for something on the dusty ground under his street lamp. The good neighbor rushed out to help.

"Nasrudin what have you lost?" he asked.

"I have lost the key to my safe."

"Let me help," the man cried. Together they pored over the dusty ground for some time. At last the neighbor said, "Nasrudin, we have been looking for ten minutes and have covered every inch of ground. Are you sure you lost it right here?"

"Oh no," said Nasrudin, sitting up. "I didn't lose the key here. I lost it in the house."

"You lost it in the house? If you lost it in the house, why are you looking for it out here?"

"Well, because the light is better here, of course!"

We laugh at Nasrudin's folly, yet most of us are at any given moment behaving in much the same way. We all have emotional, physical, spiritual needs that give us a sense of longing, urgency, and desire. If we do not stop to give full attention to what we are feeling and needing, we may go about fulfilling our desires in ways that are less than nourishing, filling or comforting ourselves with food, sex, drugs, TV, shopping, and work. This only works temporarily and adds another layer of pain to our lives.

How can this story help us, beyond expanding our awareness? If we allow it to get under our skin and into our psyches, it can be there to remind us of what we are doing. It can bring us back to the present moment to consider that for which we are truly searching.

Stories are meditative. They can help us to slow down and remind us to focus our awareness in the present moment. The story of the wild strawberry is an example from the Zen tradition.

A man is walking through a field when he looks back and sees that a tiger is chasing him. He runs to the edge of a cliff, grabs a vine, and jumps over the cliff and out of the tiger's reach. Clinging to the vine, he hears a roar below and sees that another tiger waits at the bottom of the cliff to devour him. Above, two mice begin gnawing on his vine.

Suddenly in front of him he sees a bunch of wild strawberries growing on a small shelf of rock. He pops one in his mouth. How delicious! ❦

This is the story of our lives. The tiger of our past chases us with guilt, regret, and longing, but we cannot turn and change it. The tiger of fear awaits us in the uncertainty of the future, as does certain death, but we cannot change it. However, in the present moment we can control how we meet the world. We can choose to delight in our surroundings and to fully drink from life's cup. We can have peace, but never by changing the past and never by trying to stave off the future. It is in each moment that we can stop on our vine and taste the sweetness of the present moment.

How does this help us towards healing and spiritual connection? Being present in the moment means drinking in the experience of life. Feeling alive. There is so much beauty in the world around us that we cannot help but be in awe, and feel wonder. This sense of awe connects us to the mystery of life. Like the field that must be continually tended, keeping our awareness in the present moment is a lifetime's challenge. In the process, we become much more aware of what our minds are going on about and where healing is needed.

This story can also help us to meditate and to reduce stress. If we remind ourselves of this story when we are sitting in meditation, we have an image to bring us to the present moment with an element of peace. When we are feeling stress, we can slow down and focus on the elements of the present moment. Try this some time when you are feeling stress. Ask yourself the following questions while breathing deeply and slowly: What do you see around you? What is there to smell, feel, touch, taste, and hear? These elements have the power to bring us back into our bodies, where we can breathe and relax and put things into perspective.

There once was a bird that flew round and round, asking the other birds, "Could you help me to find the sky? I am looking for a place called the sky."

"You are in the sky," they replied.

"Oh, no, this is not the sky," the bird cried.

"This is only air. I am looking for the sky." So saying, she flew off impatiently. ❦

As many spiritual masters have said, "Stop looking, and see." The divine presence is not locked away somewhere else, but is in each place and in each breath. The way of life that is required to truly understand this will make us healthy and peaceful beings. A story like this can turn our heads 180 degrees. We must contemplate the story and apply it to daily life, over and over again. If we do, we will find greater health and well-being.

Developing a healthy respect for the mystery of life is important to spiritual awareness and health. Learning to live by the adage "Things are as they should be" requires surrender to life. I use an image of a great tapestry that is our lives, or perhaps even the many lives that we each have on our journey toward oneness with the life force. When we look at this tapestry we may only see the underside, a jumble of seemingly disconnected strands and colors, where messy loose ends hang and tangle. It is only from heaven that one is afforded a view of the upper side of the tapestry, where all the strands weave together to form a bigger picture that makes sense.

How can we practice surrender? Here is a story from the Sufi tradition that has helped me:

It was a hot summer day and Nasrudin had been working in his garden. He decided to rest under the shade of a large walnut tree. Making sure that no one was about, he removed his turban to cool his bald head. As he relaxed, he meditated upon the beauty of nature and the great wisdom of Allah. Observing a fine pumpkin in the garden, he smiled to himself. "Allah, your ways are great indeed, but if I had been creating things, I would have done a few things differently. Take for example this grand pumpkin growing here upon a spindly vine on the ground, and then consider the tiny inconsequential walnut growing upon that great and lordly tree. If I were in charge I would have reversed it. I'd put the walnuts on the spindly vine and let the pumpkins grow from this magnificent tree." So saying, he sat back, closed his eyes, and began a delightful reverie of all the things he would do differently if he were designing the world.

A gentle breeze stirred the branches above him. Suddenly a walnut fell from the tree and landed with a thud on his bald head. As the pain spread, he rubbed the lump that had begun to swell on his scalp. Then an understanding smile spread over his face. He bowed down toward Mecca.

"Oh, Allah," he murmured, "forgive me. Suppose I were arranging things? I should just now have been hit on the head by a pumpkin. Ah, Allah, great is thy wisdom indeed."

This story can help us by reminding us of the folly of trying to completely control our lives and the people in them. What things and events in your life do you wish were different? Decide what is in your power to change and what must be accepted with grace and serenity. Can you accept your body size, physical limitations, life circumstances, and the people who surround you? Imagine what it would be like to actively choose to surrender to present circumstances. You may find yourself flooded with relief. Trying to control our lives requires one heck of a lot of energy!

The spiritual search is health enhancing. When we feel in a state of dis-ease, whether mentally or physically, our spiritual outlook will govern how well we are able to manage the circumstances and to heal. The spiritual search calls us to ask important questions that allow us to change that outlook: Why are we here? What is truly important in life? How do we relate to others? What is the nature of our relationship to a creator, and how can we change that? In the process we become better equipped to face the challenges of life.

One of the stories that has helped me most on my life's path is the following Buddhist tale.

A monk and his student are sitting on the bank of a river. As they sit, a scorpion ambles by and falls into the water. The monk pulls it from the water and is stung on the hand. A second time the scorpion falls into the water, and the monk retrieves it with the same result. When this happens a third time, the student cannot restrain himself.

"Master," he cries, "why do you keep trying to save that beastly scorpion? Can you not see that it is just going to sting you?"

"Yes, I see that it is going to sting me," the master replies. "It is the dharma [the nature] of a scorpion to sting. But it is my dharma to save."

When we become clear about what we truly need to be doing on this planet, much of our stressful behavior falls away.

A spiritual outlook can help us become more accepting of ourselves and lets us know that we are connected to others and to a larger cycle of reciprocity between human beings. The ability to ask for help is crucial in the healing and growth process. We need to believe that it is only human to be, and to admit to being, vulnerable at times in our lives. We cannot heal if we are spending all of our energy berating ourselves for being less than perfect.

So how do we get these stories under our skin so that they come to memory when we need them most and not just in hindsight? Our hunger for the good story often drives us to plow through story collections like children in a candy store. We read one after the other, tasting the unique flavor of each enough to say, "Mmm, I like that one, or so-so," often bypassing altogether those that have already been tried. This way of tasting stories is like reading a description of the story on its door, rather than opening the door to be deeply touched by it. This is the way of our con-sumerist culture, but stories call us to be with them in a more time-honored way.

When I was first introduced to stories, I would read through collection after collection at a rapid pace, waiting for the perfect story treasure to jump out at me. Occasionally something would touch me, but many other valuable stories passed me by because I had not taken more time with them. Stories need time to sink in so that their images may connect with our hearts and imaginations, and so personal meaning and learning may arise. Once these connections are made, the images and ideas can become a part of our psyche, available to us when needed.

Some of the stories that I included in this chapter may have been familiar to you. Did you have the urge to skip over them? Before you pass over a tale that is familiar, ask yourself what it means to *know* a story. If it means that the story serves as your teacher on an ongoing basis, then it can be said that you know it. Too often, however, we are quick to be bored by stories already heard, or we pass over them in a collection. Before the advent of the printed page and the television, sto-ries were told repeatedly so that they would not be forgotten and lost forever. These tales were also interpreted for us by storytellers, all giving their own spin. What have we lost by not knowing the stories "by heart" and sharing them with others?

There is buried treasure for each one of us inside our own hearts and in everything around us. Stories can help us to see and experience it. As

Thomas Moore, author of *Care of the Soul*, wrote, "Our lives rest on a cushion of stories." Why not build up your cushion. Take the time to get to know wisdom stories, the familiar and new, so that they may be there for you, tapping on your shoulder like the wise advisor, saying, "There's another way to experience this. Remember the story about ..."

SUGGESTIONS FOR GLEANING THE TREASURE FROM STORIES

1. Create a weekly ritual. Find a time of the week when you can usually be in the same place at the same time, perhaps a Sunday evening. Read one wisdom tale, aloud to others if possible.

2. Tell the story to as many other people as possible during the week, either in person, by posting a photocopy (one only please, including sources) on your office bulletin board or in your community bulletin, or by circulating it in an e-mail among friends. This will allow the images and ideas in the story to become common language among the people with whom you live and work.

3. Let the story ripen inside you. Go for a walk and tell the story to yourself. Let each of the main characters tell it from his/her own perspective.

4. Get the story into your psyche by making associations with the images in the story to commit it to memory. Memories are stored by association, sensory and emotional associations being the strongest. Try these methods:

   (a) In a quiet setting, close your eyes and drop into the story setting. Walk around in it, exploring the story using all of your senses, observing characters and emotions as you go.

   (b) Sit with someone else close by, knee-to-knee. With eyes closed or downcast, take the other person with you to the place where the story happens and paint a vivid picture of the place for them, walking them through the story.

5. Tell the story as if it happened to you. Put yourself in the place of one or more of the characters.

6. Make up a modern-day version of the story and share it with others. Write about the messages of the story and how they relate to your life. Imagine yourself digging for the treasure that you desire

7. Recollect times in your life when you grappled (or refused to grapple) with the issues in the story. Share these stories with others and urge them to share their stories of grappling with you as well.

8. Explore the symbols and metaphors in the story, finding your connection to them. If, for instance, there is a door in your story, pretend that you are describing a door to a Martian. "A doorway is an opening, a threshold between two worlds, something that must be opened, something that can be locked, something that can keep things in or out, etc."

9. Be creative. Find practical ways to remind yourself of a story's wisdom. Draw a picture of a strawberry and put it on your car dash or desk to remind you to come back to the present moment. Get your friends to say to you "It is as it should be" when you complain about something. (Promise not to disown them!)

10. Shape the tale for a more formalized telling. This process of choosing a perspective, a focus, and a sense of characters and place personalizes it and will help get it under your skin.

Story wrestling: Healing through telling Hasidic stories

Doug Lipman

HASIDIC STORIES ARE, intrinsically, healing stories. From the 18th-century beginning of this Jewish mystical sect, stories have been a key way to pass on the spiritual and emotional teachings of the movement's masters. As a result, writings about the power of Hasidic stories have focused on their healing effect on the listener.

But what about the effect on the teller? What form of transformation can come from the process of learning, adapting, and telling stories from Hasidic tradition? This question led me to undertake an experiment that would change my approach to healing through Hasidic stories.

A pattern of healing experiences

I have told many Hasidic stories. Perhaps a third of them have been important healing stories for me, each in different ways. But there's a usual pattern. I tell a story to a number of rehearsal buddies and coaches, who listen, make suggestions, and help me reevaluate what the story means to me. I tell the story to a variety of audiences. Then there's usually a problem or two I have to solve. Solving the problem leads me to healing.

Sometimes the problem is obviously emotional. Perhaps a part of the story seems flat; this usually indicates a place where I'm suppressing my emotions. Or a story is so emotional for me that just telling it brings me to tears. In either of these cases, I find that the most efficient way to work on the story is to work directly on the feelings. I find what I need to cry about, laugh about,

rage about, feel terror about, etc. Often I tell the story to someone who has agreed to be there for me while I process feelings. I tell the story — not for my listener, but as a trigger for my own unprocessed emotions. I have always found that following such a session, or perhaps many sessions, I am able to tell the story more vividly, with fewer of my own raw feelings intruding.

Other times the problem seems technical in nature. Perhaps I can't imagine an ending. Or a character never develops fully. In one case, I felt chronically out of touch with the audience as I told the story; this turned out to indicate an emotional issue for me about my relationship to my listeners.

Still other times I remain unaware of a story's emotional importance to me. Then months or even years later I realize, "Oh! That story was an image leading me on in my emotional growth."

For example, the Hasidic tale "The Forgotten Story" speaks of a follower of the Baal Shem Tov (the founder of the Hasidic movement) who, upon his teacher's death, is given the job of wandering from place to place telling stories about the Baal Shem Tov. His term of exile comes to an end that was preordained by his teacher; later events make clear the original purpose of his wanderings. For many years this was a "signature story" for me, one to which I felt deeply connected. Only later did I realize the comfort and guidance I got from this story. At the time I began telling it, I felt like I was out on a limb, expanding my audiences beyond the relatively safe world of telling to children in schools and into the confusing and frightening (to me) world of telling to adults. It seemed presumptuous for me to offer myself as someone who could offer spiritual meaning to adults. In that context, this story provided an image of a reluctant storyteller who, nonetheless, was serving an important purpose that would one day be revealed. It gave me a way to acknowledge my feelings of inadequacy while asserting the importance of my role.

An experiment in healing

As I prepared to write this article, I considered describing in detail one of the healing experiences I just mentioned. But that felt cowardly. Why not describe an ongoing process of healing instead of one encased in the safety of the past?

So I decided to work with a new story — one whose effect on me had not yet come to my awareness — as an experiment in healing. I would take this still somewhat raw story and try to accelerate the healing process. Instead of allowing healing to occur as a by-product of my artistic involvement with the story, I would experiment with intentional use of the story for healing.

I was aware of potential difficulties with this approach. One of the advantages of story is that it can provide a metaphorical approach to an issue I am not ready to face head on. Metaphor has its own pace and I knew I was pushing it. But I hoped the immediacy of the experience would counter any inconclusiveness of the results.

The story I chose was from a translated Hasidic manuscript — Abraham J. Heschel's *The Circle of the Baal Shem Tov* (Chicago: University of Chicago Press, 1985), pages 59-61. What follows is my final version, after my adaptations.

⤞Rabbi Gershon's Dream⤝

DOUG LIPMAN

Rabbi Gershon wrote to his brother-in-law: "My family and I are coming to see you. We will visit you on our way to move, finally, to the Holy Land."

Rabbi Gershon's desire to emigrate was not unusual. Any pious Jew in Eastern Europe during the 1700s wanted to live in the Holy Land. The land itself was holy. The air was holy. People who moved there said it was like getting a second soul.

What was unusual was this: As eager as he was to move to the Holy Land, Rabbi Gershon knew he would not begin his journey without his brother-in-law's blessing. Why? His brother-in-law was the famous mystical rabbi known as the Baal Shem Tov. If the Baal Shem Tov would give his blessing to Rabbi Gershon's journey, he could be sure it would be a success.

Therefore, Rabbi Gershon traveled overland across Eastern Europe to Medzhibozh, the city where the Baal Shem Tov lived. When Rabbi Gershon arrived, the Baal Shem Tov greeted him warmly, ushering him to the quarters the Baal Shem Tov had prepared for him.

When he entered the quarters, Rabbi Gershon's mouth dropped. The Baal Shem Tov had prepared an entire apartment for Rabbi Gershon and his family. Why such a spacious dwelling for a short visit? The next day, Rabbi Gershon rested from his journey. Whenever he heard someone walk near his door, though, he looked out — in case it was a messenger from the Baal Shem Tov, summoning Rabbi Gershon to receive the Baal Shem Tov's blessing.

But the Baal Shem Tov never called.

Rabbi Gershon was a great scholar, so he spent the next, unexpectedly free days studying the Talmud. He went to the house of study, where the other scholars sat, studied, and debated together.

The Talmud has no "page one" — to remind us that there is no beginning and no ending to study of the Torah. At the center of each page of Talmud is a passage from the Torah. Around that passage are arranged the most revered, ancient commentaries on that passage.

Around those commentaries are slightly more modern texts that comment on the ancient ones.

Studying a page of Talmud may take a day or a week or longer. Often a group of students will spend a year studying a single tractate.

So Rabbi Gershon spent his days studying the ramifications of passage after passage. This way, several weeks passed.

Then one day a messenger appeared at the house of study, asking Rabbi Gershon to meet the Baal Shem Tov in his office.

When Rabbi Gershon arrived, he saw the Baal Shem Tov's grandson seated across from the Baal Shem Tov himself. That was unusual. Rabbi Gershon thought, "Perhaps the Baal Shem Tov wants his grandson to witness someone being given a blessing to go to the Holy Land!"

The Baal Shem Tov said, "You know my grandson?"

"Of course."

The Baal Shem Tov smiled. "I would like you to teach him."

Rabbi Gershon was surprised. "He is coming with me to the Holy Land?"

"No," said the Baal Shem Tov. "I would like you to teach him here."

Rabbi Gershon tried to keep smiling. To teach the grandson of the Baal Shem Tov was, after all, a great honor! With as much gratitude in his voice as he could muster, he said, "Of course."

Starting the next morning, Rabbi Gershon's days in the house of study changed. He brought the grandson of the Baal Shem Tov with him. Now only a few hours each day were for his own study of the Talmud. The other hours he taught.

Rabbi Gershon devoted himself to his teaching and his studies, but each day he hoped that the next day would bring a blessing from the Baal Shem Tov — and the beginning of his holy journey. This went on for many months.

It went on so long that Rabbi Gershon had nearly completed an entire cycle of the Talmud since he arrived in Medzhibozh. It is customary, when you finish a cycle of Talmud study, that you give a banquet to which you invite your teachers and those who have studied with you. This way you celebrate — punctuate — this particular moment in your endless encounter with the Talmud's wisdom.

One day, Rabbi Gershon had a thought: This banquet would be a perfect opportunity for the Baal Shem Tov to give him his blessing! When he thought about it, it seemed clear. This was what the Baal Shem Tov had been waiting for. To have studied the entire Talmud with the constant intention of leaving the next day for the Holy Land — this was what Rabbi Gershon had needed, to be spiritually ready to depart!

Rabbi Gershon thought ahead. "If I wait to finish my studies before setting the date for the banquet, that will cause a delay of several days. Instead, I will set the date now. That way the banquet can happen the very day my studies are over! At last, I will receive the Baal Shem Tov's blessing and begin my journey into greater holiness!"

Rabbi Gershon calculated the exact day he would finish studying. He set the day following as the date for the banquet and continued his visits to the house of study. But the night before the banquet, he had not yet finished the last tractate!

So Rabbi Gershon studied the entire night. After morning prayers, however, he was so tired he could not continue. He had to nap. So he lay down. He dreamed.

He dreamt that he arose from his bed and walked out into the city. Soon, he found himself in the woods on the city's outskirts.

When dark fell, he was lost. He spent the night in the forest.

The next morning he wandered through the woods. He saw no sign of a road nor of another person. He spent that night in the woods as well.

The next day he saw no feature that could orient him. He wandered, always finding himself deeper in the woods. But he had to get back to Medzhibozh. The Baal Shem Tov would be waiting for him, at his banquet. He could not keep the holy Baal Shem Tov waiting!

By the last light of day he saw the figure of a man in the distance. He shouted. The man answered his call. The two of them ran toward each other, meeting in the darkening forest.

"I am so glad to have found you," said Rabbi Gershon. "I have been lost three days. But I have to get back to Medzhibozh! The holy Baal Shem Tov himself is waiting for me!"

"I am in a bigger hurry," said the man. "I am the caretaker for three children in Brody. Their father, a wealthy man, expects me to teach them. I have been lost in these woods for three days. I must find my way back to Brody!"

"Since we are both lost," said Rabbi Gershon, "let us journey together in the morning. Perhaps we will find our way to one of our destinations." So the next morning they wandered off together.

Later that day they saw a building in the distance. They ran toward it. As they came closer, they saw how large and grand it was. They recognized it as a yeshiva, an advanced school of Torah study.

As they walked up to the door, they heard the sounds of Torah study from within. They stopped to listen. What Rabbi Gershon heard pleased him. This was a high level of study!

Inside, they listened as the rosh yeshiva (head of the yeshiva) lectured on the Torah. He was revealing secrets of the Torah neither had ever heard.

When the rosh yeshiva finished speaking, the two men approached him. "We are lost. I must find my way back to Medzhibozh," said Rabbi Gershon.

The man from Brody said, "And I must find my way back to Brody."

The rosh yeshiva looked at them. "Medzhibozh? Brody? I know of no such places."

Both men said, "We just left there a few days ago!"

The rosh yeshiva said, "I can only tell you this: There is no other world but this one. I advise you to stay here."

"No! We must keep looking!"

"In that case," said the rosh yeshiva, "continue on this road. You will find another yeshiva a day's walk from here. Perhaps they can help you."

Late the next day the two men approached an even larger building. It was magnificent! From within they heard the sounds of Torah study and stopped on the steps to listen. Rabbi Gershon was so pleased with what he heard, he could scarcely rouse himself to enter.

Once inside, they listened to the rosh yeshiva lecturing. He revealed powers hidden in the words of Torah, powers that Rabbi Gershon had never suspected.

After his lecture, they approached him. "We are lost," said Rabbi Gershon. "I must find my way back to Medzhibozh."

The man from Brody was still staring at the passage of Torah the rosh yeshiva had just explained. At last he said, "And I must find my way back to Brody."

The rosh yeshiva looked at them. "Medzhibozh? Brody? I know of no such places."

Rabbi Gershon said, "We just left there a few days ago!"

The rosh yeshiva said, "I can only tell you this: There is no other world but this one. I advise you to stay here."

"No! We must keep looking," said Rabbi Gershon. But the man from Brody said nothing.

"There is another yeshiva," said the rosh yeshiva, "a day's walk from here. Perhaps they can help you there."

In the morning, Rabbi Gershon left the yeshiva. But the man from Brody said, "No. The study is so sweet here, I cannot bear to leave it."

Alone, Rabbi Gershon found his way to the third yeshiva. It was a palace! Coming upon it, Rabbi Gershon heard the sound of teachings from within. Even before he was close enough to understand what was said, the sweetness of the sound nearly overcame him.

Inside, he heard the rosh yeshiva speaking. As the rosh yeshiva spoke, Rabbi Gershon saw the Divine Chariot flying through the air.

When the rosh yeshiva had finished, Rabbi Gershon approached him. "I must get back to Medzhibozh. I walked out from there days ago. I met a man from Brody, who was also lost. We came to two yeshivas before we came to yours."

The rosh yeshiva said, "There is no other world but this one."

Rabbi Gershon said, "But I must return! The Baal Shem Tov himself is waiting for me!"

At this mention of the great rabbi's name, the rosh yeshiva looked sharply at Rabbi Gershon. Then he sighed and spoke to his students, "Then bring me the map of all the worlds."

In a moment, the rosh yeshiva was poring over an enormous book. After many minutes he looked up from one of its pages and spoke to Rabbi Gershon. "There does seem to be a small world — a mostly corrupt one — where there are two places named Medzhibozh and Brody. But my advice to you is to stay here."

"No," said Rabbi Gershon. "How can I keep the holy Baal Shem Tov waiting?"

At this, the rosh yeshiva pointed to two of his students, saying, "Take him, then." They each grabbed Rabbi Gershon by one of his arms, took him to a door, opened it, and pushed him through it into the darkness.

Rabbi Gershon felt himself falling. He fell and fell, then landed in his own bed.

Opening his eyes, he saw from the clock that his entire dream had lasted merely 30 minutes. In fact, the Baal Shem Tov was just entering his room.

Rabbi Gershon said, "I am so glad to see you! I was lost for days. In my dream, I was afraid I would miss my banquet!"

"I know," said the Baal Shem Tov. "But I am worried about the man from Brody. What happened to him?"

"He stayed at the second yeshiva."

The Baal Shem Tov grew quiet. "His soul was very great. We needed him in this world. But he chose to stay there."

Rabbi Gershon was silent a long time. At last he said, "I see. So I will be staying here to teach your grandson?"

The Baal Shem Tov smiled. ❧

Adapting the story

This story fascinated me. I was taken by Rabbi Gershon's dilemma. He wanted to go to Palestine, but he also wished to remain in the presence of the Baal Shem Tov. I was intrigued by his insistence on returning, in spite of the obvious heavenly nature of the three yeshivas.

Yet this story had obvious difficulties. What was I to make of the ending? I was fascinated with the predicament of Rabbi Gershon, but the story in the manuscript ended with the final statement about the man from Brody. Like most traditional tales, this was one I couldn't tell without changing. Nonetheless, I couldn't know how to change it until I decided what it meant to me.

What does this tale mean to me?

After outlining and telling the story to a willing listener, I asked for appreciations: what worked in the story, what moved the listener, any images that seemed "alive." Finally, I talked aloud about what the story meant to me. I concluded that, for me, the most important thing about this story was that Rabbi Gershon learns to accept the holy in the here and now, to accept his role where he is.

Next, I created an ending that fit this conception, adding the two paragraphs beginning "Rabbi Gershon was silent a long time." I told the story several more times, always trying to give the story a clear emotional focus based on my understanding of what mattered in it.

Beginning the intentional process of healing

All this had happened before my decision to use this story as an experiment in healing. To begin the experiment, I scheduled a series of sessions with helpers who would listen to me talk aloud.

In my first session, I asked myself, "What was the emotional pivot for me in my process of adapting this story?" As soon as I asked the question, I knew the answer. It was my choice of Rabbi Gershon's lesson: to find the holy in the here and now rather than look to far-off horizons.

Then I asked myself, "What does that choice of lesson tell me about myself? What message am I giving myself by interpreting this story in that way?"

An answer came immediately to mind — and I hated it. You see, at this period in my life I am simultaneously pursuing my work in the storytelling community and also trying to help bring the transformational power of storytelling into the corporate world. My hated thought was that this story's lesson for me is to abandon my efforts at this expansion. For me — this thought said — coaching other storytellers is like teaching the Baal Shem Tov's grandson. Trying to gain acceptance in the corporate world is like hurrying off to the Holy Land.

Why did I hate this answer? When I imagined making the choice to "stay where I am," I felt despair. Was this my inner healer talking, or my inner tormentor?

I resolved to explore the feeling of despair. In a second session I tried to feel the despair fully. I felt it in the pit of my stomach. After some minutes of shaking, I had a thought: I tend to feel that I must either save the world single-handedly or forfeit my right to exist at all. This is a chronic feeling that has surfaced in more than one difficult place in my life.

Toward the end of an hour of shaking, talking, and occasionally crying, I had a realization: Maybe the core issue is just about noticing that I'm okay. That led to a new question: How could I use the imagery of the story to help me notice that I'm fine without heroic achievements? This, in turn, led me to the idea of "talking to" Rabbi Gershon. As a metaphor, the story could allow *him* to be the one who had this problem, not me. So I said to the character, "Gosh, Rabbi, maybe you don't need to be any more holy than you are!" This made me laugh for quite a while. Soon I could feel myself beginning to be more relaxed about the entire issue. This reinforced my belief that the "lesson" I am trying to teach myself through the story is not to pull back my efforts in the corporate world. But as this session ended, I still felt unsure about how to proceed.

During my next session I told the story again from scratch and got appreciations from my listener. I asked myself, "What's the issue here for me?" My mind returned to the issue of having to be a savior or else having no right to live. Immediately I thought, "I hate this issue!" So I said "I hate this issue!" aloud several times. I began to laugh and shake. I continued to say it, and it continued to produce laughter alternating with shaking. From time to time thoughts came into my mind, sometimes about the other areas of my life where this issue plays out. I shared the thoughts with my listener.

Now a new thought came into my mind: "I am so pleased to give this issue to Rabbi Gershon!" It seemed that putting my attention directly on the issue would "sink" me — but I felt safer attending to *his* situation. For a while I experimented saying things like "Now *you're* in trouble, Rabbi Gershon!"

Somewhere in this process, I began to think about my father. One image kept coming up: I was about 12 years old, sitting at the dining-room table with my father as he talked to me. My father is a warm man who relates easily to all people. Yet we had a set of conversations in which he claimed that he and I were "more intelligent" than other people. I remember, as a child, feeling torn between wanting to be special and wanting to belong to the general human race. I ended this session with the determination to work further on this childhood feeling.

Several weeks passed before my next session. I reviewed where my feelings about the story had led me. Then I tried to use the image of Rabbi Gershon to resolve my childhood dilemma. I said, "You're nothing special, Rabbi Gershon. But everything about you is just fine." This produced more shaking, as well as tears. After several repetitions of this phrase, my scheduled time was over.

At my next session I began where I had left off. "You're nothing special, Rabbi Gershon" produced explosive laughter. I added an alternative ending to it: "But everything you do matters." This resulted in yawning and shaking. I welcomed these physical processes, since I have found over the years that, just as I cry to recover from grief, I shake and laugh to recover from fear — and I yawn to recover from physical injuries, including habitual tensions. I continued to repeat both forms of this phrase for several sessions. Each repetition produced sustained laughter, yawning, shaking, or tears. I had found my way to releasing a deep vein of hurt!

Somewhere in the second or third hour (spread out over several sessions) of using this phrase to produce emotional release, I began to remember childhood experiences of my mother's reactions to people who "thought they were better than us." I realized that my mother, raised on a small farm in rural Michigan, was often critical of people she suspected of having any sense of class superiority. Suddenly I understood that, as a child, I had been caught between two forces: my father's desire to be "more intelligent" than others, and my mother's strong condemnation of arrogance. She never objected to my father's version of feeling superior, but I felt caught between their strong feelings.

For one entire session I talked about my memories of a young man who would visit my parents occasionally. He would seek my father's approval by bragging about his accomplishments. After he left, my mother would say how much she hated his attitude. During this session I began to say to the young man, "You're nothing special, but I love everything about you."

Where am I now? I do not feel that the issue is fully resolved for me. But I believe that I have turned an important corner. The phrase "You're nothing special, Rabbi Gershon. But everything about you is just fine" at last provides a safe refuge from an emotional crossfire. It allows me to imagine, in terms that work for me at this moment, being both ordinary and loved.

I haven't finished the job of healing, but I believe I have found an approach that will, in time, heal this piece of childhood confusion and hurt. In the end, I expect to be able to think in relaxed fashion about what has previously been a difficult issue. And I am sure that this growth will also add depth and flexibility to my telling of Rabbi Gershon's story.

Story beacons

What does all this tell us about Hasidic stories and healing? These stories give the teller a chance to wrestle with unhealed emotional hurt.

Are Hasidic stories unique in this way? I think not. In fact, I have found that *any* story can be fodder for this process. My unconscious "healer" doesn't care where a story comes from, only that the imagery fits my needs. Personal stories, historical stories, fairytales, even jokes can sometimes contain images that shine to me, like lighthouses, through the fog of unhealed emotional hurt.

Following the light of such stories can guide me as I excavate and remove the remains of unfinished struggles. To be sure, I can follow the beacon of a story by listening to it and talking about my responses. But the process of learning, adapting, and telling a story can put me into an even more active relationship with its images. Telling is a dynamic event that molds the story while transforming the teller.

A collection of Hasidic stories compiled by Doug Lipman can be found at the Hasidic Stories website (www.HasidicStories.com).

TEACH
YOUR
CHILDREN
WELL

Storytelling and resiliency: Why children need stories

LINDA FREDERICKS

A FORMER WORK colleague of mine, Dr. Mary Davis, had been invited to an Indian reservation to give a talk on health promotion. She came dutifully armed with flip charts and overheads and gave a carefully structured presentation that included recent health statistics, research findings, and practical observations. At the conclusion of her talk she invited questions and comments from the audience. Several people raised their hands and asked questions about certain information she had shared or practical strategies that they could use.

After several moments, an older man sitting at the back of the room slowly rose to his feet and looked at her steadily. In a quiet voice, he said, "All the things you say have long been in our stories. We must simply love our children and tell them the stories again."

Those simple but poignant words have come to my mind often as I think about the power of storytelling. Stories are, after all, the most ancient, most compelling, and most intuitive form of communication, and the means by which values and culture have been transmitted from generation to generation since the beginning of humankind. Whether the stories come from Hans Christian Anderson, an African *griot*, a Native American elder, or a Hispanic *contadora*, they all contain the secrets of living life with honesty, compassion, courage, and love. Stories help to bind people together, forge family and group

identities, and create a sense of common culture and understanding. Any group —whether a family, classroom, workplace, or civic organization — is defined by the stories that are known and shared among members.

Parents and other family members are usually the first and often the most important storytellers that children know. Stories that are shared by parents or grandparents may provide endless guidance and inspiration to the child and be remembered for a lifetime. When I conduct storytelling workshops for educators and other adults, I am always struck by the vividness of memory and emotion that people have for the stories that they were told as small children.

When family members, teachers, and other trusted adults tell stories to children, they are providing far more than entertainment. They are supporting the healthy development of children and conveying the most profound of life's lessons. Through stories, children see that they are not alone in facing difficult and complex life issues. Through stories, they understand that there are other more productive ways of thinking, feeling, and acting that allow them to face actual situations with greater strength and wisdom. Stories provide a nonjudgmental means by which young people can safely examine ideas and feelings. Time-honored stories from many cultures teach young people about the qualities that shape relationships and sustain healthy human interactions.

The process of storytelling may also enhance basic academic skills. Once they have heard or read a story, children of all ages are usually eager to discuss what they have learned, so a parent or teacher can use storytelling to help children develop critical thinking skills. They can promote writing skills by encouraging young people to record their own stories, impressions of stories that they have heard, or even a play based upon a familiar tale. Children who hear stories will often improve their reading skills because they are interested in reading other related stories and information.

Stories can also increase tolerance and understanding of people from other cultures. Through the medium of story, the listener can safely explore what all human beings have in common as well as how they differ from each other. Stories have the power to gently remove the child from his or her usual reality and, for a time, immerse the listener in a different time and place. Through imagination, each child can venture beyond the boundaries of individual experience and know what it is to share in another person's travels or feel another's sorrow or celebration. Few people return from an imaginative journey to another culture without retaining a greater appreciation for the unique wisdom and experiences of its people.

The importance of cultivating imagination should not be underestimated and has profound implications, not just for academic learning, but for behavior as well. Several recent studies have shown that children who lack imagination are not only prone to school failure, but are also far more susceptible to violence. Such children cannot imagine alternatives to their problems; they tend to remain stuck in a single way of seeing or doing things.

Imagination is not a luxury, but a need that every child has. Children who possess imagination clearly have very different experiences from those who lack it. They have the ability to imagine, and therefore act upon, different solutions. They can see beyond the limitations of their present circumstances. They are aware of the impact and consequences of their actions. They can form relationships that are lasting and satisfying. Imagination — fostered through play and storytelling as well as through other creative expressions such as music, dance, and art — is one of the greatest gifts that caregivers and teachers can bestow upon young people.

Strengthening "self-righting" tendencies

Research and writings in the areas of resiliency and human development shed further light on why stories are so important and irreplaceable in the lives of children. In their pioneering research on resiliency, Dr. Emmy Werner and Dr. Ruth Smith conducted a longitudinal study (reported in their book *Overcoming the Odds: High Risk Children from Birth to Adulthood*) with children who were at highest risk for developmental problems: children whose parents lived in poverty, abused substances, suffered from mental illness, and/or were physically violent. The researchers were able to identify four basic internal characteristics possessed by resilient children, "self-righting" tendencies that moved them toward normal adulthood under all but the most persistent adverse circumstances. These self-righting tendencies are:

- A sense of purpose and of future
- Problem-solving skills
- Autonomy
- Social competence

The characteristics associated with resiliency are precisely the qualities that are embedded in the storytelling process. Most stories that are passed from generation to generation teach young people that they have a bright future, that they are not alone, and that each individual has a special and unique purpose in life. At the same time, stories frequently deal with conflict and reveal the necessity of persistence in the face of obstacles and hardships. Familiar tales such as "Cinderella" or "The Ugly Duckling" not only portray the main characters facing a series of difficult trials, but also show that the willingness to go through adversity is what allows the characters to become mature beings and triumph in life and in love. Stories provide a kind of internal map that demonstrates to the listener how others have gone on life's journey, where they have met with certain hardships and obstacles, and how they have negotiated the difficult passages.

Dealing with life's challenges is at the very heart of traditional stories, whether they are fairytales, folktales, myths, or legends. Bruno Bettelheim emphasized in his classic book *The Uses of Enchantment* that such tales teach the child that "a struggle against severe difficulties in life is unavoidable, is an intrinsic part of human existence—but if one does not shy away, but steadfastly meets unexpected and often unjust hardships, one masters all obstacles and emerges victorious." The great stories from throughout the world teach listeners that there is hope even in the darkest of circumstances, and that every person has reserves of possibilities and potential, of love, courage, and compassion.

Time-honored stories from virtually all cultures teach young people how to make decisions by discerning between good and evil, false and genuine, outer appearance and inner truth. In stories, as in life, all decisions have consequences, and the tales often contrast the aftermath of wise decisions with decisions that are foolish, uninformed, or downright malicious. The stories seem to challenge each listener by saying "Look what happened to this person after she made

this decision. What would you have done under similar circumstances?"

Storytellers must also become story *selectors*. It is important to note that not all stories are worth telling, and not all tales carry messages that support resiliency. Some traditional tales uphold oppresive social structures or frighten children into "good" behavior. So all storytellers — whether they are teachers, counselors, therapists, parents, or others — need to choose their selections carefully and be mindful of the needs and capabilities of their young audiences.

Good stories — both traditional and contemporary — promote social competence by showing the young person which qualities cause relationships to thrive, and which actions will sow distrust and discord. Stories convey the importance of truth and honesty in relationships, and emphasize the role of respect and caring between friends, family members, nations, young and old, teachers and students, humans and their environment.

Yet at the same time that stories promote the crucial importance of relationships, they also teach young people the need to go out on their own and discover their identity. It is no accident that so many of the most beloved children's tales — such as "Hansel and Gretel" or "Beauty and the Beast" — have to do with leaving home and making one's way in the world. All children are faced with issues of autonomy, and the stories guide them in understanding that the creation of a unique identity is a normal and healthy human need. As Bettelheim commented, "Young people intuitively comprehend that while stories may be unreal, they are not untrue; that while these stories do not happen in fact, they do happen as inner experience and personal development; that these tales depict in imagery and symbolic form the essential steps in growing up and achieving a healthy and independent existence."

The Gift of Good Advice

A FOLKTALE FROM NEW MEXICO RETOLD
BY LINDA FREDERICKS*

Once there were three men, poor farmers, who lived in a time of drought. They struggled day after rainless day to make the dry earth yield enough food for their families, but all of their hard work met with failure.

Plants withered and died before their eyes. In time, they realized that they had to leave their homes and find work so that they would be able to send money back to their families. It broke their hearts to leave their wives and children, but they knew that they had no choice if their families were to be saved from starvation.

They carefully packed a few bags of precious food, some jars of water, and a few pieces of clean clothing for the long journey to the nearest village. After saying farewell to their families, they set out on the road with heavy hearts and desperate hopes.

After they had walked for several days along the dusty road, they spotted someone walking towards them. As the figure came closer, they could see it was a *viejo*, an old man, carrying something on his back. As he drew even closer, the farmers saw that the *viejo* was carrying three bags of money!

The farmers greeted the old man and excitedly asked him, "Where did you get those bags of money? We are looking for work right now, and if

some job can pay bags of money like that, we want to know about it!"

In a creaky but wise voice the old man replied, "Oh, I didn't get this money from some job. I got it by following good advice. In fact, I have a proposition for you. I will give each of you a bag of money, or I will give you three pieces of good advice."

Two of the farmers laughed at the old man. "Money or advice? What kind of choice is that? You've been out in the hot sun too long, old one! Give us the money!" These two men grabbed a bag of money each and congratulated themselves on their good luck.

But the third man had been raised to respect his elders, and he had a feeling that the *viejo* knew some important wisdom that might be helpful as he looked for a way to make money. He knew that one bag of money would not go very far and that it would soon run out. Good advice, on the other hand, could last a lifetime.

When he told the old man that he chose the three pieces of advice, his *compadres* laughed even harder. "Now you are as loco as this old man. Will advice feed your children?" they sneered.

But the third man did what he felt was best. The old man took him aside, leaned forward, and whispered this advice into his ear:

"First, keep to the road, the well-traveled road. Do not take any shortcuts, for they may lead to danger.

"Second, mind your own business. Keep quiet and only watch the affairs of others.

"And last, think before you act. Don't do things without first looking carefully."

The farmer had hoped that he would get better advice than that, but he thanked the old man anyway. The travelers continued on their way. The two farmers who had chosen the bags of money could not stop laughing about how foolish their friend had been.

Then they came to a fork in the road and had an argument about which way to turn. The first two farmers thought that the shortcut over the mountain would be the better path. "If we take the long road, it will be dark before we get to the city," they insisted.

The third farmer remembered the first bit of advice that the old man had given to him. "I think it would be safer to take the longer road," he said quietly. "It is more traveled."

The other two farmers laughed at him once more. "What do you know? You know so little you turn up your nose at money and take instead a few words from a crazy old man. We're going to take the short path, and we'll arrive in the village in time to eat and rest before you even get over the mountain. We are not going to waste any more words trying to convince you." With that, they said *adios* and started to walk upon the short path.

It jut so happened that a gang of thieves had been hiding in the forest close to the short path

that day, robbing any person who came over the mountain. The thieves attacked the farmers, stole their money, and beat them so badly they could hardly walk.

Early the next morning the third farmer arrived in the small city and was surprised that his friends were not there. He worried about them and sensed that he had been right in following the old man's advice to keep to the main road. Many hours later, the other two farmers stumbled into the village. Their clothing was torn and bloody and their bodies were covered with cuts and bruises. They cried to their friend about how they had been beaten and robbed of all their money.

After the third farmer found a place for his friends to stay and heal from their wounds, he walked around the village and tried to find a job. The owner of an inn said that he needed a man to help in the kitchen. The job paid very little, but it was at least enough to buy food for the farmer's family. The farmer was grateful to have found some work.

The days turned into weeks, the weeks into months and then into years. The farmer liked the work and found that the innkeeper was a kind and honest man. Yet there was one thing that bothered him. The innkeeper was *muy gordo* — quite fat — and ate large meals several times a day. Yet his wife was small and thin and ate little but fruit and tortillas. The farmer was very curious about this, but he remembered the second piece of advice that the old man had given to him and so he decided to mind his own business.

After he had worked at the inn for three years, the owner of the inn called him over for a talk one day.

"I am a rich man, thanks to this place," he began, "but I am getting older and am tired of working. I have more than enough money for my family and me to live on. So I have made a decision: I am going to give you this inn."

The farmer was so shocked that at first no words came out of his mouth. Finally he was able to stammer, "But ... but ... why me? You have so many employees who work for you! I don't understand."

The owner smiled and answered, "I am giving you this inn because you have minded your own business. I know that you have always been curious about my wife and why she is so thin and eats only tortillas. You might even have thought that I was keeping her from eating the foods that she liked. In truth, I wish that she could enjoy food the way others do. But as a young woman she became very ill, and since that time all that she has been able to digest are simple foods like the ones you have seen her eating.

"Yet, you never asked about her and only did your work. Years ago I made up my mind that when the time came, I would give my business to the person who could mind his own business. I knew that a person who did so could also mind the business of the inn and manage it well. You are that man."

The farmer was overcome with joy. He knew with certainty that he had been right in his decision to follow the advice of the old man, for now his whole family would be able to live with him and help him run the business. He could finally take care of his family in the way he had always wanted.

The innkeeper gave the farmer one of his horses so that he could return quickly to his family and share the wonderful news with them. He had not seen his family in the years since he had first left to find work. His heart ached to see them and hold them in his arms again.

He finally came to his home and tied the horse to a post. As he approached his house, he looked into a window. The smile on his face quickly disappeared. His body shook with rage. For there, in the kitchen, was a young and handsome man embracing his wife!

"So this is the reward I get for working day and night all these years, for sending back here every peso that I earned!" he thought bitterly. He reached for his *pistolo*, determined to kill both his wife and the stranger. But then he remembered the last bit of advice that the old man had given to him, "Think before you act." He slowly put his gun away, threw open the door, and entered his house.

His wife excitedly ran up to him, as did the handsome stranger. "*Mi esposo querido* — my dear husband — are you not glad to see us? Why do you just stand there? Do you not recognize your own son? Look how he has grown in the years since you've been gone!"

The man began to sob, not only with the joy of seeing his beloved family again, but with the realization of how close he had come to slaying his own wife and child because of a tragic misunderstanding.

His family rejoiced at his return and the story of his good fortune. The farmer was now a rich man, and he and his family lived happily ever after. He was also able to hire the other two farmers to help him in his business. Never again did they laugh at any advice that he gave them. ❧

EXERCISES TO ENCOURAGE RESILIENCY

This story is one of my personal favorites and one that consistently delights audiences. I believe that listeners are drawn to it because they recognize the farmer's resilient spirit. Then unnamed hero of the story is able to trust in his own decisions in spite of the mockery of his two friends. He can think of long-term benefits and not just immediate rewards. He shows respect to an elder and is able to use the advice that he has been given, even though at first he can't understand its importance.

This story can inspire valuable discussions around personal responsibility and resiliency. Obviously the three pieces of advice are valuable in certain situations, but not in all. For example, there are times in everyone's life when it is necessary to leave the "well-traveled path" and find new ways of acting, thinking, and being. At the same time, there is a great deal to be learned from the experiences of others who have negotiated some of life's more difficult passages and emerged with profound understanding. And there are times when "shortcuts" can indeed lead to danger, as in the case of recreational drugs. With the second piece of advice, "Mind your own business," there are clearly times, as in cases of abuse or domestic violence, when one must take steps to assist the victim. And though the third directive, "Think before you act," is generally a sound practice, there are instances, as in certain emergency situations, when even this directive does not apply.

It is important to probe these distinctions with listeners and discuss when these pieces of advice

make sense and when they don't. I like to ask questions based upon the three pieces of advice given in the story, such as: When is it appropriate to "stick to the well-traveled path"? When doesn't it make sense? When should you mind your own business? Are there times when it is better not to mind your own business? Have you ever regretted acting on something before you have thought about it? Are there times when it is necessary to act without thinking?

The following activities can be used with this story or others to cultivate resilient capabilities in young people.

IF I COULD DO IT AGAIN

Ages: Middle school, high school

Objective: To increase critical thinking skills by allowing students to gain insight, understanding, and the ability to act in more appropriate ways.

Directions: Tell a story in which an important character at first makes a large mistake and then is given a second chance. Two good examples are "Great Joy the Ox" in *Stories of the Spirit, Stories of the Heart* by Christine Feldman and Jack Kornfield, and "A Blind Man Catches a Bird" from *Children of Wax: African Folktales* by Alexander McCall Smith.

After sharing the story, ask participants to remember a time in their lives when they did something they later realized was a mistake. Have them write a brief description of that experience, and then ask them to write the words "If I could do it again, I would ..." Direct participants to complete the sentence and then ask them, if they are agreeable, to share with the group the ways in which they would react differently in that situation next time. Thank group members for their willingness to speak about an episode that could be difficult or embarrassing, and congratulate them on their courage in facing that situation again and doing it in a more productive way.

COMMUNITY INTERVIEWS

Ages: Middle school, high school

Objective: To cultivate an appreciation for resilient characteristics in others by having participants interview someone in their community who has successfully coped with a difficult situation in life.

Directions: In any community there are countless stories of people who have had to cope with death, disease, or other traumatic events, but who have somehow learned to live and love again in spite of — or perhaps because of — that significant loss. Young people need to hear these stories and know that ordinary people in their home or community have at times shown extraordinary courage and strength. Such stories will encourage and inspire students as they face the struggles of their own life, learning that they are not alone and that they too have inner resources.

After students have read a story that describes overcoming difficult circumstances or coming to terms with a devastating loss, ask them to think of an adult or elder in their community with whom they feel comfortable speaking — perhaps a teacher, parent, grandparent, coach, neighbor, youth group or religious leader. Ask the students to explain to the person they choose the reasons for conducting this interview:

- To better know how to deal with hardships in their own life

- To understand the kinds of difficult issues that others have had to cope with in their lives

- To learn the process by which people healed and recovered

As a group, create a short list of interview questions. These might include some of the following:

- Can you talk about an experience in your life that was hard for you?

- How did you feel at the time?

- What did you do in that situation?

- Were there other people who helped you through that time?

- How did that experience change your life?

- What did you learn from that experience?

- What would you say now to someone going through a similar situation?

Remind students to thank their volunteers for their time and thoughts during the interview, and to consider sending a thank-you card. Have them write a description of the interview and discuss the most important learning that came out of their interview that could be applied to their own lives.

TREASURE BOX

Ages: Elementary, middle school, and high school

Objective: To reinforce resilient capabilities of young people by exploring inner strengths.

Directions: After telling a story in which a main character has overcome a serious problem, have people sit in a circle. Bring to the group a small, empty box made of any material, ornate or simple.

State that the character in the story faced a difficult predicament, yet she or he was able to draw on inner "treasures" of patience, wisdom, and kindness to bring great fortune. Ask participants to remember a time in their lives when they have been faced with a hard situation.

After everyone has a situation in mind, ask each of them to think of one or two inner strengths that they were able to draw upon to help them through that tough time. Tell them that you will pass the box around; when they receive the box, they are invited to open the lid and "let out" the treasures that they were able to find inside themselves. Ask them to share those treasures with others in the group in just a few words or sentences. Only one person speaks at a time, and there will be no discussion as the box moves around the circle. After the box has gone around, thank participants for sharing their "treasures" with other people.

NOTE: It can also be fun to put some objects into the box, such as colored stones, small candies, or feathers, that participants can take out and keep as they pass the box around the circle.

The Magic Brush

A FOLKTALE FROM CHINA RETOLD BY ROSE OWENS*

IN A FARAWAY PLACE and a faraway time there once lived a young boy named Ma Lien. He suffered economic and emotional hardship. He experienced discrimination. He had the courage to dream. Ma Lien's dream became reality largely through his own efforts. These words might also describe someone in the here and how. This timeless quality in the story "The Magic Brush" opens the possibility for Ma Lien to become a role model for listeners who need emotional survival skills. "The Magic Brush" is a special story containing hidden wisdom. And equally important, it can simply be enjoyed by both teller and listener.

Long ago in China, so long ago that if I had been there then I would not be here now, there lived an orphan boy named Ma Lien. Ma Lien lived in a small hut at the edge of the forest.

Every day Ma Lien would gather wood in the forest and sell it at the market to buy food. There was never any extra money, but he managed to get by.

A famous artist came to the village. "If you pay me," he said to the villagers, "I will teach your sons how to paint." And so an art school was begun.

Within Ma Lien's heart was a dream. He wanted to draw and paint. If he could paint, he would be able to paint the beauty that he saw — the graceful birds, the sleek, shimmering fish, the trees, the forest creatures.

Ma Lien had a plan. He went to the famous artist. "Honored artist," he said, "I would learn to paint. I have no money, but I will gather wood for your fire. I will clean your house. I will cook your food."

The artist was insulted. "Go away," he said. "I do not teach poor orphan boys."

Ma Lien refused to give up. He lingered near the open door and listened to the art lesson. The artist saw him and chased him away. So Ma Lien climbed the tree outside the artist's home. This was even better. Now he could both hear and see. But Ma Lien leaned over too far and fell noisily to the ground. "Go away!" said the angry artist. "It is stealing to take lessons that you have not paid for!"

Ma Lien's head hung low as he returned to the forest. His heart was heavy and full of sorrow. He sat in the dust near a small pool. How could he ever achieve his dream if he could not have lessons? Was this the end of his dream?

But the dream within Ma Lien's heart would not die. Within himself, Ma Lien felt a determination. "I will learn to paint," he said. "I will teach myself."

So Ma Lien knelt down by the pool and smoothed a place in the dust. Taking a stick, he began to draw the fish that he saw in the pool. Day after day Ma Lien looked carefully at the beauty around him. Day by day he drew pictures in the dust by the pool. Day by day his pictures became more lifelike, more beautiful, more real. The animals in the forest gathered near to watch Ma Lien draw. And when Ma Lien left a picture in the dust, the animals carefully walked around his pictures that they might keep the beauty of them.

Every morning, Ma Lien got up very early in order to have enough time to gather firewood and still have time to draw. One day he was so tired that he fell asleep by the side of the pool. An old Chinese gentleman came into his dream. He was wearing a long, green brocade robe. His hair and beard were white. In his hand the old gentleman carried a golden brush.

"Ma Lien," he said, "you have desired to paint. That is good. You have been diligent in your practicing. That is good. Use this brush to paint. But promise me that you will paint for the good of the people."

In his dream, Ma Lien took the brush and promised. Then he awoke. He yawned and stretched. "What a queer dream …" With wonderment, Ma Lien looked at the golden brush that he held in his hand.

That day Ma Lien took his bundle of wood to the market and sold it. But instead of buying food, he bought ink and rice paper. This day he would go hungry, but he would paint! He hurried home and spread the rice paper out on the table. He dipped his brush into the ink.

"What shall I paint first?" He decided to paint a fish, the first thing he had ever drawn. His fingers were sure as he painted the fins, the scales, the tail. For had he not practiced these strokes over and over again in the dust by the pond? As Ma Lien finished the last stroke on the tail, the fish slid off the paper and into a bowl of water. For the magic of the brush was that whenever Ma Lien finished the last stroke, his painting would come to life.

Ma Lien had fish for dinner that night. He found that his life was better with the magic brush. He painted chickens that laid eggs. He painted fish and other food to eat. Life was good.

But as Ma Lien wandered through the village, he remembered the words of the old gentleman, "paint for the good of the people." Ma Lien saw the people carrying heavy buckets of water from the river. He painted a well with cool, fresh water. He saw a farmer pulling a plow through the hard earth. Ma Lien painted a water buffalo to pull the plow. Life became better for all the people in the village.

Now, when something remarkable happens, it doesn't take long for word of it to spread. In the next village over, they said, "Have you heard of Ma Lien and his magic brush? Whatever he paints becomes real." And in the next village over, they said, "Have you heard of Ma Lien ...?"

And soon the Emperor himself heard of Ma Lien and his magic brush. "Send for Ma Lien," he ordered. "Ma Lien should paint only for me."

Ma Lien did not want to go to the Imperial City. But no one says "no" to the Emperor. So Ma Lien went to the palace. When he arrived, Ma Lien bowed low before the emperor.

"Ma Lien," said the Emperor, "I want you to paint me a mountain of gold and a golden dragon."

Ma Lien's heart was anxious. He was worried. He bowed low and replied, "Your Excellency, I have promised the old gentleman who gave me this brush that I would use it for the good of the people. I am sorry, but I cannot see that a mountain of gold or a golden dragon would be for the good of the people."

The Emperor was furious! He seized the golden brush and had Ma Lien cast into prison. "I will paint for myself!" he said. And dipping the brush into the ink, he began to paint a dragon. He was not pleased with the picture that began to appear on the paper, for his hands were unskilled and angry. A heart that is greedy and angry cannot produce beauty. "Perhaps it will look better when it is done," he muttered.

As the last stroke was finished, a strange creature hopped off the paper. It looked more like a stunted rooster than a dragon. It gave a queer squawk, pecked the Emperor on the nose, and ran into the forest.

Then the Emperor knew that he needed Ma Lien. He sent for him. "Ma Lien," he said, "I was wrong. Of course you must paint for the good of the people." He gave the golden brush back to Ma Lien. "I have been thinking," said the Emperor, "that my people work hard. Would it not be for the good of the people if there were an ocean

here? At the end of a long day, they could walk along the shore and listen to the soothing sound of the waves."

"Yes," Ma Lien thought. "An ocean would be for the good of the people."

But he did not completely believe that the Emperor had changed. The words that came out of the Emperor's mouth were correct, but the Emperor could not conceal the greedy glint in his eyes.

Ma Lien bowed low, dipped his brush in the ink, and began to paint. He painted the swirling waters of the ocean, the rise and fall of the waves, the white foam as the waves broke upon the shore. And when he finished the last stroke, the ocean rolled off the paper. The people walked along the shore and listened to the murmur and crash of the waves. And it was for the good of the people.

"Ma Lien," said the Emperor, "my people are hungry. There are fish in the ocean. Would it not be for the good of the people if they had a boat so they could catch fish and be hungry no more?"

Ma Lien thought about the fish. Yes, a boat would be for the good of the people. So he picked up his brush and began to paint. But he still did not trust the greedy emperor. Stroke by stroke, the boat began to take shape.

"Ma Lien," said the Emperor, "my people need beauty. Give the boat red silk sails. Put gold trim on it."

Ma Lien painted the red silk sails and the golden trim. As the last stroke was finished, the boat slid off the paper and into the ocean. There it was, gently rocking back and forth in the waves. The Emperor and his courtiers hurried on board. The boat rocked gently back and forth, back and forth.

"Ma Lien," called the Emperor, "paint me a wind. Paint me a big wind!"

Ma Lien began to paint. He painted the swirling, angry winds. He painted a veritable storm. As he finished the last stroke, the wind whooshed off the paper and through the air. As it passed over the ocean, it caught the red satin sails of the boat, carrying it so far out to sea that neither the boat nor the Emperor and his courtiers were ever seen again.

Then the people needed a new Emperor. They asked Ma Lien to be their new Emperor.

"No," he said, "let me go back to my village."

And he did.

And if you should happen to go to China and travel through the countryside, you may find a certain small village. At the edge of the forest, you may see a small hut surrounded by a peaceful garden. Graceful birds alight in the trees to sing beautiful songs, and shimmering fish swim in the pool. Should you ever happen to see this hut, you will know that you have found the hut of Ma Lien, where he lives in peace and harmony and paints for the good of the people. ❧

Stories as tools for coping

ROSE OWENS

THE GIFT OF A STORY is one way to share coping strategies that may help individuals who are experiencing an emotional crisis. Emotions sometimes seem to overwhelm us as we are confronted by death, divorce, loss, anger, abuse, violence, bullying, teasing, etc. Within any environment, there are individuals who already need these tools and children who will need them at some time in the future. Hawaiian storyteller and teacher Diane Aoki reminds us that "sharing stories is a way to plant a seed of some kind which may not bear fruit immediately but may sometime. A seed that is never planted will never grow — an option that is never considered can never be chosen." We all are affected by the emotional forces that surround us — we need to be given tools to help us cope. Sharing a story may help listeners develop the inner tools they need to cope with life's present complexities. Participating in a story develops the imagination and helps listeners perceive ideas and thoughts they might never have had on their own.

One story will not magically resolve a crisis. A storyteller is not a healer with miracle cures, nor is a storyteller a psychologist. The teller simply has a story to share. This story may have been selected carefully because it has wisdom embedded in it. However, the role of the storyteller is not to provide therapy or moralize, but to offer the gift of story, allowing the listeners to participate in the process and to choose what they will receive and internalize. A storyteller may carefully choose a tale that has bits of hidden wisdom — one that she believes an individual or a group of listeners needs to hear — but she knows, of course, that what is finally heard is actually determined by the listener.

Even though a story cannot be a magic solution, it is important to understand that stories do have the power to help healing occur — for stories can help us connect with each other and with our inner self. The process of selecting stories with embedded "inner wisdom" that will provide coping tools involves reading and testing many different tales. Myths and traditional folktales are excellent sources for such stories because they contain powerful metaphors that have been polished over time.

These metaphors allow individual listeners to internalize as much or as little of the analogy as they are comfortable with.

"The Magic Brush" is an example of a story that carries hidden resources. Because Ma Lien is a poor orphan boy, the village artist refuses to teach him. Having tried and failed to obtain knowledge and training through a traditional path, Ma Lien refuses to let his dream die. He decides to teach himself. Using the simple tools he has available — a stick and a patch of dirt — Ma Lien practices drawing the creatures he sees in the forest. When an old Chinese gentleman miraculously gives Ma Lien the gift of a magic golden brush, Ma Lien is true to his promise that he will "paint for the good of the people." The boy uses ingenuity to outsmart the evil Emperor. By the end of the story, Ma Lien understands what is best for his own good as well as the good of the people.

The story of Ma Lien is a many-faceted jewel. Each storyteller or listener may hear other messages, but here are some samples of what my listeners and I have found in this story:

- **Believe in yourself.** Ma Lien knew he was capable of becoming an artist.

- **Don't allow others to limit your choices.** The artist refused to teach Ma Lien, so he taught himself.

- **When one plan doesn't work, try another plan.** Since he could not receive art classes, Ma Lien decided to practice on his own.

- **How hard you are willing to work is more important than how much money or influence you have.** Ma Lien was a poor orphan boy, but he was able to succeed because he worked hard.

- **Doing the best you can with what you have brings rewards.** Ma Lien drew with a stick in the dirt. He was rewarded by increased skill and then with the gift of the magic brush.

- **We should help others.** Ma Lien used his brush for the good of the people.

- **Keep your promises even when it is difficult.** Ma Lien refused to paint for the selfish Emperor and was cast into the dungeon.

- **Wealth and power do not guarantee happiness.** Ma Lien chose to return to his village to paint and help his people.

The storyteller's role is to offer the gift of story — not explain what the story means. Using a "lecture format" to impart the bits of wisdom embedded in a story can be like turning off a light switch. I have seen and felt the wall go up between my middle-school students (12-to-15-year-olds) and myself when I attempted to discuss a sensitive issue. But when I tell them a story, I feel them relax and settle into the tale. There is no stress, no expectations. If we choose to discuss a story, I will explore options and possibilities with the listeners rather than telling them what that story means.

New York storyteller Sue Tannehill suggests that we can "offer stories of characters who survive and thrive by their wits ... sometimes it's the only weapon a kid has!" In these types of stories there is no magical intervention — no granting of magic wishes — that allows the character to survive. The resolution comes through the actions of the hero or heroine. In "Tipingee," a Haitian folktale, a small girl escapes evil by outwitting both her selfish stepmother and the witch. Another story, "Nadia the Willful," portrays a young Bedouin girl who must cope with the grief of losing her brother. At first she denies his death and feels angry, but these attempts to cope with her grief are unsuccessful. As the tale unfolds, Nadia draws upon her own memories to tell her brother's story and to finally bring healing to herself, her father, and her tribe.

Personal stories provide opportunities to share examples of the resilience of the human spirit. The stories of our lives can provide evidence that others have faced adversity and survived. Because a fire destroyed our living room and coated the rest of our home and belongings with soot, my family lived in a rental home for seven months while we rebuilt. Sharing stories about this experience has helped me connect with listeners, to prove that adversity can be overcome. My family, my home, and I all survived, and life goes on. Storyteller Sheryl Karas, an author from Santa Cruz, states that people "tend to gravitate toward stories that speak to experiences they have had and are trying to work out or world experiences they want to make sense of." Stories about self-reliance may help the listener conclude that people can find ways to improve their lives.

The Littleton High School massacre was splashed across the media for days. Because my middle-school students were trying to understand it, we spent some time discussing the tragedy in our classroom. When comments and questions continued to emerge, I knew my students had not resolved their concerns and I sensed that they felt vulnerable. One boy in particular carried a map of Littleton High School in his pocket. He frequently pulled it out, studied it, and talked about it. He was accomplishing little work. I decided to offer my students some stories. I carefully chose three stories that I felt might give them the opportunity to internalize the message they needed or to discuss their concerns.

I began by sharing an Aesop fable, "The Bundle of Sticks." I brought in a bundle of sticks and allowed the students to "experience" the story as I told it. In this fable, a father asks each of his children if they can break a bundle of sticks. They can't. Then, when the bundle is separated, he asks each child to break the stick he holds. As a storyteller, I offered them the tale as possible support. The story may have told them, "We need to stick together. When we tear each other down, we weaken our community. We can accomplish more when we work together as a group than if we act individually."

The students listened intently as I told "The King's Hawk," the story of a young ruler who impulsively acts in anger. The king becomes angry with his pet hawk when it repeatedly knocks a cup of water from his hands, and he kills the hawk. When his drinking cup falls into a crevice and cannot be retrieved, the king climbs to get a drink from the upper pool. He finds a dead poisonous snake in the water. His loyal hawk, who had been trying to warn him of the danger, has been rewarded with death. Although the young king realizes that his anger was not justified, and he experiences sorrow for his actions, it is too late. What he has done in anger cannot be undone.

To conclude the program I shared "The Story Spirits," a tale from Korea about revenge. A young Korean boy loves stories, so every night his old servant tells him a new tale. The young man feels that these stories belong only to him, and he selfishly confines the story spirits in a leather bag. The story spirits want revenge and plan to kill the young man on his wedding day. He is saved by the intervention of the old servant, who overhears the plotting of the story spirits. This story was selected to open the possibility of discussing revenge. Is revenge justified? Are there other solutions when someone has been wronged?

I believe the best stories are those that help us see the complexities faced by other people — tales that connect us with each other. As Mary Pipher writes in *The Shelter of Each Other*, these stories "heal the polarization that can overwhelm us all and ... calm those who are frightened as well as those who hate. These stories would offer us the possibility of reconciliation. We need stories that teach children empathy and accountability, how to act and how to be. Children are hungry for stories that help them feel hopeful and energetic ... these stories will shelter us all."

Early Childhood Interventions The Parent-Child Mother Goose Program

The heart of Mother Goose: Lullabies, lap-rhymes, and stories

ALLISON M. COX

SOME OF THE HOME-VISITATION nurses and family support workers at the health department told me that they were overwhelmed. Their job was to visit high-risk families with babies or young children, assess their needs, offer support, and connect them to resources.

What does "high risk" mean in this context? These households were trying to survive on a low income. In some, the head of the house was a teen mother, while other households were led by elders who felt drained as they tried to raise their grandchildren. Some of the people spoke little or no English, and many had not finished high school. Some of these parents had horror stories about what life was like for them as they grew up, so they had fled from their relatives, but now they were socially isolated and, understandably, not very trusting. With no positive role models available, these parents, many of them single women, had little confidence in their ability to parent their children or to improve their lives.

I had worked with these families as a social worker in the health department's obstetric clinic, so I knew the challenges facing the nurses and family support workers. Caseloads were high, needs were many, there never was enough time or staff to go around. We needed to find more successful ways to support these families on their way to becoming self-sufficient and help them connect to necessary community resources. And then one day, I received a call from storyteller Nan Gregory in Vancouver, British Columbia, that offered us another way to think about encouraging resilient families. "Allison, I think you may want to come up here in August for a training course that is coming to the West Coast for the first time. It is designed to teach people to run a Parent-Child Mother Goose Program."

The Parent-Child Mother Goose Program has proven successful in working with the families of newborns up to age four. These days, many families have moved distances apart, so the tradition of sharing lullabies, rhymes, and stories across generations is often lost. The Mother Goose Program aims to teach these lost arts. Because of the playful nature of the program, it appealed to parents who had previously avoided recommendations to go to parenting classes.

The Parent-Child Mother Goose Program suggests that each group meet with two teachers, once a week, for ten weeks. All classes are offered for free. Teaching is directed toward the parents. Children's participation is determined by their stage of development and inclination that day. There are no toys at the sessions, and we don't give out handouts until the end of the ten weeks of class. This teaches the parents that all they need to know to engage their children can come from within themselves.

What have been the results of this program?*

- Parents see that they can positively affect how their children behave and learn.

- They develop more realistic expectations of their children just by observing other children of similar ages and the modeling of the group leaders.

- They learn skills to help them cope with their cranky, fussy children that are a wonderful alternative to the frustrations that lead to abuse.

- Parents report that they now use songs, nursery rhymes, and story with their children in place of disciplinary measures that tended to escalate the situation in the past.

- The children in these classes showed marked improvement in language and pre-literacy skills.

- Even though there was no official agenda to educate the parents about health and parenting issues, these topics arose naturally, out of the conversation between the parents at the meetings.

- Cultural sharing was sparked as different women would excitedly comment, "Oh, we have a rhyme just like this in Cambodia (or Mexico or Russia ...)!" Then everyone would learn rhymes in yet another language.

- These families developed a new network of friends.

- We also developed future community leaders by encouraging group participants to become assistants to help train future groups, or even to become trainers themselves.

When we started these groups in our community, we found that older siblings began asking if they could also come to the group to learn the silly rhymes, soothing lullabies, and new stories that their mothers had been telling at home.

Over and over we found that if we start out simply and offer families enjoyable and safe ways to come closer to their children and the community, huge steps can be made to increase both the parent's and child's self-esteem.

The next three articles describe how the Parent-Child Mother Goose Program has worked in various cities across Canada.

The parent-child Mother Goose Program

CELIA BARKER LOTTRIDGE

SOME YEARS AGO a social worker, whose job included the difficult duty of taking children out of destructive home situations and into care, observed that if he told stories to the children as he spent time with them, their relationship changed. He ceased to be the man from the agency and became a real person, a person who gave the children something and shared an enjoyable moment with them.

Barry Dickson, the social worker, talked about this experience in a class on nursery rhymes Joan Bodger and I were teaching for the

---

* The results reported here are based on information from: Celia Lottridge and Katherine Grier of the Parent-Child Mother Goose Program; a program evaluation in Edmonton, AB, by Barbara Sykes, Ruth Wolfe, Louise Gendreau, and Lynda Workman; and the experiences of Allison Cox while training staff and families of Pierce County, WA, in these programs.

Storytellers School of Toronto. "It's really the parents I work with who should be telling stories," he said. "They are the ones who need to connect with their children." I remember this moment very well, even though it happened in the early 1980s, because Barry's insight combined with Joan Bodger's knowledge and initiative led to the pilot project that became the foundation for the Parent-Child Mother Goose Program as it now exists.

Joan and I were both storytellers, but Joan had the added background of having worked with Head Start and other remedial early education programs and was a Gestalt therapist as well. She felt that the power of story to connect teller and listener could also be found in nursery rhymes when they were used with the very youngest children, and she believed that helping parents connect or bond with their children when they were still infants would have the most significant effect. If parents who did not bond well with their babies were given simple ways to build the connection with rhymes, it might well prevent problems from developing later.

And so in 1986 a pilot project began with groups of high needs parents who did not appear to be bonding well with their infants under one year old. The project operated under the auspices of the Children's Aid Society, was funded by its foundation, and was taught by Joan, myself, and Katherine Grier, another experienced storyteller. Because our major objective was to help the parents and infants build a real connection, we focused on teaching interactive rhymes, the kind parents have used with babies since time immemorial. Some of these rhymes have the idea of really looking at the baby built into them:

Ring the bell (Gently tug on a lock of the baby's hair)
Knock on the door (Softly tap on her forehead)
Peek in (Look into her eyes)
Lift up the latch (Touch end of her nose)
Walk in (Touch her lips)
Let's go down cellar and eat apples (Run your fingers down to her tummy and tickle gently)

Other rhymes encourage warm and gentle physical contact:

Trot trot to Boston (Bounce baby gently)
Trot trot to Lynn (Same action)
Look out for the rose bush (Same action)
You might fall in! (Let baby fall a little way between your knees and then lift him up for a hug)

And others build on a baby's delight in feeling with all parts of her body:

Shoe the wild horse (Tap bottom of baby's bare foot)
Shoe the mare (Again)
But let the little colty (Again)
Go bare, bare, bare (Stroke the bottom of the foot firmly enough not to tickle)

Our purpose was to teach the rhymes in such a way that the parents would remember at least a few of them and use them in their everyday lives. The adults' response was not very positive at first. They came because they were encouraged to and because they did want to do things that would help their children, if they could, — but they were fairly silent and unenthusiastic. The babies, on the other hand, loved it. If the parents were reluctant or unsure, we would "borrow a baby" and bounce and hug. The baby's response often encouraged the parents to have a try.

As the sessions went on, we saw that not only were the babies responding to the beauty and fun of the rhymes, but the parents were as well. They began to come into the room with the anticipation of having a good time and doing something satisfying. We could see that the experience of hearing the rhymes and spending time talking about how they could use them was doing something positive for the adults in themselves, not only because it was good for the babies.

We soon realized that these women needed attention and fun as much as the babies did and that giving them concrete activities to help them relate more strongly to their children was only part of our task. These were people who lacked, in various ways, the ability to connect to other people, to find the strength to cope with the problems of their lives, or to find genuine moments of pleasure in their day-to-day existence.

If we were to help the adults do more for their children, we needed to add goals such as helping them feel connected to us and to the group as a whole. We needed to make their time in the program a pleasure rather than a task, and we had to do whatever we could to give them some sense of perspective and strength. Since the group was not a therapy group, as such, and we were teaching the program as storytellers, not as therapists, we decided to use what we knew about the power of story and tell stories to the adults.

The result was exciting. Initially, the adults were surprised that we would tell stories to them, but they enjoyed having a part of the hour that was especially for them. We chose stories we were sure they would enjoy and to which they could relate. Within a few sessions, many of the participants were asking to hear their favorites again. We could see them relax and focus and laugh and sigh. Sometimes the stories would give rise to discussion, often about relationships between men and women or the experience of finding oneself alone in the world. We never directed the discussion but simply responded to whatever came up. It was clear that storytelling added an essential dimension to the program.

When the pilot project concluded, Katherine and I felt that this powerful model could benefit families in the wider community. The result is the Parent-Child Mother Goose Program, a non-profit agency serving a number of low-income neighborhoods in Toronto. Our participants may include parents who lack crucial parenting skills, some without confidence in their ability to be good parents, many who are isolated for any number of reasons, and a few whose response to their children's behavior is inappropriate in some way.

Our general objective is to help these parents develop new ways to relate to their children, gain internal resources that they can draw on in difficult times, and learn alternatives to inappropriate responses in dealing with their children. We hope to encourage the use of language with children from an early age and to build a supportive group that parents can rely upon for friendship and help. Our groups are teaching groups, not therapy groups, and most often we do not know what specific problems our participants have, unless they choose to tell us.

Our experience, starting with the pilot project and continuing since the inception of the Parent-Child Mother Goose Program, is that storytelling helps us achieve these objectives for a number of reasons. First, the story is something we give adults simply because we think they will like it. It is, in a way, a gift to people who often are given very little, although a lot is asked of them "This story is for you," we say. "You don't have to remember it or do anything with it. Just enjoy it."

Second, we choose stories, almost always folktales, that have content relevant to the lives of the people we are telling them to. They are stories in which people learn to take care of themselves, where they overcome such hardships as being unloved or poor, and where humor gives perspective on the relationships between men and women. We avoid "and they got married and lived happily ever after" tales unless we are looking for a laugh. Many of the stories have strong women as their heroes because most of the adults we work with are women. We also look for stories that reflect the ethnic backgrounds of the participants. Often this helps people remember stories from their earlier lives, and they may share them with us.

Third, we don't decide what a story means. We believe that every story has many layers and each listener will find the layer that is most meaningful to her.

Fourth, we value the stories as part of group experience. Our groups are made up of people who may have little in common except that they all have young children. They come from different backgrounds, often originally from different countries, and speak a number of different first languages. There may be a wide range of ages. Some participants will be single while others have partners in parenting. In a Parent-Child Mother Goose group, these disparate people build up a common culture of rhymes and songs they have learned together and they all experience the same stories. This group experience tends to foster a supportive group feeling in an unforced manner. We can see the participants growing comfortable with each other as they share the laughter, beauty, and wonder of the material we use.

Fifth, in our programs the stories are part of life. We all know each other. We sit around in a circle with cups of coffee and babies on our laps. Most of the time we have no separate room for child care so the walking children will be playing with one of the teachers or helpers in another part of the room. It is often noisy. But we persevere and usually the story comes through. We believe that the message this gives is that even in the midst of distractions, it is right and good to take a moment for something that matters to you.

Sixth, and perhaps most important, as we learned in the pilot project so long ago, in order to help people who are in some way wounded to be better parents, we have to do something to help them as whole people, not just in their behavior as parents. Sharing oral stories has inherent healing qualities because of the caring experience of being told a story, because the stories offer perspective and images of strength that each listener can hear as she needs to, because the stories have a pattern in which the characters go through difficulties and emerge to a better life, and because the stories are beautiful, entertaining, and funny. They feed the spirit.

The Parent-Child Mother Goose Program is now offered in many communities across Canada and the United States as a result of training workshops we have developed. The people we train are often more used to working with children than adults, and very often they have never told stories before, so at times they feel uncomfortable. We offer follow-up workshops on storytelling and help those we have trained link up with storytellers in their own communities who can offer further training and support. We have published a book, *You Can Tell a Story: A Handbook for New*

Storytellers, and we continue to offer storytelling suggestions in our newsletters. Invariably, experienced Mother Goose teachers, like the participants, find the storytelling to be one of the most satisfying and valuable parts of the program.

For more information about the program, write, fax, or e-mail:

The Parent-Child Mother Goose Program
720 Bathurst Street, Ste. 402
Toronto, ON M5S 2R4
Canada
Phone: (416) 588-5234
Fax: (416) 588-1355
E-mail: mgoose@web.net

The stories in the rhymes

Sandra Carpenter-Davis

There was an old woman
Tossed up in a basket
Seventeen times as high as the moon.
And where she was going
No one would ask it
For under her arm she carried a broom.
"Old woman, old woman, old woman,"
quoth I.
"Whither, oh whither, oh whither so high?"
"To sweep the cobwebs from the sky."
"Can I go with you?"
"Aye, bye and bye."

As a STORYTELLER with a background in social service work, I was delighted when several years ago I began teaching with the Parent-Child Mother Goose Program. My job was to encourage parents or caregivers and their infants or toddlers to play and interact using rhymes, songs, and stories. Many of the participants, mostly mothers living in a primarily low-income neighborhood, spoke English as a second language. Customs and child-rearing practices were varied. Yet there was something about rhyme and song and story that was universal. There were themes common to all cultures: food, soothing crying babies, animals, body parts.

Slice, slice. (Make a slicing motion on baby's arm or belly)
The bread looks nice. (Pat baby's body or shoulders)
Spread, spread. (With open hand, make a spreading motion over baby)
Put butter on the bread.
On the top, put jam so sweet. (Rub top of baby's head)
And now it's good for me to eat! (Nibble baby's belly, hands, neck, cheeks)

And, of course, the stories resonated with everyone, whether this was a story for the adults to enjoy or a children's tale they might learn and tell at home.

I have been teaching programs and workshops using rhyme, song, and story for several years now and have a favorite exercise that I first learned in the Parent-Child Mother Goose

Program. The exercise is simple: create a story from a rhyme. It is a natural progression to move from rhyme to story. So many rhymes are little stories, and fleshing out the details is a simple task. The exercise introduces powerful images and poetic language and empowers each participant to create a story.

Participants work in small groups of three of four. This allows each person to contribute more easily; often participants for whom English is not their native language, and others who have been shy or quiet, become very vocal. The room comes alive with the delightful noise of women playing with words and expressing their personal visions of what they imagine when hearing a particular rhyme. The stories generated may be funny and even silly, sometimes sounding like a television soap opera. Or they might take on the form of a classic folktale or nursery tale. Often several stories emerge. The noise in the room escalates and the teacher(s) move from group to group with suggestions on how to bring each group story into shape.

A group can choose to tell the story it has created in any of several ways. Though each person is encouraged to tell a part of the story, sometimes participants are reticent and feel more comfortable if one member narrates the story on behalf of the group. Often these same people will spontaneously jump in with comments as the narrator tells the story. There may be members in each group who simply want to tell their own story, and that is never a problem. The more stories and voices heard, the better. It soon becomes clear that we all create different images or pictures in our minds. Seldom do the stories sound alike. Yet certain themes often recur when using a particular rhyme.

The following nursery rhyme generates some interesting stories:

Peter, Peter pumpkin eater
Had a wife and couldn't keep her.
He put her in a pumpkin shell
And there he kept her very well.

Peter may be a mouse who has house troubles till he finds the pumpkin. Then he and his wife and children all eat until the pumpkin is empty and they can live inside the shell. But often someone will suggest a story of marital discontent, with a controlling husband putting his wife in a pumpkin shell. This interpretation can lead to an interesting discussion. Though issue-centered discussion is not the focus of the Mother Goose Program, such discussions occur frequently and are encouraged.

Here are two more rhymes about relationships:

My little old man and I fell out.
I'll tell you what 'twas all about.
I had money and he had none.
That was how the row begun.

And:

On Saturday night I lost my wife,
And where do you think I found her?
Up in the moon, singing a tune
With all the stars around her.

This following rhyme always generates a lot of discussion:

Today is the day we give babies away
With a half a pound of tea.
If you know any ladies who want any babies,
*Just send them around to me.**

---

* "Today is the day we give babies away" can be found on Rosalie Sorrel's CD *Be Careful, There's a Baby in the House* (Green Linnet GLCD 2100). I avoid using this rhyme if I believe there may be group members who have children in the care of children's services.

The stories inspired by this rhyme may be funny or sometimes even sad, but inevitably the talk will turn to the frustration every mother feels when her baby is "driving her crazy." This rhyme, more than any other I know, gives parents permission to express these feelings. The discussion of sleepless nights and colicky babies lets other mothers know they are not alone. Mothers share examples of what has worked or not worked for them. That most mothers feel tired a good deal of the time is an important fact that is seldom acknowledged by doctors and other health care professionals. The stories unite us in a common experience.

Sometimes discussions carry over from week to week, and parents offer each other support not only in the group, but outside the group as well. Quite often a mother will volunteer to take a new group member to another program in the area, and I have seen several friendships form that led to the exchange of caregiving services and even to the sharing of living accommodations.

Perhaps it is because the program is not seen as directly about parenting skills, but rather as an enjoyable parent-and-child play program, that the rhyme, song, and story lead so naturally to discussion. People are validated in any way that they contribute to the group, and generally the level of comfort grows with each class. This is probably the greatest secret behind the program's success.

Oral literacy: Learning while listening

MERLE HARRIS

AS A MOTHER, I found that reciting rhymes, singing songs, and telling stories to our two young sons was as beneficial for me as it was for them. I learned quickly that it is impossible to recite a rhyme with an angry voice, and that reciting a silly rhyme with actions calmed me, gave me time to think, and side-tracked the boys. When I was given the opportunity to start the Parent-Child Mother Goose Program in Edmonton in 1994, I discovered many more truths about the role of the oral tradition in today's society.

In one of the first pilot programs I ran, there was a very young mother, with a baby and a toddler, who was a natural with the rhymes and songs. She interacted with her children and noticed and commented on other children's reactions. I mentally noted she would make a wonderful facilitator when her children were older. At the end of the first ten-week session we handed out a little booklet with the rhymes and songs we had learned. I spent time tidying up, handing in keys, and making arrangements for the next session and got into the parking lot a good half hour after everyone left, but there she was waiting for me. She handed me back the booklet, saying it would not help her as she was not able to read. But she knew all the rhymes and used them with her children. She had come to love telling them stories, some she heard at the program and others she made up for them. She said for the first time she felt she could ensure her children were ready when they got to school, and she added that she knew she needed to learn to read but it would have to wait till she had more time.

Right then she needed to learn how to be a good mother.

I learned an important lesson because that young mother had the courage to tell me she could not read. It made me realize there are many parents who are either illiterate or alliterate — some because they speak another language, and others who have just fallen through the cracks over the years. As a result, I have encouraged teachers in the program to interview parents when collecting information and write it down (rather than handing out forms of any kind).

We also encourage the parents to use rhymes, stories, and songs as often as they can. Doing this promotes oral literacy, which is the child's ability to understand that words have meaning. Parents can easily recognize the meaning (and the strength) of oral literacy when they see a small baby suddenly tighten its arms, or tucks its chin in, anticipating the tickle that is going to accompany the next words in an oft-shared rhyme. When small children constantly hear the same rhymes and songs, often accompanied by actions, words become concrete things. Each time they hear "up" and they are lifted up in the air, or "down" and they get dropped down, the magic and power of language is reinforced. Oral literacy prepares all children, and especially those whose parents are unable to read to them, for the huge task of learning to read and write because language has come alive for them. They know the sounds and meanings of many words, they anticipate tickles, hugs, and endings, so when they first see those rhymes written down, there is a recognition and the words on the page will make sense more quickly.

I was involved in a Parent-Child Mother Goose Program with a group of parents who had grown up in extremely dysfunctional homes and had few parenting skills. The two facilitators were wonderful, and the mothers were soon joining in with the rhymes and songs, especially when the babies and toddlers reacted to the bouncing rhymes.

One week the staff put some bright pictures and rhymes on the walls, but none of the mothers took their children over to look at them. They just sat and waited for the circle to begin. I was asked to tell a story that morning, and I thought of the Jewish folktale about the young man who wanted to be a janitor at the synagogue but did not get the position because he could not sign his name. I thought that maybe these mothers didn't take their babies and toddlers to look at the pictures because they did not want people to know they were not able to read the words, so I decided to change the tale to feature a woman — "Miriam's Story." I hoped that in some way I was telling them they could be good parents without being able to read.

I popped into the supermarket one day later that summer, and one of the mothers was also there. She came up to me and asked if I remembered her and introduced me to her seven-year-old daughter. She told me she hoped Miriam's story would become her story, as she too could not read or write. She had been required to take literacy classes when her daughter was five, but when she read to her daughter, her daughter would laugh at her, saying she knew more words than her mother. In the past her daughter would never sit still for her, but now she loved having her mother tell her stories.

Programs such as the Parent-Child Mother Goose, which encourage parents to tell their children stories, recite rhymes, and sing songs, are necessary. For some parents, reading well enough to hold their child's attention requires a great deal of learning. When these parents are bombarded with messages that "Children need to be read to if they are going to become successful," they must feel utterly hopeless. Reading is important, but if, through storytelling, nursery rhymes and lullabies, we can teach them the other three Rs — rhyme, rhythm, and repetition — perhaps we can ensure that their children will become fluent readers in their own time.

Miriam's Story

MERLE HARRIS

Many, many years ago, a young woman from a large, poor family left home and went to a nearby town to look for work. She had no formal education and no real skills — just a desire to provide for herself.

She offered her services to the local seamstress, but the seamstress needed someone who could sew without being taught. She tried at a small restaurant, but they needed someone who already knew how to cook or bake. However, the owner suggested she go to the city hall where the mayor was always looking for employees.

She went and asked for work, and after the mayor questioned her about her abilities, he said the only position he thought she was suited for was to take care of the plants around the city hall. It was a small job and the pay was low, but she gratefully accepted the position.

"Good," said the mayor. "I'll draw up the papers. What is your name?"

"Miriam," replied the young woman.

The mayor handed her a piece of paper and asked her to sign her name on the line at the bottom. Miriam picked up the pen and made a large "X" on the line.

"That's your signature?" asked the mayor.

Miriam, feeling very embarrassed, explained that she had not learned to read or write.

"Well, I'm sorry," replied the mayor, "but if you can't sign your name you can't have the job."

Miriam begged and pleaded, but the mayor held firm and she left city hall. She passed the busy market. Seeing all the fruits and vegetables for sale made her realize how hungry she was, but she had no money to spend.

As she was passing the small fields on the edge of the town, she noticed an elderly couple working in their garden. It was filled with the most beautiful flowers Miriam had ever seen, and she had an idea. She stopped and asked them if they had ever thought of selling their flowers at market. They replied they were too old to make the journey and sit at market, and she offered to go for them.

In no time at all, the three of them had cut and bundled up bunches of the flowers, and Miriam returned to the market with the flowers and a pail of water. She spread her shawl on the ground and gently placed the pail of flowers on top, and all the flowers were quickly sold.

When Miriam returned to the couple, they insisted she keep half the money and asked if she would like to help them regularly. They reached an agreement. Miriam would have a room in their barn, help in the flower garden, and take the fresh flowers to market weekly. In exchange, they would feed her and she would get half the takings.

Miriam became a fixture at the market, and the flowers sold out each week. It was only a matter of months before Miriam needed to buy a wheelbarrow to get the flowers to market, and then a cart drawn by a donkey, and within a year she had a stall of her own.

When the old couple died, they left their small holding to Miriam, who seemed to have a way with flowers. She started to experiment with new varieties and cultivars, and her stall at the small market became known for its unusual flowers. She married a young man who had bought flowers from her, and with his help the small farm became a successful greenhouse where people came to buy both plants and cut flowers.

The years passed and they had children who loved helping Miriam in the greenhouse and at the market stall. Miriam's greenhouse had grown, and she had become an authority on flower cultivation. Her cut flowers were carried by florists in big cities, and Miriam was invited to talk at flower shows around the country.

Miriam and her family became rich over the years, and she watched with great pride as her children went through school and graduated from university. As Miriam and her husband grew older, their children became more involved in running the greenhouse.

One day, Miriam decided that before she retired she would like to give something to the town that had brought her such happiness and success. She bought a piece of land between the city hall and the market and designed and planted a wonderful park, filled with the newest varieties of the most colorful flowers. There was a fountain and a stream, arbors and pergolas dressed in roses and vines, and benches dotted here and there where people could sit and admire the flowers.

The mayor, young and newly elected, organized a formal ceremony in which Miriam could give the park to the people. The mayor decided that a plaque should be placed near the fountain so that visitors would know how the park came to be. He had the plaque printed, and just before the ceremony he asked Miriam to sign it.

Once again, Miriam picked up the pen and made her large "X." The young mayor could not contain his amazement. "Why, you cannot write your name! Just imagine what you could have done if you had been able to write."

Gently and proudly Miriam replied, "As I look at my park, I realize that if I had been able to write, I would still be the person watering the plants." ❧

STORIES
GO TO
SCHOOL

The Odyssey Project:
Adolescent pregnancy prevention through storytelling

ALLISON M. COX

WE WERE SURPRISED when the Washington State Department of Health called the local health department to ask us to apply for an adolescent pregnancy prevention grant. Our staff had discussed the possibility of requesting a grant, but had decided there wasn't enough time to design an adequate proposal. We had wanted to suggest an intervention with children *before* they reached adolescence, since the goal was prevention.

Our health department was already aware that the city of Tacoma and the surrounding county had some of the highest rates of teen pregnancy in the state, and we also knew that teen pregnancy is a problem across the entire country. The United States has the highest rates of teen pregnancy and births in the western industrialized world. Four in ten young women become pregnant at least once before they reach age 20 — nearly one million a year. Eight in ten of these pregnancies are unintended, and 80 percent are to unmarried teens. Two-thirds of teen mothers have a history of sexual abuse. The consequences are generational. Less than one-third of teen mothers complete high school, and 80 percent are on welfare. Children of teenage parents are more likely to perform poorly in school, are at greater risk of abuse and neglect, and are more likely to end up in prison or as teen mothers themselves.

Much of my work as a health educator was focused on using storytelling for health promotion and disease prevention. My supervisor and co-workers were encouraged by the successes we had encountered using storytelling as a medium for public health efforts, so it seemed a natural progression to adopt this format to engage children on the difficult subject of pregnancy prevention.

The state Department of Health agreed to fund a pilot project using storytelling with high-risk Grade 4 students. We proposed that our team (including two health educators with social work and psychology backgrounds, and a community health organizer with experience in adolescent health) would meet with the students twice a week to share and process stories focusing on risk factors predisposing youth to teen parenthood. Stories would explore themes related to self-esteem, continued school involvement and attendance, teen pregnancy, substance abuse, domestic violence, peer pressure, hygiene, and positive decision-making. The stories would also emphasize refusal skills.

The children would learn to tell stories to their younger peers as well. We made sure the processing activities that followed the stories matched the multiple learning styles of the students, (e.g., auditory, kinesthetic, or visual). We invited community mentors, drawn from the cultural groups represented by the students, to come and share their own personal stories and discuss the importance of education to prepare for both careers and parenting. We intended to follow these students for two years, until they completed Grade 5, and to assess the results each year. We decided to call this undertaking "The Odyssey Project," since it would be both an adventure and a two-year journey for all involved.

Finding the schools

Our next step was to find two schools in the county that would agree to be our experimental and control groups. We had to locate schools in similar neighborhoods, with comparable class size, and a similar ethnic mix. The experimental school would hear specifically selected stories dealing with identified themes on a weekly basis. The Grade 4 (and later Grade 5) classes at the control school would have occasional storytelling (two to three times a year) that matched curriculum goals of those classrooms, as well as some smoking prevention information that was offered to all county schools. We narrowed our search to those areas where the local health department had placed a Family Support Center on a school campus due to high risk in that community (such as poverty, violence, substance abuse). This ensured that we were reaching a portion of the population that most needed the intervention and that we had already established some ties within the school and the community.

Then the district superintendent of public schools imposed a requirement that health department staff could enter a classroom only if the agenda of stories and activities could be closely matched with the curriculum taught by the Grade 4 teachers. I took a deep breath and agreed. "There are enough stories in the world to meet both our goals and yours." After another

month of searching, we found two schools in the same district that agreed to be our experimental and control sites.

Obtaining parental consent

Because we planned to administer pre- and post-program surveys and interviews of all students in both experimental and control groups, we needed parental consent. At the principal's suggestion, we sent home a letter to the parents explaining the project and noting that a copy of the assessment tool was available in the principal's office if they wanted to read it. Even though the purpose of the project was explained, several parents had concerns, wondering why the local health department wanted to collect data on their children and worrying that they would be reported to Social Services if any "problems" were found. To assure the parents of our good intentions, we developed a number code for each child and promised that only numbers, not names, would be used on the surveys collected.

Designing the curriculum

We searched for stories with risk reduction themes that paralleled the weekly focus of the Grade 4 classes. During the first session of the week, the "Odyssey ladies" (as we were now known) shared stories and the students learned and practiced storytelling. During the second visit, we engaged in activities to process the stories. We developed a list of activities involving art, movement, song, games, puppetry, crafts, journaling, discussions, special guests, family history, costuming, writing letters, and more. We also developed an extensive list of themes:

- Weighing risks
- Abstinence as an acceptable choice

- Helping and cooperating with others
- Understanding, respecting, and accepting differences in others
- Responding to difficult choices in a resourceful manner
- Recognizing abuse
- Understanding individual self-worth and maintaining a positive self-image
- Alternatives to violence to achieve goals
- Dealing with peer pressure
- Communities caring for each other and working toward common goals
- Making decisions using facts rather than rumors
- Making the community an enjoyable and more interesting place to live
- Developing personal strengths, intelligence, and kindness
- Acting with respect, fairness, and generosity and refraining from greed and jealousy
- Treasuring people rather than possessions
- Recognizing family strengths and weaknesses
- Accepting difficult changes and living through adversity
- Fears and trials of pregnant teens
- Adversity often brings people together
- Pretending to be a different person just so others will like you only creates confusion and lies
- Family traditions and tales teach about our past and move us toward the future
- How a parenting teen's future and responsibilities compare to those of teens who decide not to parent while they are in school

- Following one's dreams, and turning dreams into reachable goals
- Succeeding through belief in oneself
- Understanding cultural differences

Children's perspectives

Surprisingly, no parents ever asked us if we were going to talk with their children about birth control or sex education (which was not our agenda unless the students brought it up themselves). The children raised many topics that might have curled the toes of more conservative community members: drug use, physical abuse, neighborhood violence, sexual promiscuity, and more were mentioned by the class during discussions. Rarely did anyone giggle or gasp — this was real life for these children. We talked about what mattered to them.

When the students told personal stories, sometimes the hard realities of their world came forth.

- When the Odyssey staff asked for stories about respecting nature, a 10-year-old boy told a story about the drug dealers in the house on the corner who had tied up their dog and used it for target practice. He said he had learned that "animals shouldn't be treated that way."

- During stories of bravery, a nine-year-old girl told of throwing a metal toy truck at the face of a man who was climbing in her apartment window. She grabbed her little brother, locked him and herself inside her mother's bedroom (her mother was at work on swing shift), and dialed 911 as the intruder tried to break in the door. The police came and apprehended the burglar, who was stumbling about due to a wounded eye.

- The class was drawing scenes that came to mind after I told a Japanese story, "The Tale of the Oki Islands," about a girl whose parents had been sent to a prison island and her adventures as she sought to find them. I stopped at a Cambodian student's desk and asked her to tell me about the picture she was drawing of two tiny figures walking in a great empty field. She turned to me and said simply, "This is the day my sister and I walked to Thailand."

The Odyssey staff and the teachers of these classes agreed that we would allow the children to tell their personal stories as well as the folktales, legends, myths, and literary stories we were teaching them. We suspected that many of them had nowhere else to talk about these issues. Odyssey had become a safe place to share and test negotiating the waters of an often-frightening world.

Family boundaries

Many times I wondered if we would get a call the next day from a concerned parent, but the calls never came. I believe it is because these children wanted the Odyssey ladies to keep coming back, so they may have been selective about what they shared at home. This belief was reinforced by the responses from several parents when students took home a set of questions they were to ask their families for our oral history project. The questions included:

- What was your favorite toy as a child?
- Does your child's name have a special significance?
- Who is the oldest of all your relatives?

At least five families said that this was none of our business and told us to stop asking so many questions. Again we encountered the fear that we were trying to invade their lives.

The students, however, just found other family members to ask and learned a wealth of information about themselves and their past. I heard excited cries of discovery:

- "My great-great-grandfather was the first doctor in the state of Washington!"
- "I never knew that I was Native American. My mother said that she is half Cherokee."
- "My grandma came over in a big boat all the way from Poland."
- "My dad says we are going to go back to Hawaii as soon as we have saved enough money. He's going to show me where he grew up."

Learning to tell

Most of the children in the Odyssey Project had never attempted to tell stories before, and only a few said that storytelling was part of their lives at home. So we started from square one, teaching the students about the components of story (beginning, middle, and end). We went over the building blocks of storytelling, such as posture, tone, cadence, volume, etc. The shy children were drawn out with puppets and masks. One child was so bashful that the words could not escape her lips, so we gave her the task of leading the listeners in movements that went with the story. We discussed the difference between the stories that they understood and the simpler stories that they could tell to the younger grades.

Telling to kindergarten, Grade 1, and Grade 2 occurred several times a year. Every student had a chance to tell an individual or tandem tale at least once a year. The Odyssey classes also led the younger children in call-and-response stories at assemblies. Students were encouraged to write their own stories and kept copies of their favorite tales in their notebooks. All stories had to be practiced in front of their classmates before being told to the younger classes. The rest of the class would offer feedback regarding the best part of the telling and what else might be added to improve it. The immediate feedback of applause and approval was inspiring to these students, some of whom had rarely felt successful at their endeavors in school before.

Cultural relevance

We were gifted with classes that were ethnically and culturally diverse. Some of the students were originally from Japan, Mexico, Vietnam, Venezuela, Russia, Germany, Cambodia, Samoa, South Africa, Korea, and Thailand. There were usually a few of the children in each class who spoke little or no English at all, and the school system could not afford translators for each class, so their fellow students were often their only translators. We involved these students by inviting them to tell a story they had learned in their own language, while their classmate/translator told the story in tandem with them, translating line for line. Children who usually sat in class, understanding very little, finally had a voice. Some of them were speaking with their peers for the first time. This proved so successful for our Hispanic students that some of them went to the school library to find more storybooks in Spanish so they could tandem-tell additional stories to the kindergarten class.

We invited mentors from the community who spoke the same languages and came from the same countries as our students to share personal stories of immigration, education, and choices regarding planned parenting. They emphasized the importance of retaining their own language and culture while learning to read, write, and speak English as well. We learned how to say hello, goodbye, and thank-you in multiple languages and kept notecards with these words on the front board. When I told stories from one of the ethnic groups represented, students often appeared proud that a story from their culture was shared. I would sometimes incorporate the original language into the story and ask the children to translate for me. The class learned quickly that I was delighted to hear "I went home and told that story and they said that you told it wrong!" This meant that we would get to hear yet another version of the story.

Long-range projects

Besides the weekly activities, there were long-range projects. Some, such as compiling personal notebooks, creating the family history quilts and collecting recipes for an Odyssey cookbook, have already been mentioned. Other projects included:

- **Designing a T-shirt.** Students drew pictures representing the Odyssey Project, and the staff and children together chose a picture of a multiracial group of children holding hands, with a caption in colorful lettering that read "Believe In Yourself." Every child was given one of these shirts at the end of the year.

- **Compiling a memory book.** This book contained favorite quotes, drawings, and stories as well as spaces for the children to collect phone numbers and addresses to keep in touch over the summer. Each student received one of these.

- **Planting a tree.** We planted a tree on the school grounds, accompanied by a plaque stating that the Odyssey class had contributed the tree.

- **Creating a time capsule.** This time capsule, which was to be opened in 10 years, contained a collection of stories and favorite objects from the Odyssey classes.

Assessing our progress

The Odyssey Project grant was renewed for an additional two years. At that time the Odyssey staff recommended that we start our intervention at a younger age. Our surveys had shown that too many children had solidified their attitudes before Odyssey had a chance to intervene. The second two years of this project began with Grade 3 students, who were followed through Grade 4, giving the project a total of four years running.

The evaluation component of this project was difficult at best. The turnover rate of the students attending this school made it impossible to collect consistent data. Each year only 13 to 17 of the original 30-plus students who had started in the fall remained in the classroom by June. Because the population was so transient — one of the facts that put this population at high risk — it became difficult to gather results. Often students would be in class one day and, without warning, would move to a new school the next. Such is the life of parents escaping abusive partners, of a family's inability to pay rent, of children who are sent to live with another relative because mom's boyfriend doesn't like kids, etc. By the third year of the project, the health department began to shift resources in specific directions that did not include adolescent pregnancy prevention or the Odyssey Project, so there was a bittersweet end to four years of work.

Understanding the results

The health department's senior epidemiologist's final evaluation of the recorded interviews was, "The students who were exposed to storytelling engaged more in the first person and active voice than those children without this experience. These patterns are tantalizing and warrant funded research in more depth." A small measurement at best — and yet encouraging that these children are now more able to speak for themselves. Did we make a difference in whether or not these children will grow into pregnant or parenting teens? I don't know. Did we make a difference in their lives? I believe that we did.

For several years after the first group of fifth graders left the school and the Odyssey Project, these students returned to school periodically to ask about the Odyssey ladies. "Are they still telling stories here?" they'd ask. The school principal responded to a newspaper reporter's queries about the effects of the project by explaining, "There's a lot less trouble on the playground among those classes involved in the Odyssey Project." When I went to schools across the county during the last two years of the project, some of the students who had moved from the Odyssey school into new school districts would be in my audience and become my ambassadors. One time, students in a middle-school class groaned when they were told that a storyteller was about to perform. "We're not little kids — why do we have to listen to stories?" But a girl in the last row jumped up and said, "I know this lady — she's the Odyssey storyteller. You're going to like this. She's real good."

I believe we were effective in creating a safe environment for these children to explore who they were as people and to help shape dreams for possible futures. We talked about real issues in their lives and gave them the space to form their own opinions. The Odyssey staff offered the students tools for survival, for negotiating through a world that for many of them was fraught with peril. We had fun. We hammed it up. We took risks, we survived, and we thought of so many ways that we could work together to make our world a better place. Through it all, story was the thread that bound us all together. It's what kept these children involved and asking us to come back again. The only time that the students ever tired of hearing us tell them stories was when they'd call out, "Hey, am I going to get time to tell my story now?"

SOME SAMPLE ACTIVITIES

Interviews: We tell the story "Slower Than The Rest" by Cynthia Rylant, about a girl who is slower to learn than her classmates, but teaches them an important lesson with the help of her pet turtle. The theme of how classmates are treated if they are different is developed further by having students interview each other. Students pair up with someone they don't know very well. They then introduce each other to the class and share something new they learned about each other from the interview.

Exploring Gender Roles: In Charlotte Zolotow's story "William's Doll," William wants a doll. His brother keeps teasing him and his father keeps buying him "boy's toys" until his grandmother finally gets him a doll when she comes to visit. The class discusses those things that are supposedly for one gender only and what happens when these stereotypes and biases are broken. Students are instructed to write down personal goals for themselves, and then imagine and write down what their goals might be if they were the opposite gender. We ask if the goals change? Why or why not?

Growing Up: We tell the students "Baby Rattlesnake" (collected by Lynn Moroney, told by Te Ata), a Pawnee tale of a baby rattlesnake who insists that he won't wait until he is older to get his rattle, even though he is warned that he will get himself into trouble. Students discuss what activities they are now old enough to accomplish that they could not do before, and what activities must wait until they are older. How old do they need to be and what else will they need to do to prepare themselves? We give them diplomas (designed by Odyssey staff) and have them fill in on blank lines a list of those things that they had to wait for but are now competent at accomplishing. Students share their own lists with the class and display their diplomas around the room.

Puppets: We tell "War Between the Sandpipers and the Whales," a Pacific Islands' tale (included in Margaret Read MacDonald's *Peace Tales*) about how fighting can escalate to harm all involved. The tale provides a cogent parallel to the gang violence that occurs in these students' neighborhood. Students make stick puppets from their own drawings of sandpipers and whales and practice telling the story as a group. When they feel ready, they share this story with younger students.

Setting Goals: In "Maria" (from Walter Dean Meyers' *Sweet Illusions*), Maria's father, who immigrated to the U.S.A. to better his family's life, feels as though all the dreams he had for his daughter are now dead since she has told him that she is pregnant. This story illustrates the fear and trials of being a pregnant teen. We use the exercise included in this same book: students imagine themselves as Maria and write: 1) what their life will be like in ten years if they give up hoping and trying, and 2) what their life could be like if they "get it together." The students share their insights with the class, followed by discussions.

Family Stories: We tell "The Quilt Story," by Tony Johnston, in which a pioneer mother makes her daughter a quilt that becomes a family heirloom as it is enjoyed by various family and pets. We create a class quilt. The students take home family interview sheets over a weekend. Back in class, each student uses cotton sheeting and fabric crayons to create a square. The squares depict what students learned of their family and culture. Volunteers then sew the squares together to create a background to use for storytelling presentations.

Celebrating Diversity: We tell students the story "Everybody Cooks Rice," by Norah Dooley. In the story, a child visits various houses in the neighborhood looking for her little brother. During her search she learns about her neighbors, who are from various ethnic backgrounds, and notices that they each prepare rice in a different way. Students and invited family members and guests taste several varieties of rice dishes prepared by staff. Students are given recipe forms to take home and record a favorite family recipe. A class cookbook is then compiled.

Cucarachita

A Mexican folktale retold by Maureen Pedone[*]

THE FAVORITE STORY of the children in the Odyssey Project was "Cucarachita" — the story of the little cockroach girl. Storyteller Olga Loya first recorded this traditional folktale in 1991 and plans to release her version of "Cucarachita" as a children's picture book in the future.

—*Allison M. Cox*

Una vez (one time) there was a little bug and her name was Cucarachita (little cockroach). Cucarachita lived in a casa grande (big house) with her madre y padre (mother and father).

She had lots of beautiful frilly little cockroach dresses to wear and lots of little cockroach Barbie dolls and cockroach toys to play with.

Now you would think that anyone who lived in a *casa grande* with a *madre y padre* who loved her and had lots of clothes and toys would be happy, wouldn't you? But Cucarachita wasn't happy at all; she was very sad. And the reason she was so sad was because Cucarachita thought that she was *muy fea* (very ugly).

Her *madre* would say, "Ay, Cucarachita, you are not *fea*, you are *muy bonita* (very pretty)."

And her *padre* would say, "Cucarachita, you are *muy bella* (very beautiful), like *la reina de la bellesa* (a beauty queen)."

But Cucarachita would say, "That's not true.

You have to think I am *bonita* because you are *mi familia* (my family)." And no matter what anyone said, they couldn't convince Cucarachita that she was not *fea*.

She would go up to her bedroom and look into her *espejo* (mirror) and say, "*Ai*, look at me — I am so *fea*! My *pelo* (hair) is kinky and frizzy and sticks out all over my head! And my *pestanas* (eyelashes) are short and stubby. My *boca* (mouth) is too teeny tiny. And me — look at me! I am so *bajita* (small). I hate to be *bajita*! I want to be *alta* (tall)."

One day Cucarachita was out taking a walk and she passed by a beauty parlor. And she thought, "I'll bet there's something in there that can make me look beautiful." So she went inside and found just the thing she needed. She bought herself a beautiful *peluca* (wig). It was long and black and curly and it looked beautiful! Cucarachita was so proud. She walked home, patting and fluffing that *peluca* and feeling pretty good.

When she got home, she looked into her *espejo* to admire that new *peluca*. It looked great. But her *pestanas* were still short and stubby, her *boca* was still teeny tiny, and she was still *bajita*. Then she remembered something else she had seen at the beauty parlor.

"That's just what I need," she thought.

The next day, Cucarachita went back to the beauty parlor and she bought some *pestanas postisas* (fake eyelashes). She put them on and they were wonderful. They were so long that they curled up right over the top of her head! Oh, Cucarachita was so proud! She walked home patting and fluffing that *peluca* and fluttering those *pestanas postisas*, and she felt really good. But she still had a teeny tiny *boca* and she was still *bajita*.

One day, Cucarachita was in her room looking through a magazine — a beauty magazine,

which was the only kind she ever read. As she turned the pages, she saw an ad. It was just what she needed. She got all the money out of her piggy bank and went to the drug store. And she bought herself some *lapis de labios* (lipstick). She painted great big huge *labios rojos* (red lips), and they looked great! Cucarachita felt good! She walked home patting and fluffing that *peluca*, fluttering those *pestanas postisas*, and blowing kisses with those huge *labios rojos*. But she was still *bajita*.

A few weeks later, Cucarachita was invited to a very important party. She went to a department store to buy a new dress, and while she was looking through the dresses, she saw something on a shelf on the wall. Shoes! They were just what she needed. So she bought a beautiful pair of *zapatos de tacones altos* (high-heeled shoes). Oh, Cucarachita was looking good now! She walked down the street patting and fluffing that *peluca*, fluttering those *pestanas postisas*, blowing kisses with those huge *labios rojos*, walking tall on those *zapatos de tacones altos*, calling, "*Hola! Hola!*" to all her friends. She looked good, and she felt like a million, million dollars! And you know, because Cucarachita thought she looked good, so did everyone else she met.

She was walking along, and down the street came Gato (cat). He took one look at Cucarachita and thought she was *muy bonita*. He walked up to her and said, "Meow, Cucarachita, you are *muy bonita*. Will you marry me?"

And Cucarachita said, "Well, if I marry you, what song will you sing to me at our wedding?"

Gato smiled and rubbed his whiskers, and he opened his *boca* and began to sing. Oh, he howled and he yowled and he made such a terrible noise he nearly frightened poor Cucarachita out of her wits!

And Cucarachita sighed, "Oh, that is not the

song I want to hear. I'm sorry, I cannot marry you." And she walked away.

Well, Cucarachita was pretty happy — she looked good, and she had received a proposal of marriage. She strolled along, looking good and feeling fine, and down the street came Lobo (wolf). Oh, he was something — *alto y fuerte* (tall and strong), with snapping black eyes and shiny white teeth — he was *muy guapo* (very handsome).

Lobo took one look at Cucarachita and said, "*Ai, chica* (hey, baby)! Will you marry me?"

And Cucarachita said, "Well, if I marry you, what song will you sing to me at our wedding?"

Lobo winked at Cucarachita and he opened his *boca* and began to sing. Oh, he howled and he yowled and he made such a racket he nearly frightened poor Cucarachita out of her wits!

And Cucarachita sighed, "Oh, that is not the song I want to hear. I'm sorry, I cannot marry you." And she walked away.

Cucarachita felt like the queen of the world! She looked good and had received two proposals of marriage — there was no stopping her now! She walked along, feeling good, and down the street came Ratoncito (little Rat).

Ratoncito was quiet and shy, and he saw Cucarachita and thought she looked very nice. And he said, "Cucarachita, will you do me the honor of becoming *mi esposa* (my wife)?"

And Cucarachita said, "Well, if I marry you, what song will you sing to me at our wedding?"

Ratoncito smiled and he got out his guitar. He opened his *boca* and began to sing. He sang about *amor* (love) and *beldad* (beauty), and he sang about beautiful starlit nights. And his song was so romantic that Cucarachita nearly fainted with delight.

"*Ai*, that is my song. *Si* (yes), I will marry you," she said.

And so Cucarachita and Ratoncito were married, and they went to live in Ratoncito's *casa*. And they were as happy as happy could be. The things Cucarachita liked to cook were the very things Ratoncito liked to eat, and the songs Ratoncito liked to sing were the very songs Cucarachita liked to hear.

But then Cucarachita began to grow afraid because she knew that, sooner or later, Ratoncito was going to see her without all her makeup. And she was afraid that when he saw the way she really looked, he would frown and call her "*tarasca*" (ugly old hag).

One day she took a deep breath and gathered all her courage and went into *el bano* (the bathroom). And she pulled off that *peluca*, took off those *pestanas postisas*, washed off those huge *labios rojos*, and last of all she took off her beautiful *zapatos de tacones altos*.

Cucarachita went out and stood in front of Ratoncito. He looked at her from her *cabeza* (head) to her *dedos del pie* (toes) and said, "Hmm." Then he looked at her from her *dedos del pie* to her *cabeza* and said, "Hmm."

Finally he said, "You know, Cucarachita, when I asked you to marry me, I thought that you were *muy bonita*. But today you look different. I don't know what you have done to yourself, but I have never seen you look more beautiful. And you know what? I like you much better this way. Now you are truly *bella*."

Cucarachita was so happy because she knew that Ratoncito was not looking at her with his eyes, he was seeing her through his *corazon* (heart). And Ratoncito and Cucarachita lived together very happily for *muchos, muchos anos* (many, many years). ✤

TELLING "CUCARACHITA" TO THE ODYSSEY CLASSES

Allison M. Cox

When I told "Cucarachita" to the Odyssey kids, I made some adaptations to the tale to fit with the goals of our project. In our version, Cucarachita finished school before she got a job, and then she saved her money to buy all the "stuff," an important message we were emphasizing to these students. The class suggested that Cucarachita did all her shopping in one trip to the mall — much to their delight, we went with this suggestion.

When Gato and Lobo sing for Cucarachita, we made this a participation part of the story so that our students could engage their younger classmates when they retold the story by having them yowl and howl together. We had Cucarachita rebuff the approaches of Gato and Lobo, not only because they had terrible voices, but also because these suitors did not treat her with respect. When Cucarachita refused their offers of marriage, the cat and the wolf each stuck their tail in the air and walked off in a huff because "no one ever told them no before!" — another addition of the class.

Ratoncito sings to Cucarachita that he will help with cooking and washing the dishes before they go on their nightly moonlight stroll. We added this to teach students the importance of partners helping each other rather than adhering to rigid role definitions.

Cucarachita still shone through all these incarnations and was requested again and again. The children even made shadow puppets of her in hilariously high heels, "big hair" wigs, and eyelashes as long as she was tall!

Listening is the other half of telling: Teaching students with story

KEVIN D. CORDI

I HAVE BEEN TEACHING for over 12 years, and during those years I have heard all about the ways to help reconnect kids to learning. I have listened to the endless arguments for "Back to Basics," "Tough Love," "Discipline Approach," and ceaseless others. However, over the years I have come to realize that the best methodology for helping children learn is through the gift of story.

When children do not have a place to tell their stories, they remain unheard and possibly hurt, neglected, and confused. How can a student ever seek to learn when he or she has had to remain silent? Every child or teenager has an endless supply of stories to tell and is eagerly seeking others to listen to them. I learned this lesson years ago when a young student named Jennifer Wooley at East Bakersfield High School asked me to start a storytelling club at our school. I had just finished completing a Masters degree in Storytelling and Education, learning various techniques to employ storytelling in the curriculum, but it was the need of this young teenage girl that convinced me students need a place to tell their stories.

A week later, four students and I sat together in a dank basement, planning to tell ghost stories for a half an hour. That half hour became three or four hours, and we told not only tales about ghosts, but also personal stories of everyday life and of school foibles such as dropping books or being called on in class. We even told about missing grandparents and recounted the favorite tales we had heard when we were younger. After that late afternoon of stories, Jennifer announced next week's meeting and I knew that, with my guidance, the students were teaching themselves.

An idea takes hold

On that day, Voices of Illusion, "the first full time high-school storytelling troupe" (according to the National Storytelling Network), was created, inspired by a successful middle-school troupe coached by storyteller/teacher Robert Rubenstein. We met daily and discovered we loved telling and listening to stories. We soon grew in membership and were much in demand all over the state and community. Over ten years later, I now have the distinction of being the first full-time high-school storytelling teacher in the country. In addition to having Voices of Illusion at Hanford High, where we perform over 50 shows a year, we now have a Junior Voices of Illusion. I teach the art of telling stories to almost 300 students a year. I have also started a nationwide program that has registered over 50 other storytelling groups at schools and libraries, and I currently serve as the chair for the National Storytelling Network's "Youth Telling" special interest group.

Some students feel more comfortable telling personal stories because this is the first time someone has really listened to them. When students tell their own stories, they often will talk about fears they have had (and secretly still feel) as a child, the mishaps of school life, and even about relationships and breakups. Others find comfort in folktales. Some girls will choose stories where a young princess outwits the evil king, or a boy may choose a story that speaks of true love or the thrill of a quest.

Regardless of the type of story they choose, they are telling *their* story. As one of my students once told me, "Every story you tell has a little bit of you in it." This is true. If a student tells "The Tortoise and the Hare" or a story where a child is laughed at because of a limp, it may be a way to reveal him or herself to others. Whether it is the simple fact that the student believes "Slow and steady will win the race" or knows the embarrassment that comes from having to look different, wear glasses, walk with a limp, etc., the story is the one that student needs to express.

The environment of the storytelling event, whether it is in the classroom or after school, allows students to feel comfortable sharing their stories. After each story is told, the class or group members take turns offering positive feedback regarding what they liked about the story and the telling. Comments of a critical nature are not given unless the teller asks. Sometimes students simply want to be heard. Eventually students will seek guidance and criticism, but only when they are ready. The only rule I have is "No one makes anyone feel uncomfortable for any reason."

Students find their voice

Jose, now graduated, had a terrible speech problem, according to his elementary school teachers. As he immersed himself in fantasy tales and folktales, Jose began to realize that he could not only write stories, but tell them as well. With every story Jose told, he improved. His confidence in his ability grew until he was able to oversee the storytelling club. Jose even flew with me to Albuquerque, New Mexico, and helped establish a new storytelling club. He soon had gained enough confidence to do over 200 storytelling shows, and more importantly, his reservation about communicating disappeared. Sure, if you listen closely, Jose still has a slight speaking difficulty, but it is not enough to overcome his desire to share with others.

Shannon came to class, carrying an old book, with her family following close behind. Shannon handed the book over to me and shared The book was the personal writings of her uncle, the legendary Native American actor, Chief Dan George, memorable in many films including *Little Big Man*. Even though her uncle's story was so very important to her, it wasn't until Shannon was in our storytelling club that she realized she also had the ability to tell the stories of her people.

Although extremely intelligent, Chris missed many days of school, acted out in class, and generally was labeled "a non-achiever." When he came to his first Voices meeting, I told the story "When Did Polar Bears Learn To Dance?" and he listened intently. It was a story about a father who did not listen to his child; instead he sent him to the beach, where his imaginary friends, the Polar Bears, would listen to him. After the fourth meeting, Chris asked if he could tell my story. I didn't know why he was asking about this particular story, but I told him he was free to tell it. It was not until later that I discovered Chris' father was a musician who was never at home, and this story touched him because it related so closely to his own life. Even though these words were never spoken between us, when Chris tells the story, you can hear his connection to the tale.

Juan joined a gang when he was very young. He was soon involved in many illegal activities, but wanted desperately to change. He joined my storytelling group as a teenager. Even though the tattoos he wore identified him as a gang member, my students ignored the emblems and instead just listened to his stories. Juan soon published a story in a national storytelling journal. "Turning Around" was about his striving to build a better future.

One of my students recently shared with me that she had tried to commit suicide. She told me that while she realized it was a mistake, life was still touch-and-go for her. I listened to every word of her story. I told her I cared about her, but mostly I just listened to what she had to say. Two days later she dropped one of her classes to be in my storytelling class. Each day she finds more of her voice, and because the class praises every story she brings to them, she is increasingly comfortable with herself.

Hearing the story behind the story

I wonder how many times a student wants to talk but can't? I imagine how much healing could occur if we only provided a place for students to tell their stories. Why is it uncommon to listen to our student's problems? Unfortunately, even the most concerned teachers or counselors are not given enough time in their schedules to simply listen to students. In this day of "standardization," we neglect the uniqueness of each student. While the nation is concerned about making sure each child rises to meet some national standard, all children have concerns of their own, concerns that are being neglected. While the academic skills are valuable and even necessary, it is imperative that we take the time to listen to our students talk about their promises, problems, and concerns.

When I was in England I visited a class simply called "Communication." This class consisted of the "troublemakers," and generally was a place where members could discuss their problems. I attended for a few weeks, and I noticed that while their conversation was hard, their respect for each other was encouraged and valued. It is this communication that caused them to have fewer difficulties at home and in school. When someone really listened to them, problems were reduced. Perhaps it is time to provide a place for our students to simply talk. Why not a place to tell stories?

During this journey to England, I also learned about a program called "The Listening Post," which invited elders to simply come and sit down with the students in a tough school district. After a few months of having elders listen to students, rates of violence and vandalism dramatically decreased at the school.

Michelle Austin, a recent graduate, spoke of how storytelling helped her deal with losing a boyfriend. "Stories help you to realize that if other people can get through that same ordeal, you can, too. One of the stories from *Chicken Soup for the Teenage Soul* helped me get through my breakup. It made me realize what my problem was and that it should not be my only concern. Just because it happens does not mean that life will not go on, and I was reassured that I can be happy again."

Dawn Escobar shared that storytelling has helped her find friends and understand her feelings. "Stories have a way of letting kids relate to their own lives. It helps me by letting me express my feelings through a story. Through stories I have made many friends and am able to understand their needs. By telling a story, I can look at a problem or escape from it. Storytelling can be an escape from everyday life."

Stories as guideposts

Ever since my life has been immersed in stories, the healing they offer has naturally evolved to become a tool I use with my students. I have learned to honestly respond with stories when students tell me of a difficult or a promising time. Even when I am "off duty," you can find me engrossed in the telling and learning of tales. When a student has to deal with the death of a friend, I consult stories such as the Ghanian folktale "The Cow Tail Switch," or I may share the wisdom story "This Too Shall Pass." When a teen needs to understand the value of a true friend, I seek the counsel of the ages. I examine everything from Biblical parables to Zen meditation tales, and I have found honest inquiries or even answers to their situation. When students feel lonely, depressed, ignored, stupid, hurt, or even arrogant, there is comfort and gentle guidance in our stories.

I have allowed the stories to help me make decisions in my own life. I have learned from shrewd legendary tricksters like Coyote, Raven, or Brer Rabbit. I marvel at the humorous wisdom of the foolish people of Chelm. I believe in the truths passed on by Aesop and respect the sagacity of parables, morality tales, and cultural folklore.

I am now known as the teacher who tells stories, and I covet the title.

Spread the word

For the work of story to continue and grow, the following basic guidelines will prove helpful to teachers, parents, and others who care about kids:

1. **Make time for kids to tell their stories.** Create a storytelling club in your hometown, make storytelling an integral part of the classroom, set aside some time in the evening at home. Designate this as storytelling time, free from assignments and other work — a time simply for children and teenagers to be heard.
2. **Avoid being judgmental of the stories and the teller.** Students must first know they can trust you with their stories and that you will not judge their appearance, interests, and values. After you have established this climate of trust, students will be assured that their choices are respected, valued, and understood, and they will be accepting of your ideas and opinions. The stories you model will also help them deal with choices in their lives.
3. **Involve other kids and adults.** The more others feel a part of the program, the more community will be established for the group of storytellers. Invite guest tellers (youth and adults), and enlist the help of parents and other adults to tell or assist in your club.
4. **Allow time for your work to grow.** Kids are not used to being listened to — let it build.

In order for change to occur, listening needs to begin. Once a child or a teenager realizes that adults value and hear what they have to say, real communication can begin. Let us set aside our differences and rely upon that universal need we all possess to guide us, the need to tell our stories. Together we can make a difference.

For more information about starting a storytelling connection in your class, school, or library, contact:

Voices Across America
1400 North Harris Street
Hanford, CA 93230
www.youthstorytelling.com

ADOPTING FAMILIES

Family trees

Reneé Díaz de León Harvey

As an adoption social worker, it is my responsibility to forge a solid relationship with special needs children, aged 3 to 14, who have been abandoned or abused by their biological parents. By the time I meet these children, they have been made legal wards of the juvenile court, and the legal rights of their parents have been terminated permanently. I strive to gain their trust and guide them to accept new adoptive parents. Usually these children have been in several temporary foster homes, and they often exhibit difficult behaviors because of the trauma and loss they have suffered.

When I started in this job, I often took children to local parks because these were practical, peaceful places for us to get to know each other. I found myself sharing my zeal for stories and my affection for trees with the children. Weaving folklore and facts, I taught the children how important trees are because they give us oxygen, food, shelter, shade, books, beauty, and inspiration for stories. Originally I told stories primarily to bring "my kids" pleasure. If I could teach them something valuable about nature, or influence their language skills, that would be a bonus. However, I began to notice that many of the children responded most strongly to the characters or parts of stories that reflected their own struggles. Since stories had been a staple of my childhood and I had experienced them as sustenance

to my spirit, I began to cautiously experiment with little stories that incorporated a problem or event in their lives.

Gradually, there in the realm of our imaginations and in the natural verdant protection of pines and maples, chestnuts, dogwoods, yellow chains, and a dozen others, the stories of Greenie, a little tree who is taken from his home in the forest, sprang to life. Starving for some safe way to experience and sort out the events and feelings that have caused them so much pain and confusion, the children seemed nourished by these explorations of loss and sorrow, discovery and transformation. They relished these stories and seemed never to tire of going on an adventure with Greenie. Although Greenie was sometimes confused and often frightened, he never, ever gave up and always found ways to solve his problems. Within himself he had good ideas, but he learned (usually the hard way) how important it was to ask the elements or animals, and occasionally humans, for help. Sometimes the only thing that worked was magic.

I have made up numerous Greenie stories in order to offer children ways to experience and resolve the feelings and events of their wounded lives. Greenie's trouble remembering or his all-too-vivid memories, his angers, his struggles, his fears, and his dreams are always similar to those of the children who hear his stories.

Once, when I was in Wright Park with a nine-year-old girl named Jenny, a Vietnamese family — mother, father, and three girls about the ages of six, eight, and ten — came and joined us on the grass. I was telling a silly yarn about a flea and a mouse who try to outsmart a cat and hitch a ride to a fiesta. After we finished laughing, Jennie asked me to tell the story of Greenie.

I started the story as I often did with the phrase: "A long time ago when the flowers still sang songs ..." One of the little girls blurted out, "Flowers never sang songs," to which Jennie sighed and said, "It's like a long time ago when things were perfect, like when I lived with my mom and she made me pancakes for breakfast."

No matter how traumatic their abuse has been, most children idealize their "life before" with their birth parents. The use of this kind of symbolism in a story can be an effective non-linear technique to express that concept and offer the opportunity to experience it emotionally in a safe context. This is a simple example of the way images in stories give life to understanding. I was surprised only at how Jennie articulated this, not that she had connected intuitively to the imagery in the story.

As the small circle of listeners was drawn into the story, there were no further interruptions. Both the Vietnamese parents appeared to be in a trance, and I wondered how much English they understood. However, as Greenie was moved from place to place and his roots scraped against the concrete, the young mother began to weep. The father covered his face. I was scarcely able to finish the story. We sat in silence for some time

until the mother whispered, "We lose our parents, our home, our country." After some gentle urging she told us some of their experiences of war and exile. With a knowing wisdom, the oldest daughter said, " It helps my mother to tell the stories." With a smile, the mother — Myong was her name — confirmed that to be the truth.

For a long time we sat together, an unlikely knot of people bound by the tapestries of the stories in which we all saw ourselves. I was deeply touched by Myong's stories and suggested she consider contacting some friends I had in the Vietnamese community who were working to support and preserve their culture. She seemed doubtful that her painful tales could be of value, but did ultimately make connection with a group that welcomed her storytelling as a valuable contribution.

Jenny was deeply affected by this family's experience and related to them instantly. We discovered that the sisters would be going to Jenny's school in the fall, and eventually the four girls became good friends. Even when Jenny moved to her permanent family, she and the Trangs maintained their friendship.

I remember I once took five-year-old Ryan to the park in autumn, when a small red-leaf maple that he had found especially sheltering during the summer months stood leafless and barren. Stiff and solemn, Ryan was a little boy who usually locked his emotions inside. But that afternoon he looked stunned and cried, "What happened to it?"

I started to give him the scientific explanation for trees losing their leaves, but then I felt inspired to tell him this little story:

Greenie enjoyed having the birds play in his branches and sing their songs. But one day they all flew away and left Greenie alone. He was so sad, he cried his leaves to the ground. The next morning a little brown bird flew back and promised Greenie he would return in the spring. Two squirrels told Greenie they believed the little bird would keep his promises. Sure enough, the next spring Greenie woke up one morning and the little brown bird was sitting on his shoulder, singing this happy little tune: "In the Fall I fly away. In the Spring, I come to play."

"Yes," cried the squirrels. "Winter, spring, summer, fall — we are your friends through them all." ❧

Retreating to his usual blank expression, Ryan listened to the story and appeared unmoved. He wanted me to tell him the story two more times and then he just sat staring at the scraggly tree. He didn't like the idea of pretending to be Greenie or of drawing a picture of him. As I almost never ask children questions like "How do you feel?" or "What do you think?" unless they indicate a desire to talk about the story or convey a response that begs for discussion, I said nothing to Ryan.

Even when I create a story specifically for a child with the hope that it will offer solace or the opportunity for inner movement, I give the story as a gift, demanding nothing in return. Children often need to hear a story several times in order to process its meaning for themselves, so one of the surefire signs that it has power for them is if they want to hear the story again and again. It is impossible to know how or when or what story will touch a child. The best strategy is to listen carefully to what the child tells you and watch for cues. From my own struggle to talk less and listen more, I have strengthened my knowledge of when to intervene or guide a child toward exploration. There are many effective tools — playacting the part of story characters, drawing, devising games, etc. — that can be employed if they seem appropriate. I do believe very strongly that simply telling the story and allowing the child to experience it with no agenda is vitally important. I have learned to trust the intrinsic power of images and metaphors of story to woo the heart and mind into discovery, to heal and to restore.

Ryan and I puttered through the park for a few more minutes, but before we left he mumbled, "Goodbye, Greenie," and put his face against the thin trunk of the maple. A few days later, Ryan's foster mother called me jubilantly. "Ryan cried," she announced. "For the first time, I mean really cried, good strong cleansing tears. I found him on the back porch with his pajamas on, arms stretched out, the tears streaming down his little old-man face. He said he was crying like Greenie."

What a delight it was to take Ryan to the park the next spring and show him the little maple festooned with leaves and birds.

Working with foster parents and adoptive families

As the children in my charge continued to experience enriching adventures through tales and fables, foster and adoptive parents began to make comments that validated the importance of these stories as a valuable source of nourishment. This was not surprising, but what I did find astonishing were the many remarks that indicated these adults' desires for someone to tell them a magical story or two. Again and again I heard, "Well, when are you going to tell us some stories?" or "I wonder if hearing stories would help me as much as it has helped my foster kids?"

Gradually, I gained enough confidence to introduce storytelling into the foster parent training classes as well as the adoption preparation classes I was conducting. At the time, I was working with a group of parents who were struggling with their anger at and frustration with the children upon whom they so ardently wanted to lavish care. Helping foster parents acknowledge and accept these feelings is an ongoing challenge, as they are an especially tenderhearted and devoted class of caregivers whose skills and self-esteem are intrinsically tied to patience and understanding. Ironically, they could accept the children's misbehavior as a natural consequence of the children's traumatic lives, but had trouble justifying their own "negative feelings."

So I began searching for stories that would offer opportunities to explore these feelings and provide a model for solutions. I discovered that many cultures around the world tell stories that depict parents struggling to deal with children who are difficult or different in one way or another, whether as a result of physical disfigurement, disease, deviant behavior, or some other reason.. A common motif is returning the child to nature to be cared for or absorbed into the universe and transformed into a different living thing — a tree, a river, a plant — which, in turn, is returned to parents and tribe. There are some variants in which parents seek help from nature or animals when dealing with their children. As a result of the advice from or experience with these beings or forces of nature, the parents come to realize the value of the child, and their tender feelings for the children are reawakened.

Drawing on an old family story that my relatives carried from Spain and credit to a Moorish storyteller, as well as on other variants I have found such as "The Ugly Child," I adapted the ancient tales of child abandonment in the following version, "The Tree of Creation." This story is specifically designed to address the dynamics of parental anger. I reserve this story for adult listeners and recommend that my foster parents and adoptive parents find other stories to share with the children. This adaptation was influenced by my own poignant memories, bestowed by my mother, who had often told me how impatient my short-tempered father became with me when, as a baby, I cried or fussed. He would rush out of the house, seeking the solace of the garden, and go to the tree that he and my mother planted to commemorate my birth. Within minutes he would return carrying a leaf or a blossom, which he said reminded him of the beauty and preciousness of his daughter.

Because trees have always been a source of strength and meaning for me, and since the little tree Greenie has nurtured transformations within so many children, I continued using the symbol of a tree to germinate growth and change in these foster and adopting parents.

The Tree of Creation

Reneé Díaz de León Harvey*

Once upon a time, long, long ago, yet not so long ago, there lived a child who had a heart full of love, a head full of ideas and dreams, and all the ways of a growing child. In essence, he was an amazing and wondrous little human being.

And yet sometimes his parents, although they loved him dearly, found him so difficult they felt they could not bear to live with him for another hour. One day, after the mother had fed the child, washed the pots, swept the floor, and started the soup for the next meal, she settled down in her chair to rest for a minute. But the child whined for more food. The mother didn't see how the child could still be hungry, but she gave him some bread. As he grabbed it, she was surprised to see how different the child looked. It seemed to her that the child's mouth was bigger than it had been before, and somehow misshapen. The bread was not enough, and the child pulled on her skirts and demanded more. His hunger seemed like a wild thing and the mother felt as if it would devour her, so she put the child in his bed. He howled and raged so loudly and for so long that her head felt as if there were shards of glass splintering inside.

As soon as the father arrived home, the mother told him of the child's terrible behavior, but the father wasn't too concerned. He went to see the child, who had escaped his bed and was sitting by the hearth, covered with ashes, playing with a gourd. The father held out his arms to the child, his son, but the child, fascinated by the gourd, ignored him and continued shaking the rattle. Laughing, the father scooped the boy up in his arms, but the child wiggled and screamed to be free. And so it went for the rest of that evening and the whole next day. Nothing the parents did or said pleased or comforted the child.

"He is not sick," growled the father." Just willful."

The mother sighed. "He's different. He doesn't love us anymore. I wonder what we have done wrong?"

At that moment the child looked up at the parents and stared at them, and it seemed to them that their child knew something they did not know and saw something they could not see and they felt afraid. "Let's get rid of him," said the father, "before he causes us any more trouble." The mother wrung her hands and cried, but she followed the father and together they took the child to the forest and left him.

At first the child was frightened, but he soon discovered a large purple seed. He smelled it, licked it, shook it, and was about to throw it away, but some feeling told him that this odd-looking furry seed was something more than it seemed. As he had seen his parents plant before, the child buried the seed in the ground. Within a short

174

time, a sturdy, graceful tree sprang up from the earth.

The child called out:

Grow, grow, my bountiful tree,
Grow fruits and nuts to nourish me.

And indeed, the tree grew delicious fruits and nuts, which the child ate with pleasure. And the child's hunger was satisfied.

When a torrent of rain lashed through the forest, the child called out:

Grow, grow, my guardian tree,
Grow thick branches and shelter me.

And indeed, the tree developed thick, arching branches, and the child stayed dry and warm.

Eventually the child fell asleep, but in the middle of the night he awoke in fright and cried out:

Sing, sing, my sweet singing tree,
Sing a song like my mother's for me.

And indeed, the tree lullabied the child with songs of leaf and wind, and he was soothed.

The next day, when the child became restless and lonely, he called out:

Grow, grow, my strong, proud tree,
Grow a branch like my father's knee.

And indeed, the tree molded and shaped a branch like the father's knee, and the child climbed on and was transported to the wondrous places in the father's stories and was delighted.

Now in the meantime, not a night had passed before the mother's heart began to feel as empty and barren as a river without water, while the father's mind whirled like rocks swept around in a storm. There they sat, in their silent, lonely, tidy, little house, wondering what in the world had possessed them to take their beloved child to the forest. Full of remorse and regret, they rushed back to the woods and began to search. At the place where they had left the child, the parents discovered a magnificent tree, rich with fruit and sweet with flowers. Enchanted, the parents climbed up onto the tree to smell the flowers and taste the fruit. Suddenly the child, who had been watching from high in the tree, called out:

Bow down, my fine, good tree,
Bow down and uncover me.

And indeed, the tree shuddered and sank close enough so the parents could see the child. The parents looked at the child staring up at them, and it seemed to them that this was the most beautiful child they had ever seen, the most precious child in the whole world. The mother remembered how the child had blossomed when she had first held him close to her body. And the father remembered the faint little mewling that evolved into a lusty cry. Still standing near the tree, the parents began to tell the child the story of his birth and of each awe-filled day that had followed as he grew. Soon they were filled with the joy and wonder of that time. Weeping, the mother begged the child to forgive them, and the father held out his arms and lifted the child down.

And the child called out;

Dance and sing, my magical tree,
Honor this reunion of my parents and me.

And indeed, the tree swayed and whispered and showered the child and his parents with flowers and songs. And there was forgiving, loving, and understanding.

In harmony, the mother, the father, and the child returned home. And whenever the child began to look different to the parents, they would travel back to the forest and stand before the Tree of Creation and call out:

Heal, heal, our fine, wise tree,
Heal our hearts so our eyes can see.

And indeed, the tree would soothe the parents and sing to them and shower them with flowers and fruits and, most important of all, with memories of the child's arrival. And the parents would rush home and find the child as precious as the day he was born. And so it was. ❧

After using "The Tree of Creation" in several trainings, I learned through trial and error that this story was most effective when used in conjunction with music. The melodic messages seemed to bypass the defenses and reach deep within the listeners. It was almost as if the music would sing the story in the heart and soul and then instruct the mind about what was really important. I have played classical music as well as Irish and Mexican lullabies before telling the story.

After telling the story, I asked the listeners to write down uncensored feelings, memories, or issues that the story awoke in them. I reassured the group that this free-writing would be private, and they would not be required to share unless they so chose. Inevitably, the response was enthusiastic and insightful.

One issue that surfaced repeatedly in every class was the foster/adoptive parent's usually illogical, but persistent, fear that the child's behavior was a result of something they had done wrong or of their not being a good enough parent. To obtain a new perspective, I sometimes suggested we do a round robin about "What we did wrong to our kids," in which all the parents added a reason that explained their failure. We had a lot of fun with this, and by the time we got from "I was born in Texas and I talk funny — not like *my* mom" to "I spread the peanut butter on the bread too thick — that's not the way my family makes sandwiches," we were all laughing. We had been reminded that things are not always as they seem, and we often do not have as much control as we would like.

Foster parents' inability to handle the challenges that a child posed, and their subsequent decision to ask for the child's removal, was one of the most emotionally charged issues discussed. A successful tool perfected over time was to ask the parents to take turns creating stories about who was to blame for the placement failing — the child, the social worker, society, the court, themselves. From this vantage point they could sometimes see how inaccurate, useless, and unsatisfying blame is as an explanation. It motivated them to seek more complex clarifications. Roleplaying another's viewpoint was also a fruitful exercise.

Of all the stories I have told, "The Tree Of Creation" has offered the brightest pathways for parents to explore the demands of caring for difficult children. Ultimately, their explorations yielded rich and powerful revelations. One of the most significant discoveries that continued to appear was the foster/adoptive parents' reluctance to acknowledge that their anger was often related to their ferocious incomprehension of the biological parents' transgressions against helpless children.

However, facing their own feelings of frustration helped the foster parents close the distance between themselves and the child's biological parents. "I guess one of the reasons that I hate admitting that I get angry at Michael is that I don't want to think I am like his mother in any way. But maybe if I was a 16-year-old mom who was an incest victim and lived in a one-room apartment with no friends, and no car — maybe I *would* have a hard time with a screaming baby." This young foster mother, caring for a "crack" baby who cried inconsolably for hours, went on to say, "Actually, the truth is, even with all the help I have, this baby, as much as I love him, is driving me crazy."

For most caregivers, acknowledging angry urges was one thing, but identifying with biological parents who abandoned or injured their children was quite another. Perhaps the most monumental challenge foster and adoptive parents face is the tendency to dehumanize these parents and characterize them as monsters. Because story and music gave them a safe and structured environment where they caught glimpses of their shadow sides, most, though not all, were able to recognize that as humans they shared more commonalties than dissimilarities. "The Tree of Creation" and other stories contributed to the understanding that our goal was not to excuse abusive behavior, but only to move away from a place of total condemnation. Only then could foster parents honestly respect the original connection that the children in their care have to their biological parents, while still honoring the importance of their own relationship to the children.

"The Tree of Creation" sparked many ideas about how parents could help themselves remember "the blessed nature of our children." In several groups, the parents decided to write stories about their own foster children, and then they incorporated these stories into their family time. In the case of the children who went on to adoptive placements, the parents recorded their special stories in the child's Life Book. Similar to a baby book or childhood memory book, Life Books often contain the only photos or records of their family of origin or of their multiple foster home experiences.

Various versions of the Greenie stories were included in the Life Books, and to youngsters like Ryan, who had waited three years for a family to adopt him, these stories represented many of the struggles and successes of their journey.

Ryan's example confirms the power of story to offer solace and solutions to the spirit.

Gradually, as he became attached to his adoptive family, Ryan created happy endings for the little tree and declared, "Greenie is growing strong by a river that sings." (Ryan's new home was in a rural area close to streams and a lake.)

Two years later, long after I had formal contact with Ryan, his mother sent me a photocopy of a picture he had drawn for her as a Mother's Day gift. A family of trees with branch-like arms joined together. Birds perched on the trees and the sky was filled with musical notes.

The Pincoya's Daughter

A FOLKTALE FROM CHILE RETOLD BY
CELIA BARKER LOTTRIDGE*

WHEN I FIRST HEARD this story, I thought of mothers I have worked with who were trying to regain custody of their children and who felt such a mingling of resentment and gratitude toward the foster parents who cared for their children in the interim. I was also reminded of the many grandparents in our community who are raising grandchildren while their own sons and daughters are trying to cope with any number of hard situations. As much as these elders love their grandchildren, they tell me, "Retirement time was supposed to be more restful than this!" Here is a perfect tale to offer ways to understand these ongoing issues in our community.

—*Allison M. Cox*

In another time, an old woman lived by herself in a little stone house by the sea, far south along the coast of Chile. She was very old, so old that all of her family had died or gone away, and the people in the village nearby hardly remembered that she was there.

The woman was too old to keep a garden, but it didn't matter because the sea gave her everything she needed. She spent her days walking slowly along the beach with her basket, gathering shellfish from the tidepools and seaweed and driftwood from the beach.

The old woman loved the bright days when the sky was blue and the waves were gentle, but she was not afraid of storms. When the wind blew and waves pounded the rocks, she sat by her little fire and thought of what she would find on the beach the next day. For after a storm there might be fish in the tidepools and treasures cast up on the beach—an iron cooking pot, a woven rug with one corner torn off, a piece of fishnet —

all things the old woman could put to good use.

One night there was a storm fiercer than any that the old woman could remember. The wind blew the smoke back down the chimney and tried to lift the very stones of her house from the earth. The old woman wrapped herself in her warmest blanket and kept her mind on the fine fish and useful driftwood she would find when the storm had blown itself out.

In the morning, the wind was only a breeze and the sea was calm. The old woman picked up her basket and set out to see what the waves had brought her. She was pleased, for the pools were full of fish and shrimp and the beach was littered with small pieces of driftwood the old woman could easily carry home. And in the last pool, at the far end of the beach, was the greatest treat of all — a large crab.

"That will make me a fine meal," said the old woman to herself, and she laid the crab in the top of her basket and turned back toward her little house. When she got there, she set to work at once to prepare the crab. But when she lifted off its top shell, she did not find what she expected. Instead she saw a baby. The old woman stared in amazement. Surely she was not seeing a baby. The baby gazed back at the old woman with eyes as gray as the sea on a stormy day. Then she smiled and waved her little arms.

The woman saw that the baby was small, smaller than the babies she remembered. She had red hair, as many people do in that part of Chile, and instead of legs she had a tail like a fish.

"I'm dreaming," said the old woman, and she closed her eyes and waited to wake up. But when she opened her eyes, there was the baby, waving her arms and wriggling her tail.

"What shall I do with you?" the old woman asked the baby. But the baby only smiled.

At last the old woman lifted the baby from the crab shell and placed her in a basket. Then, for the first time in many years, she set out for the village. She remembered that there was always a wise woman living in a house at the edge of the village. Surely this woman could help her.

The wise woman welcomed the old woman and even seemed to know who she was. "You have come because you need help," she said. "Tell me what it is."

The old woman handed her the basket. The wise woman lifted the baby from the basket and her eyes widened. She said nothing, but she took the baby in her arms and looked at her perfect hands and her round little face and her silvery tail.

The old woman waited, and at last the wise woman said, "This baby is one of the people of the sea, the Pincoya. She must have been washed onto the beach in the storm. You must give her back to her people. Put her on the rocks where they can find her. Leave her there and they will take her back to the sea."

The old woman put the baby back in the basket and carried her to the rocks at the edge of the water. She found a hollow where the baby could lie safely and lined it with seaweed so that it would not be rough. Then she put the baby gently on the seaweed and watched to see that she would not wiggle and fall. The baby stared at the moving water and lay still. The woman looked out over the water too, but she saw only ripples and drifts of foam, no Pincoya people.

She turned to go back to her little house, but she couldn't leave the baby there alone, so she hid behind a nearby rock and waited to see what would happen. Soon she saw a patch of red seaweed come floating in on the waves. Then she saw that it was not seaweed but hair, the long red hair of a Pincoya woman who lifted her head and looked for a long time at the baby lying in the hollow of the rocks. She did not reach out for her, but turned her head toward the beach.

She called out in a voice like a sighing wind. The old woman could not understand the words, but she had to answer that call, so she stepped out from behind the rock. Then the Pincoya woman spoke to her. She said, "Oh woman of the land, this is my child. She is very small and she is not strong. She cannot swim yet and the sea wolves are bad this year. I fear for her. Oh woman, keep her with you until she is strong. Then she can return to the sea."

The old woman said, "But I am very old. I cannot care for a baby. And what does a Pincoya baby eat? I cannot care for a baby."

"You have cared for her already," said the Pincoya mother. "She only needs to be safe. I will bring food and put it on this rock. Feed it to her and care for her until she is strong. Please, do this for my child."

The old woman looked at the baby, who looked straight back at her with those gray eyes. "I will do it," she said. "I will do it for you and for the baby."

The Pincoya mother put her hands to her heart as if to say thank-you. Then she sank beneath the water. The old woman shook her head. "Whatever I knew about babies I have long forgotten," she said, almost to herself. Then she lifted the baby from the rock and laid her again in the basket and took her home.

She made a bed for the baby beside her own, and every day she fed her the tender strands of sea plants the Pincoya mother left on the rock. She carried the baby out to the beach and put her on the sand to play while she gathered mussels and seaweed for her own soup for dinner. The baby rolled on the sand and splashed in the edges of the waves. She played with shells and starfish and squawked back at the seagulls. Every day she seemed to grow bigger.

The old woman often put off her gathering to sit on a rock near the baby and watch her play. She rolled pebbles to her and listened to her laugh. She showed her the flowers that grew along the beach and the lizards that lived among the rocks and other things a sea child might never know of. And the old woman began to remember songs she had sung to her own babies very long ago, and she sang them to the Pincoya baby to put her to sleep when the sun went down.

The baby loved to listen to the old woman's voice, and she watched with bright gray eyes all that the old woman showed her. But all this time she was growing. She no longer fit into the basket,

and the old woman carried her in her arms, or the baby flipped along beside her as she walked slowly down the beach. One day the old woman looked at the baby's sturdy little body and strong tail, and she knew it was time for her to go back to the sea.

So the next morning she lifted the baby in her arms, meaning to carry her to the rock where the Pincoya mother would find her. But instead of going toward the rock, her feet carried her along the narrow path to the village, to the wise woman's house. The wise woman was sitting in the sun beside her door, and she reached up to take the baby from the old woman's arms. She held the baby on her lap and bounced her and listened to her laugh. And she waited for the old woman to speak.

"See how strong this baby is," said the old woman, "and how happy. Surely she should stay with me. Surely she should not go back to the sea."

"She is strong and she is happy. You have done well. But she is a Pincoya baby and her own people need her. She will grow up to be one of them. You must return her to her people." And the old woman knew that what the wise woman said was true.

She took the baby in her arms once again and carried her back to the rocks. She set her on the sand while she gathered seaweed to make the hollow comfortable. Then she lay the baby in the hollow in the rock. The baby lay there quietly as if she was waiting for something.

The old woman did not hide. She stood beside the rock and soon she saw the beautiful red of the Pincoya mother's hair drifting around her as she swam. When she was near the rock she lifted her head from the water. She reached out her arms to her child, but she looked at the old woman.

"Thank you," she said. "You have taken good care of my daughter. She is strong now and the sea wolves will not catch her. We will never forget you, oh woman of the land." Then she lifted the baby from the rock and set her in the water. The baby flipped her tail and dove, and the old woman saw her hair stream out in the water, just like her mother's. Then she was gone.

The old woman never saw the Pincoya child or mother again, but her life was not the same as it had been before. Now the tidepools were always filled with fish and shrimp, and driftwood always washed up on the end of the beach near her little house. And when the old woman sat on the rocks and looked out to sea, she often saw that red that looks like seaweed, just under the surface of the water, but she knew it was not seaweed. And sometimes it seemed to her that the murmuring of the waves sounded like a song, a song that she had sung to the Pincoya's daughter 🐚.

Traditional stories that address adoption issues

Nancy Schimmel

I had been a storyteller for about 18 years when I was reunited through a registry with the daughter I had given up for adoption 37 years previously. After the first period of amazement, I began to think about stories that related to the issues I was discovering as I entered the community of the adoption triad — other birth mothers, adult adoptees, and adoptive parents.

My daughter and I corresponded for over two months before we met while I was attending the National Storytelling Conference in her home city. Later, I fashioned a program using the story of our reunion as a frame, using excerpts from our correspondence and slotting in traditional stories that illustrated some of the problems we were working through and the joys we were finding. I started by telling the traditional stories at adoption conferences, and then did the whole program. Finally, my daughter and I did the program together at two different adoption conferences. We have now been reunited for nine years and have become good friends.

These stories are all for older children and adults. I thought it would be easy to find them using the various story indexes, but most came to me through friends or serendipity. If you know of others, please let me know.

- "The Cow-Tail Switch" in *The Cow-Tail Switch and Other West African Stories* by Harold Courlander and George Herzog. A hunter fails to return from the hunt. Later, a son is born and asks where his father is. The older sons find his bones, reconstruct him, and bring him to life. The father gives the cow-tail switch to the youngest, who asked for him, because a man is not truly dead as long as he is remembered.

- "The King's True Children" in *The Beautiful Blue Jay and Other Tales of India*, collected and edited by John W. Spellman. Jealous older wives send the youngest queen's two babies — a boy and a girl — down the river, where they are rescued and raised by a fisherman and his wife. When grown, the brother follows a quest to a sacred spring, but looks back and is taken by demons. His sister rescues him, and her fame brings a reunion with their birth parents and a reward for the faithful fisherman.

- "The Lion's Whiskers" in *The Lion's Whiskers and Other Ethiopian Tales* by Brent Ashabranner and Russell Davis. A woman tames a lion in order to win the love of her little stepson. An antidote to all those bad stepmother stories and a hint ("you're not my real mother") about why they exist.

- "The Bear-Child" in *Look Back and See: Twenty lively tales for gentle tellers* retold by Margaret Read MacDonald. In this Inuit tale, an old man makes a bear cub from an ice bear's blood. He and his wife adopt the cub, but lose him when they ask him to hunt an ice bear. This is also available on Milbre Burch's cassette *Treasure on the Tongue*. A similar tale is "The Little Daughter of the Snow" in *Old Peter's Russian Tales* by Arthur Ransome. For once there is longing for a daughter, rather than a son. The girl the old couple make out of snow is active and independent. They lose her when they do not value her enough.

- "Odilia and Aldaric" in *The Giant at the Ford And Other Legends of the Saints* by Ursula Synge. An Alsatian tale in which a warrior rejects his blind daughter and she is raised in a convent. At baptism, she regains her sight. Then begins a contest of wills between equally stubborn father and daughter. Also available on Milbre Burch's cassette *Saints and Other Sinners*. Another version of the legend appears in Butler's *Lives of the Saints*.

- "Once There Was and Once There Was Not" in *Tales the People Tell in Russia*, retold by Lee Wyndham. A conceited storyteller challenges another storyteller to a contest, only to be bested by the teller's small daughter.

- "One, My Darling, Come to Mama" in *The Magic Orange Tree and other Haitian Folktales*, collected by Diane Wolkstein. Philamandré's mother despises her and loves her sisters. When a devil steals the three beloved daughters, the mother goes mad and runs away. Philamandré finds work and marries a king's son. Many years later her mother, old and mad, comes to the palace and Philamandré takes her in.

- "The Stolen Bairn and the Sìdh" in *Womenfolk and Fairy Tales*, edited by Rosemary Minard. An Irish tale in which a mother makes two matchless things to trade with the fairies to get her stolen baby back.

More stories related to adoption issues can be found on the audiotape *Warming the Stone Child: Myths and Stories about Abandonment and the Unmothered Child* by Clarissa Pinkola Estés, from Sounds True Recordings, 735 Walnut Street, Boulder, CO 80302.

EXPLORING ALTERNATIVE SEXUAL IDENTITIES

Bi-anonymous

Melanie Ray

One of the most beautiful things that stories do is recognize people. Children like stories about children, active people love an action adventure. If you appear anywhere in the story it's great, and if the one like you is the main character and outsmarts the villain, well, hooray!

If being recognized for one of your socially accepted qualities is a thrill, it is that much more exciting to be honored for something usually scorned, ignored, or considered shameful. If the heroine in one of my stories is poor, then someone in the audience who knows poverty will feel included. The world as they know it will be explored. They will see people in the tale like themselves being clever, resourceful, kind. They will see others in the audience interested in the poor characters. And the others will recognize the humanity they might possibly have ignored or looked down upon until now.

Lesbians, transgendered persons, gay men, and bisexuals are among those people who are often not recognized. Oh, yes, the bold ones, the drag queens, the "out" celebrities, the bull dykes are recognized by some, sometimes with approval. But the vast majority of heterosexual folks wouldn't know if they had polyamorous bisexuals sitting next to them at the movies unless the "bi's" wore T-shirts emblazoned with the news. After all, it isn't necessarily a conspicuous difference. So the majority of sexual "minorities" are mostly invisible to the general public.

I like to do my small part to counteract this invisibility. I like including the possibility of other sexual orientations in conversations where it's not expected. I might ask a new acquaintance, who is talking about a sweetheart without identifying them as male or female, "and does he or she live with you?" It is especially gratifying if the person seems very heterosexual. If straight, they are reminded that other sexual persuasions are out there and can be included with respect, and if not straight, they are often surprised and pleased.

In my role as a storyteller, I also tell some lesbian stories in places where they aren't expected. I always enjoy telling them to lesbian audiences, but it is wonderful to trot them out for audiences of a more general makeup, where sexual preference is not the reason for the gathering.

The first time I did this was years ago, when I worked with Nan Gregory as Wives' Tales Storytellers. We were preparing a set of stories to tell at a women's gathering. It was not a group of lesbians or feminists. Our audience was women deeply committed to family services, but the theme they asked for was women and relationships. I felt that something should be offered to reflect different sexual preferences. Nan, a woman without a homophobic bone in her body, was supportive. I found a story and we worked it up.

My heart was in my mouth (so to speak) when I told it to the polite gathering on the appointed day. I couldn't tell if the audience — taken as a whole — liked the story of spinsters finding each other in small-town New England, found it disturbing, were outraged by it, or aroused. I had to float my tale on the ever-so-slight craft of only one or two open faces in the crowd. One of them was this dark-haired, bright-eyed, half-smiling woman. She was quiet, but she looked so happy. At the end, the whole room accepted the tale with moderately warm applause.

Later, that woman told me how good it made her feel to have her sexuality acknowledged and celebrated, albeit anonymously, in that group. She cared about the group and the work they did together, but she was not "out" to these women. Having another important part of her life honored in front of them, and to see their mostly positive or at least neutral reaction, made her feel safer, braver, and a little more visible. I must say, I was quite pleased myself.

Nan and I have also told a lesbian coming-out story to all sorts of audiences, and every one seemed to find it hilarious. It is a very funny story whether you are gay or not. And it puts lesbians into a visible position beyond their own community. I tell these stories occasionally in this context — as a neutral part of a wider spectrum of tales for a general audience. But I feel a need to do more.

Confusion, ignorance, and fear can lead to violence. People are beaten and even killed because of their minority sexual orientation. There is a higher incidence of suicide among queer teenagers than among teenagers in general. Stories are needed to help remedy this situation, to help the confused find clarity, the ignorant see an "other's" humanity, and the fearful gain courage.

But I lack the repertoire. I have a personal tale or two, a few literary tales, and I know Hercules was in love with a lad who was captured by water nymphs. But there are limits to the number and scope of my own stories. Literary stories are often too long or just not tellable, and that story of Hercules has little else to recommend it.

What I really want is more folktales, stories from the rich and ancient oral tradition, the vast sea of narratives. I like to tell folktales and I think they are the best tales for any kind of healing and teaching. They have such universality in them, such powerful imagery. The protagonists are easy to identify with, perhaps because they are more archetypes than characters.

But I cannot seem to find the appropriate folktales for these issues of sexual orientation — at least not easily, and as an artist managing herself, I need easy. I want a bibliography. I want it in the subject index of storytelling source books. I want a great folklorist to do the research and guide me to the texts. Please? I have heard other tellers complain about the dearth of folktales on the subject, so I don't think it is just my busyness or my sloth that keep me from finding them, although it may well be I have been looking in the wrong places.

I do believe these stories exist. When the women's movement started, no one could find strong women in the folktales. But the strong women were there; they had just been overlooked by folklorists and collectors uninterested in strong women. We need to go hunting for these stories that have been made as invisible as we ourselves are. As the world has always held a certain percentage of people with other sexual persuasions, there must be stories about them. As some cultures do value their gay, lesbian, bisexual, and transgendered people, they must have folktales celebrating them. I'm sure we outnumber princesses in any society!

A pitifully short list of some sources for stories

- *Kissing The Witch* by Irish author Emma Donahue (New York: Joanna Cotler Books, Harper Collins Publishers, 1997). Literary retelling of 13 fairytales, told through the eyes of the unique women in these stories.

- *The Other Woman* by Colette, translated from the French by Margaret Crosland (London: Virago Press, 1993). As in the previous citation, not all these short stories, selected from *La Femme Cachee* and *Paysages et Portraits*, are on the topic, but she is deliciously inclusive.

Short stories by English author Sara Maitland, can be found in:

- *A Book of Spells* (Great Britain: Michael Joseph Ltd, 1987)

- *A Big Enough God: A Feminist's Search for a Joyful Theology* (New York: Henry Holt, 1995)

- *Ancestral Truths* (New York: Henry Holt, 1994)

- *Angel Maker* (New York: Henry Holt, 1998)

Again, gays and lesbians are not the focus, but they appear in a number of the stories as a natural part of the universe, and in some they act as the primary characters.

- *Cassell's Encyclopedia of Queer Myth, Symbol and Spirit: Gay, Lesbian, Bisexual and Transgender Lore*, collected by Randy Connor, Mariya Sparks, and David Hatfield Sparks (Continuum International Publishing Group, 1998).

≈The Tackety Boots≈

A SCOTTISH FOLKTALE RETOLD
BY HAZEL LENNOX*

I FIRST HEARD THE STORY from Taffy Thomas, who said that he heard the story from a well-known teller in Scotland, Betty White, who had died only a few weeks before. This is an excellent story for young people who are exploring their own sexuality, and also for older folk who too often fall into ways of thinking that are rigid.

> It was the end of the harvest. All the fruits and grains were gathered in, and the Laird — that's the name for the man who owns all the land — was throwing a big party for the workers.

The tables were groaning with food and drink, and everyone was making merry. The Laird stood up and an expectant hush fell on the company. "Now," he said, "ye see this bag of gold. This is for whichever one of ye can tell the best story of the night. And," he continued, pointing his finger around the room, "a'body [everybody] has to participate. If ye canna tell a story, sing a song, or show your bum, then oot ye gan."

Sandy was sitting in the corner. He looked around the room and didn't see a room full of friendly faces; he saw a room full of people he would have to work with, possibly the rest of his life. He thought to himself, "A canna dae it [I can't do it]. Ah just canna get up and tell a story." For you know, it takes a bit of nerve to get up and tell a story.

Rising to his feet, Sandy exclaimed, "Ah canna dae it. Ah canna tell a story."

"Then," thundered the Laird, pointing to the door, "oot ye gan." (Bosses can be like that, you know.)

Sandy heard the big door slam shut behind him. There he was on the outside and there everyone else was on the inside, having fun. Disconsolately, he began to walk down the path, scuffing his feet and pondering the injustices of life, and he found himself walking alongside the river. Spotting an old boat pulled up on the bank, Sandy wandered down and, taking out his pocket knife, began to pick the moss off the outside — for it was his job to look after the boats. Then, lifting one tackety boot up after the other, he stepped into the boat and sat down on the seat. Reaching under the seat, he pulled out a tin can used for the very purpose of bailing and began to bail water out of the boat.

Suddenly the boat gave a jolt and began to drift away from the bank. There were no oars, no sail, and no wind, yet the boat was moving inexorably into the middle of the river.

Sandy was most distraught and didn't know what to do, and he put his head into his hands. Just then he caught a glimpse of a reflection in the water, and she had long black eyelashes and rosy red cheeks, and looking down — and feeling down — he saw that things had changed. She saw a long silver dress and silver slippers.

By the time she reached the other side, she was in a complete state of confusion. She was struggling to pull the heavy boat onto the shore when a young man happened to come along, and seeing her struggling with the boat, he ran down to help and bent his back and pulled the boat onto the shore. Seeing that the young woman was in a distressed state, he suggested that she go to his wee cottage until she calmed down.

He sat her down by the fire and gave her a nice bowl of tattie (potato) soup and a cup of tea, and she became a little more composed. Night was falling, and there was nowhere else for her to go, so he suggested that she stay there the night, and he gave her his own straw bed in the loft while he slept by the fire. The next day she just sort of stayed around, and days became weeks and weeks became months and didn't they fall in love. (And this is where we all get to say "Aaaah" and I hold my hands over my heart.) And then didn't they have a baby! (I'm missing out a few details here for you to fill in yourselves.)

One day, they were out pushing the pram along the river path and the same old boat was pulled up on the shore. With a laugh, the young woman ran down to the boat and began to pick at the moss on the outside. Then, lifting one silver slipper after the other, she stepped into the boat, sat down on the seat. Reaching under the seat, she pulled out a tin can used for the very purpose of bailing out the water and began to bail out the boat.

Suddenly, she felt a jolt and the boat began to drift away from the bank. There were no oars, no sail, and no wind, yet the boat began to drift inexorably into the middle of the river. She leaped to her feet and reached out her arms to the shore and was crying, "Oh my man, oh my child! Oh my man, oh my child!"

The young man raced down to the side of the river and stretched his arms out as far as he could, and she stretched her arms out as far as she could, yet they could not touch, they could not reach.

She was most distraught and didn't know what to do, and she put her head into her hands and felt rough curls and a stubbly chin, and looking down — and feeling down — she saw that things had changed. He saw a pair of moleskin trousers and big tackety boots.

Sandy reached the other side and pulled the boat onto shore and he was still shrieking, "Oh my man, oh my child! Oh my man, oh my child!" And he ran up the path to the big house and burst in the door — and the party was still going on. I know it's surprising, but it's true. And he was still shouting, "Oh my man, oh my child! Oh my man, oh my child!"

Startled, the Laird looked at Sandy and noted his disheveled hair and the wild look in his eye and said, "Sandy, lad, whatever are ye haverin' on aboot?"

So Sandy went in and told them the story — just as I've told it to you — and at the end of it, the Laird fixed him with a hard look and said, "Sandy, if you're saying ye've been to the other side of the river, where none of us has ever been, then it's the best story I've heard all night. Here's the bag of gold to ye." Sandy took the gold and went over to the corner and sat down again, and he never said another word all night. 🦟

Dismantling discrimination, one story at a time

RICO RODRIGUEZ

FOR THE PAST SEVERAL YEARS I have been training sexual minority youth to go into schools and do anti-homophobia peer education. I firmly believe that most young people will listen more amenably to other young people telling their stories than they will listen to adults. I have worked with two groups in Toronto: T.E.A.C.H. (Teens Educating And Confronting Homophobia), a program of Planned Parenthood of Toronto; and Speak Out, a program of the Equity Department of the Toronto District School Board. I provide the storytelling component of a compact but extensive facilitator training. There are a few adults who participate as supporters and accompany the youth to the workshops or conferences, so the youth are not thrown to the wolves alone, so to speak — they have a queer adult to help fend off any homophobic attackers. Once the programs are finished, processing is a big component and the youth all get together to share their experiences.

The goal of the storytelling component is to help the youth learn how to tell their own coming-out stories. I tell them that they do not have a single coming-out story, but many. In fact, I point out, "Once you are queer, you never stop coming out, so every time you have to tell someone that you are gay or lesbian, there is a potential story." The training program is designed to exploit those untapped resources that will enable them to build a repertoire of stories they can draw on for different situations.

I start with simple exercises such as the story behind one's own name. "Why were you named so-and-so?" The students work in pairs and then report to the group. This is a lot of fun and gives me, as well as the group, the opportunity to listen to stories that we can draw upon to remember each other's names. We process the activity and come to some conclusions about style, learning process, language use, etc. But the most important step is that they are, from the very beginning, actually telling stories.

Then we do an exercise for the senses: a visualizing, smelling, sensing, touching, tasting, hearing exercise. I ask them to close their eyes and relax and focus on either the coming-out story or any story they would like to tell. I invite them to see it as a movie, divide it into sequences of events. I then ask them to see, smell, touch, taste, sense, and hear the story. Once they finish the exercise, I ask them to tell the sequence of events to a partner. Then they will list the sequence of events and formulate their story.

The rest of the workshop focuses on learning techniques, developing a storytelling language, telling their story to the group, and hearing feedback from their audience and myself. I always tell them to keep in mind that what they are doing by going to schools, community centers, and conferences is heroic. Exposing oneself is no easy task, and I commend and thank them for their courage. I also tell them that it is extremely important work because they are recruiting people to the cause of seeing people with different sexual orientations as living, breathing, normal human beings. The best way to do this is by building relationships with their audiences, and the most honest approach is to tell their audiences about themselves. I encourage them to include details about their musical tastes, their choice of clothing, their favorite movie, rock, hiphop, or dance stars. I suggest they include true facts, such as having anxieties about their schools, their parents, and their siblings, or what it was like for them to fall in love and perhaps to be rejected.

I have learned that it is better to wait until the end of the training session to tell my own coming-out story to the workshop participants. Some of the students told me that they felt they had to match my story or be as polished or as humorous, etc. I did not want to put undue pressure on them to come up with something that was not theirs. So my story is the last thing they hear. I usually return to one of the processing sessions later in their work, to see how the students are progressing in developing their own stories.

The Best of Both Worlds

RICO RODRIGUEZ

I HAVE BEEN ABLE TO TELL my own story in schools, anti-homophobia conferences, storytelling festivals, and other venues. Of all the places where I tell this story, schools have been the most challenging. I believe it is important to go into schools and do this work because if there is even one student questioning his or her own sexuality, stories such as mine can provide a light, a way toward understanding. There are also students and staff whose benign or malignant homophobia has never been challenged, and my story provides an opportunity for that to happen. One of the stereotypes that my story addresses is that queers are hated by their families. My story about my relationship with my mother challenges that assumption.

> *I swore I would never tell my mom I was doing drag. I just couldn't let her know about Chabuca. You see, I had gone to great lengths to convince her that being gay did not mean I wanted to become a woman.*

My mom had grown up being told that gay people were sort of "in between" and that everything would be all right once they had a sex change. I told her many times that this was not the case with me. "I am gay and I am a man who wants to stay a man," I would say. But she insisted, and several times she made some allusion to a conversation with a knowledgeable friend who had given her confirmation of what I had come to call her "primitive beliefs." She would repeat, "We were always told about the change, in fact the Church approves of it." Sometimes hearing this infuriated me and made me livid and I would scream. Other times I had my usual very rational and civilized explanation for her. But I never really had one that was good, that made me feel complete when I gave it. Until one day I closed my eyes and said, "Because I like my penis just the way it is ...." Enough to tuck it away neatly for the many nights of performances.

Well, to be honest, the whole coming-out experience had been very hard and lengthy for me. I wasn't about to embark on another one. I know, we as homos are never really done with coming out. I am resigned to the fact that I will still be coming out well past my departure from this planet. I have a beautiful Latino family and they are religious and they eat a bit of hot food and they do all those other things people think Latinos do. Well, only to a point. My family was very progressive and very liberal. In fact, we had been vegetarians when it wasn't even cool! But when it came to fags and dykes, well, they were homophobic! The truth is that once I accused them of being homophobic, and they did not even know the word existed, let alone its meaning. They simply called homos *Maricos* or *medio raros* (fags or kind of strange).

I think I was five when I realized I was gay. I knew because after my first day of school, my two older sisters asked me which girls from my kindergarten class did I like. I did not have an answer for them; I had been busy looking at the boys. But I did not tell them this because I knew they would think there was something *raro* with me. So the next day I found out whom the best-looking boys thought were the best-looking girls and I made a *lista*. When I came back home I gave the *lista* to my sisters. I should have never done it. They still tease me with those girls. In fact, they still remember their names! Now I had, of course, another *lista*, my *lista secreta*. One with all the names of all the best-looking boys in my class. Eventually the *lista* included the best-looking boys in the whole school. I was lucky and I survived just like those not-so-obvious homos are able to do. I was creative at hiding and covering up. Out of the depths of repression, the necessity for the gift of creativity cometh.

I grew up and moved to Canada, and for a very long while I was just not prepared to go through the agony of formally and officially telling my family I was gay. I had seen many friends and heard of many people going through horrifying and awful experiences. I was away at university and I only saw my family for the statutory holidays and other selected dates. So I decided to play the waiting game and to slowly sneak in. This strategy is foolproof. You get people to know and like you first, and then, wham! — you strike. It really works. Not that my family did not know me or not like me. They adored me and still do. But I'd rather avoid big dramas.

Besides, I had read a few books on the subject of coming out. They all advised not to come out to families during traditional festivities such as Thanksgiving, Easter, never on Mother's Day, and never, never, never on Father's Day. Also never on Xmas or during birthdays, and forget about weddings, that most heterosexual of rituals. They said there is just too much pressure, too much family, too busy, and I think too many weapons at the dinner table, all those knives and forks, etc.

I thought my whole life was a big hint for my family. I was artistic, I had never brought a girlfriend home, I had lots of boy friends, I was involved in issues of human rights, etc. I had even been living with my boyfriend for several years. So I thought they would clue in sooner or later. And they were, of course, suspicious. But no one ever asked any questions. They were in deep denial. I know there were thoughts, but they were quickly repressed. And I am glad they were repressing something too. In this way we all had something in common.

One day I was finally ready. I had the urge to make it official, to put an end to the rumors and innuendo, to come out of the closet once and for all, to finally be free! I had a conversation with my alter ego, Chabuca, and she told me what to do. You know what I had read in all those books about when not to do it. Well, Chabuca told me they never said anything about your own birthday. So this is what I did. On my birthday I sent a card to my mom, with a bouquet of roses. The card said: "Mom, I love you and it's a girl." So that took care of all that. I knew my mom would get it, and I knew she would tell everyone else. So I let her do the dirty work. I know this sounds like chickening out but, hey, this worked for me.

But a while later Chabuca asked me, "When are you going to tell her about me?"

I said "Never, never, ever, ever."

"Look," Chabuca said, "she has taken it real well. I mean, she is not blaming you, she is blaming herself. This behavior is quite normal and appropriate. She is trying to figure out if she left you alone with the nanny for too long. Or if they cut too much during your circumcision. At any rate, she just moved round the corner from Church and Wellesley and she is having a good time seeing all the drag queens, fags and dykes, and other weirdos go by."

I knew this was all true, but I decided to wait once again. I played the sensitive card and told Chabuca, "You and I have had all these years to figure all this out. Let's give the old lady time and not rush into things."

Chabuca agreed reluctantly and reminded me that with my mom living so close, she would sooner or later find out. Chabuca reminded me also that I was not going to be able to hide all the dresses, wigs, and makeup, and that the smell of Obsession and Chanel #5 would lead my mom to my apartment on her own. I think, as well, that behind all these sensible and rational things, there was also our fear that my mom would not be shocked at all, but that she would like to borrow the dresses and the wigs, and that she would ask me to do her makeup.

As it turned out, I didn't really have to wait all that long, and the prophecy of Chabuca was realized on a Pride Day afternoon. My friend David, my partner William, and I had decided to come out in drag for Pride 95. David was going to be a French maid, William would come out as Dame Edna, and I would bring Chabuca out. Chabuca was also going to march in the parade with the troupe members of the Popular Theatre group, where I worked as a counselor. Sean, a friend of ours who is a singer, heard about our plan and gave us a call. He asked us if we would like to be

his backup vocalists during his performance on Pride Day. We would only have to do a two-step dance and sing some "do wup shoo waps." Of course we all agreed.

So on Pride Day, after we had all done ourselves up and looked beautiful and glamorous, we started our trek to the north stage to meet up with Sean. We walked up Church Street in our pumps, and it was quickly getting painful and it was too, too hot. As we started to realize the north stage was farther north than we had anticipated, William or Dame Edna pointed out, "We are getting awfully close to your mom's apartment building." But I said, or Chabuca said, "Never mind. Mom has gone to Whitby to visit my sister."

We continued with our painful trek and we finally got to the north stage, which was situated almost right below my mom's building. With the certainty that we were safe, we jumped onto the stage with Sean. We sang three songs with him and had a blast. There were lots of people there, and Sean sounded good. At the end of the set he thanked us and introduced us to the crowd. We had told him to call us the Seanettes and also gave him our stage names. Well, he called us the former but forgot the latter and introduced us by our real names. He called me Rico Rodriguez.

Somewhat disappointed about this, but still high on the experience, we started our descent from the stage. William went first, I followed. Right then, a woman approached us. She took off her sunglasses, took one look at me, and exclaimed at the top of her lungs "RODRIGUEZ!" She was my mom and she exclusively reserves calling me by my last name when there is something wrong.

William ran as fast as he could and disappeared into the crowd. I just fainted and lost it. A few seconds later I recovered and composed myself. I could see my mom actually looking at me with those admiring, beautiful, full-of-love eyes of hers. I did not hesitate and asked her to follow me to where I had to meet the Troupe. So we started the trek back down Church Street to Alexander Street where the floats were all assembled.

On the way there my mom could not get her eyes away from me. She said, "You look beautiful, in fact better than your sisters." And I really liked that. Just as Chabuca and I had feared, she wanted the wig, the dress, and a makeup session.

At some point she stopped me and said, "When you were in my womb, I often thought you were going to be a girl."

I replied, "You are one lucky woman because you got both a boy and a girl in one."

"Yes, the best of both worlds," she said.

As we walked past Bar 501, many of the boys hanging out of that famous window started to make lots of noise. One of them jumped down and asked me, "Would you marry me?" I did not know what to say but my mom jumped in and asked him, "How much money do you have in your bank account?" The boy said, "Not much." So she pushed him out of the way with her purse.

We finally got to our destination and there we met up with William. My mom asked him not to run away again. Lots of pictures were taken of the three of us. Soon thereafter the parade began and we started to march. My mom got a set of maracas, and we danced and made some noise. When we got to Gerrard and Church, my mom gave me a kiss and told me it was time for her to go. I asked, "Where are you going?" and she said, "I have to go to Church. I am going to St. Mike's to pray for you, William, and all your friends and everyone who is here today."

I frowned a bit, but she added, "I am going to ask God not to change you one bit, and I am also going to thank Him for giving me the best of both worlds." 🙋

Other resources

MY GENERAL PREFERENCE is to tell personal stories. I am most comfortable opening up with them, and they help me develop a good rapport with the audience. But I also have a repertoire of folktales that I use. They range from the deep and serious to the humorous.

On the more serious side, I tell two versions of "The Ugly Duckling" — the original by Hans Christian Anderson and an adaptation by Peter Cashorali, author of *Fairy Tales: Traditional Stories Retold for Gay Men*. I believe this story is a metaphor for coming out. All the elements of being a "misfit" are there until there is a realization when the "misfit" meets others just like him or herself. Then individuals recognize themselves for who they are. Cashorali's books contain many other gems. I adapt these stories by adding songs and other components to them.

I also tell Cashorali's "The Golden Key," a story of personal discovery that I find both inspiring and encouraging. On the more humorous side, also from *Fairy Tales*, I tell "Beauty and the Beast" (all about leather), "Hansel and Gretel" (who meet a drag queen in the woods), and "The Two Travelers" (about the dichotomy of muscle and hairdressing queens). I choose these stories for their playfulness, but also because they include elements of the community that are stereotyped and marginalized.

DECONSTRUCTING PREJUDICE AND DEVELOPING EMPATHY

Kofi's Hat

A WEST AFRICAN FOLKTALE RETOLD
BY SUSAN O'HALLORAN

Once upon a time, there were two women who were very special to each other.
Since they were tiny children they had been the best of friends.
They never argued and they never fought.

That may not seem so unusual until I tell you that these two women were sisters. Now, as we know, sisters usually have at least a disagreement or two, but these two sisters had none. They were so close that when they grew up, they went in search of partners who also were close friends. They found two men from the same village who were brothers. The sisters married them and bought a farm together, each couple working one half of the farm. Every night, after their work in the fields, the two couples enjoyed meeting for dinner and talking about the day's activities.

And each year, the couples entered the village yam-growing contest. But no matter how hard the couples tried, they never produced as many yams as another man in the village. His name was Kofi. Every year, Kofi's yam crop was larger than anyone else's.

One night at dinner, one of the brothers had a good idea. He said, "Why don't we put our crops together and enter the yam contest that way?" So that's what they did. The next year, for the first time, someone besides Kofi won the yam contest. Well, you can imagine that losing made Kofi quite upset.

Kofi began to worry. What if the couples made more money than he did in the marketplace and he made less or none at all? What if, because they made more money, they had more power? What if, because they had more power, everyone listened to them instead of him?

Kofi was a mean-spirited man. He was vile, vicious, and venomous. He was hurtful, heartless, and hateful. He was uncharitable, ungrateful, unkind, unmerciful ... he wasn't a very nice man. So Kofi came up with a plan to cause trouble between the two sisters and their husbands. He decided to make a hat, a *fela*. He bought two pieces of cloth, one a midnight black and one a shiny, shiny red. He sewed the two pieces of cloth together so that the seam of the hat would run from his forehead to the back of his head, making one side of the hat red and one side of the hat black.

He took that hat, put it on his head, and walked down the center of the field where the two couples were working, one couple on his left and one couple on his right.

At dinner that night, the couples talked about what had happened that day.

"Did you see Kofi walking down the center of

our field?" one sister asked.

"Oh, yes," said the other sister. "How odd that he should be walking about in the middle of the day. But did you see that he wore a beautiful new *fela*?"

"Oh, yes," answered the first sister. "A beautiful red *fela*."

"Oh, no, Sister. You must have had the sun in your eyes. The *fela* was black."

"Oh, no. I am sure. For as you know, red is my favorite color."

The second brother joined in. "But I saw the hat as well. The *fela* was black."

"Red," said the first brother.

"Black."

"Red."

"Black."

They fought so hard that the couples parted without saying goodnight. The next day they continued their argument as they worked in the fields, and that night they didn't eat dinner together. The next week they didn't work the fields together. That year they didn't enter the village yam contest together, and Kofi won. Then Kofi won the year after that and the year after that and the year after that and the year after that as long as any of us can remember. ❧

Compassionate action through storytelling

Susan O'Halloran

Storytelling Creates Connection

How do we find what divides us? How do we listen to another person's or group's perspective? I believe that storytelling gives us a way to talk about potentially divisive topics. If our discussions are not grounded in heartfelt personal experience, talking about controversial subjects can easily become argumentative contests where people feel even more locked into their opposing positions. More frequently, we avoid talking about race, class, gender, sexual orientation, physical abilities, and the like altogether. However, I don't think we dodge "difficult" subjects because we don't care. I think it is more accurate to say we don't know how to care and we're afraid of stirring up even more disharmony. Stories can guide us through those fears by giving us a way to move from argument to dialogue, from a debate-team mentality ("I'm right; you're wrong") to the language of the heart ("I hear you; I'm with you").

Since 1996, I have been involved in a story project under the umbrella name of Kaleidoscope. I partner with Father Derek Simons, a storytelling fan who heads Angels Studio, a communications ministry through his religious order, the Society of The Divine Word. We shared a common vision of using storytelling to promote understanding and reconciliation around issues of difference.

The result of our collaboration has been twofold:

- We created a live performance piece called "Tribes & Bridges" (with myself, an Irish American storyteller, joined by Antonio Sacre, who is Cuban American, and La'Ron Williams, who is African

American), which deals with racism and has recently been videotaped for larger distribution. (My version of the story "Kofi's Hat," given here, is from an adaptation by Sacre, Williams, and O'Halloran of a West African folktale.)

- We have produced a series of videotaped interviews called "Kaleidoscope Voices" in which more than 40 adults and students share their diversity stories as part of a high-school curriculum on valuing differences.

In each of these two formats — professional storytelling and community interviews — the stories move listeners to a common ground of shared human experience.

Real Stories Show Our Common Humanity

In "Tribes & Bridges," the audience hears Antonio Sacre talk about getting into a fight with the class bully, Larry Sargeant. Antonio feels a certain pride that he has taken on this large, callous persecutor. However, after the fight, Antonio learns that Larry is behind in school because his father beats him and then keeps Larry out of school until his bruises heal.

In "Kaleidoscope Voices," viewers hear a grown woman talk about the ethnic slurs directed at her on the grammar school playground and then watch her well up with tears, the sting of humiliation still raw in her soul 30 years later.

In another interview, we hear the story of a young woman who only had two sets of clothes as a young girl. She'd wash one set in the bathtub each night, but sometimes the clothes wouldn't dry. She'd be forced to wear the same outfit to school two days in a row. Her classmates' teasing was relentless.

Both the live performance and taped interviews ask, "What would happen if we knew each other's stories?"

In addition to this personal sharing, we have attempted in "Tribes & Bridges" and "Kaleidoscope Voices" to go beyond telling individual stories to retelling the stories of whole groups of people. We want to tell our country's fuller history, the stories few of us have heard, the stories which can help explain why so many separations exist between groups and what we might do about these divides.

In "Kaleidoscope Voices," for example, an American Indian woman explains the concept of a sovereign nation. She speaks about how few of us learn in our current school systems about America as a nation with many sovereign nations within it. "Without this education," she asks, "how are people to make sense out of different rules or laws for one group of people from another? No wonder we have fights over things such as land and hunting rights."

In "Tribes & Bridges," La'Ron Williams describes a nurturing, Grade 3 teacher taking the brown crayon out of his hand when he wanted to color the people he'd just drawn and, without a word, handing him, instead, the peach-colored crayon marked, "Flesh." In his story, La'Ron tells of the multitude of ways the well-intentioned white staff in his mostly Black school taught him to feel ashamed of who he was, while unwittingly teaching his white classmates that their ways were "normal" (i.e., "superior").

Without diatribe, with simple sharing, we are able to tell the stories of people who have been designated as outsiders in our country and, at the same time, make the invisible lessons and privileges of the insiders more visible. One of the most frequent remarks after our live shows or after the students view the videotaped interviews is "I didn't know that." These kind of stories can help students make sense of the problems around difference that we still have today. We can't change something if we don't know it's there. Stories help us "find the hat" and see what is dividing us. Telling stories of exclusion as well as of the great sacrifices people have made towards inclusion lets students know that they have a part to play. They can be actors making a difference.

As one student said, "In our class, I learned about America being two countries at once. I thought that was great. I didn't know about the historical perspectives and systemic reasons for things. I learned everyone else's story plus more of my own." And another's comment, "Better than a lecture. I learned to have pride and felt inspired to join a club or do something about racism. Today I felt like I wasn't alone."

Kanu Above and Kanu Below

A LIMBA FOLKTALE FROM SIERRA LEONE RETOLD BY MARGARET READ MACDONALD*

Kanu Below was a chief.
He lived on this earth.
Kanu Above was a God.
He lived in the skies.

Now Kanu Below had a beautiful daughter.
He cared for her more than for all his wealth.
How he loved that child.
But one day Kanu Above reached down and took the child away.
He carried her off to the sky and kept her there.

Kanu Below wept and wept.
He could not be comforted.
In his sorrow he forgot to look over his people.
His under-chiefs began to take more and more responsibility for the village.
One day those chiefs came to him and said,
"Kanu! Kanu Below!
A stranger has come into our village.

His name is Spider.
That person is causing much trouble.
He weaves sticky webs over everyone's doorways.
He leaves webs across the paths.
People are tripping and falling.
People keep stumbling into spider webs.
You must send this person from the village.
We do not want him here."

Kanu looked up from his grief.
"I will handle this problem.
Tell Spider to come here."
To Spider he said,
"Spider, you must not leave webs across the paths.
People will trip and hurt themselves.
You must not spin webs across the doorways.
People will stumble into them.
Do you understand?"

Reprinted from *The Storyteller's Start-up Book* by Margaret Read MacDonald (Little Rock, AR: August House, 1993) with the permission of the publisher.

To the chiefs he said,
"See this Spider?
This Spider does some things we do not like.
But this Spider has much good in him.
We will keep him in the village.
We will keep him among us."
And it was so.

Two days later the chiefs came again to Kanu.
"Kanu! Kanu Below!
A stranger has come into the village.
His name is Rat.
This Rat is sneaking into people's houses.
He is taking rice.
He is taking meat.
He is taking kola nuts.
This Rat cannot stay in our village.
Tell him to go."

Kanu said, "Tell Rat to come here:'
To Rat he said,
"Rat, you must not go into people's houses and
take things that are not yours.
They are hungry too.
Do not take their rice.
Do not take their meat.
Do not take their kola nuts.
Do you understand?"
To the chiefs he said,
"See this Rat?
He does some things we do not like.
But there is much good in Rat.
We will keep him in the village.
We will keep Rat among us."
And it was so.

Two days later the chiefs came again.
"Kanu! Kanu Below!
A stranger is in this village.
His name is Anteater.

He is causing trouble.
This Anteater is digging holes in everyone's
yard.
People are falling into them and breaking their
legs.
Send this Anteater out of the village.
He cannot stay here."

Kanu said, "Tell Anteater to come here."
To Anteater he said,
"Anteater, you must stop digging holes in peo-
ple's yards.
People are falling.
They are hurting their legs.
You must stop doing this.
Do you understand?"
To the chiefs he said,
"See this Anteater?
He does some things we do not like.
But there is much good in this Anteater.
We should keep him in the village.
We must keep him among us."
And it was so.

Two days later the chiefs came again.
"Kanu! Kanu Below!
There is a stranger in the village.
His name is Fly.
He is driving everyone crazy.
He buzzes around our heads.
He bites us on the neck.
He bites us on the behind.
Send him away from here.
Get him out of our village."

Kanu said, "Tell Fly to come here."
To Fly he said,
"Fly, you must not buzz around people's heads.
This is very annoying to people.
You must not bite them on the neck.

You must not bite them on the behind.
This hurts our people.
Do you understand?"
To the chiefs he said,
"See this Fly?
He does some things we do not like, yes.
But there is much good in this Fly.
We must keep him in the village.
We should keep him among us."
And it was so.

Days passed, and Kanu was still so sad for the loss of his daughter.

One day he said,
"If only someone from our village could climb to the sky and speak to
Kanu Above.
Perhaps he could be persuaded to return my daughter."
Kanu Above was powerful.
Kanu Above was frightening.
None of the chiefs was willing to approach him.
They kept silent.
But Spider spoke up.
"Kanu Below, I could go for you.
I could spin a web and climb to the sky.
I like the way you treated me.
I will help you."

Rat said,
"Me too.
I will go.
I like the way you treated me, Kanu.
I want to help."

Anteater said,
"Don't forget me.
Let me help also.
I like the way you treated me, Kanu.

I am going to help:'

Fly said,
"And I will go along too.
I like the way you treated me, Kanu.
Now I am going to help."

Spider spun a web right up to the sky.
He fastened it to a cloud.
The four friends climbed up and began to walk around in the sky country
looking for Kanu Above.
There was his court!
"Kanu! Kanu Above!
We have come from Kanu Below.
He misses his daughter so much.
We ask that you return her."

Kanu Above glared at these intruders.
He was angry.
But he said,
"Well, sit down.
We shall see."
Kanu Above called the women.
"Go and prepare food for our guests."
But to one woman he whispered something in private.
Fly said, "This might be a job for me."
Fly followed that woman.
He watched.
The women prepared rice.
They prepared palm oil sauce.
They prepared meat sauce.
That woman took poison.
She poured it into the meat sauce.

Fly hurried back to his three friends.
He buzzed in their ears.
"Don't touch the meat.
It is poisoned."

"Don't touch the meat.
They poisoned it."
"The meat is poisoned.
Don't touch it."

The food was placed before them.
There was a bowl of rice.
There was a bowl of palm oil sauce.
There was a bowl of meat sauce.

"Thank you for the food," said the friends.
"But in our country we never eat meat."
They pushed away the meat sauce and ate only
the palm oil.

Kanu Above looked at them.
"Are these people clever? Or what?"
Kanu Above said,
"Now you may rest in this house."
They went into a house.
Kanu's servants closed the doors.
Kanu's servants closed the windows.
They were locked inside that house.
They waited one ... two ... three ... four ... five
... six days.
No one brought them food.
No one brought them water.

Rat said, "This is a job for me."
Rat gnawed a hole.
He went out.
Rat went into one house.
He took rice.
He brought it back.
He went into another house.
He took meat.
He brought it back.
Rat went into Kanu's house.
He took kola nuts.
He brought them back.

The friends ate and were healthy again.

Kanu's men saw that they were still alive.
They brought brush to set fire to the house.

Anteater said, "Here is a job for me!"
Anteater began to dig.
Fast, fast, he dug.
He dug a hole right under the wall.
The four friends escaped.

They went before Kanu Above.
They brought with them one kola nut.
"Here is a kola nut.
We give it to you.
Our house burned down.
May we take back the child now?"

Kanu Above wondered,
"Are these people clever? Or what?"
"I will bring the child," he said.
"But you must choose her.
If she is really yours, you will know her."

He sent the women to dress the girls.
There were twenty young girls.
They would all be dressed alike.
The friends were worried.
They had never seen Kanu Below's daughter.
How would they know her?

Fly said, "This is a job for me again."
He followed the women.
He watched them dress the girls.
They put beads around their necks.
They put bracelets on their wrists.
They put anklets on their feet.
They braided their hair just so.

But one girl, they ignored.

No one helped her.
She had to put on her own beads.
She had to put on her own bracelets.
She had to put on her own anklets.
She had to fix her hair all by herself.

Fly said, "That must be our chief's daughter.
She is not from this place.
They treat her poorly."

Fly flew back to his friends.
He buzzed in their ears.
"The girl who jumps.
She is the one."
"Grab the girl who jumps."
"Watch for the girl who jumps.
That will be the one."

They brought out twenty young girls.
They were all dressed just alike.
They were lovely in their beads and bracelets.
Fly buzzed around their heads.
"Not this one ... not this one ... not this one."
Suddenly he bit one girl.
"Whoop!" she jumped.
The friends grabbed her.
"This is the one.
We choose this one."

Kanu Above stared and stared.
"Are these people clever? Or what?
Well then, you may have that girl.
Take her to your chief.
And here are four kola nuts
to show my admiration for his four friends."

They took the girl and climbed down to their country again.

Kanu Below was so happy ... so happy ... to have his daughter home again.
He called all the people in the village.
"See what these four have done," he said.
"This is Spider.
You wanted to send him away.
This is Rat.
You did not want him in the village.
This is Anteater.
You did not want him around.
This is Fly.
You would have banished him forever.
Yet these are the ones who have brought back my daughter.
To me these four are without price.
It is these four who will be my chiefs in the future."

And it was so.
This is the story of Kanu Above and Kanu Below. 🕷

Speaking from the heart: Empathic rapport and the role of the oral tradition in moral development

PAUL NELSON

Empathy: The prerequisite for a civil society

Despite its prosperity and affluence, America continues to suffer from a host of pathological and social ills. Particularly troublesome is the high incidence of depression, eating disorders, suicide, drug abuse, and school violence among youth.

While a multitude of reasons have been cited for these disturbing conditions, many psychologists believe that these ills are symptoms of a deeper problem: the lack of a uniquely human trait — empathy. In his book *Emotional Intelligence*, Daniel Goleman calls our culture's empathy deficit "a tragic failing in what it means to be human," and he demonstrates how many of today's ills, especially among our young people, are linked to the emotional illiteracy that arises in place of empathy.

Empathy refers to our ability to relate to how other people feel and see the world. As we inquire into the perceptions and feelings of others, we also learn how to identify our own emotions more carefully and to sort out our thoughts, opinions, and behavioral choices. By fostering empathy, we become better at managing our feelings, avoiding harmful consequences related to mismanaged behavior, and creating more productive outcomes. An empathic concern for others gives us a better chance of creating a life rich with recognition, warm friendships, and accomplishments as we successfully negotiate the complex world of personal, social, and business relationships.

Empathy can also be viewed as the basis for a civil society, since it is the root source of human traits such as affection, compassion, courage, forgiveness, generosity, tenderness, honesty, commitment, and modesty — traits that serve to create a society that is fair, honest, respectful, trustworthy, and enjoyable. People who possess these sensibilities are often referred to as having *heart*.

Empathy is especially important for young people to learn, as it serves as the foundation for moral reasoning. As a child matures, so too does his or her ability to recognize feelings and to imagine the outcomes of specific actions — who will be hurt and who will be helped. By adolescence, the young person should understand that actions can have far-reaching, abstract consequences as well as immediate and concrete ones, and should be able to apply "moral brakes" to behaviors that may have hurtful results. Without empathy, young people become severed from the full range of human experience and blind to the moral significance of situations they encounter.

While there continue to be constructive efforts to help today's young people find their moral compass (i.e., teaching ethical thinking and developing character through values clarification and discussion of moral dilemmas), many of these educational initiatives have met with limited success. Attempts to return to the "good old days," when young people were expected to acquiesce to the moral dictates of authoritative elders and institutions, do not adequately address the core issue and usually meet with opposition from young people. According to Goleman and others, the way to reverse trends in our society toward further violence, corruption, and criminal behavior is to foster empathy rather than reinforce authority.

Empathy must bloom from within the child. To stimulate and nourish this type of perception, adults must protect and nurture empathic skills in the young person. They must start doing so early, and must consistently model those sensibilities of the heart that make us truly human. Storytelling offers us a unique opportunity to do these things.

Empathic rapport: Bringing empathy to life

There have been hundreds of studies conducted on empathy and its relationship to personality and childhood development. Based on the findings from this research, psychologists tell us that there are four actions individuals perform that establish an empathic rapport between themselves and other. This rapport is critical to foster empathy and, subsequently, moral development. The four actions are:

- **Establishing emotional resonance.** We become attuned to the feelings of others by asking questions, actively listening, participating in the give-and-take of verbal dialogue, attending to non-verbal cues, etc.

- **Engaging in perspective-taking.** We imagine ourselves "walking in someone else's shoes."

- **Displaying empathic behavior.** We model empathic behavior and those human traits that arise as a result of empathy (i.e., affection, compassion, tenderness, forgiveness, commitment, trusting, etc.). We also make word associations with those traits and behaviors. People in possession of such traits are variously described as virtuous, moral, ethical, wise, having heart.

- **Providing positive regard.** We actively validate another's experience by giving that person attention, eye-contact, praise, etc. This is an especially important response if we are trying to provide a sense of security and self-esteem within a growing child, both necessary for the development of empathy.

These four interactions, not surprisingly, are at the heart of the oral tradition. For countless generations, this tradition has brought people together to talk, listen, and engage in empathic rapport. It has been instrumental in sustaining clans, tribes, and societies where family affiliations are strong and supportive, and where pro-social behavior thrives.

Narrowly defined, the oral tradition refers to the passing on of historical facts, values, ethics, and cultural norms from one generation to the next through stories, myths, legends, fairytales, parables, poems, and songs. More broadly speaking, it can be defined as virtually any interpersonal exchange between a teller and listener where personal stories are shared in an intimate way. In both cases, the teller and listener actively explore, acknowledge, and validate their feelings in a safe, nurturing environment. By choosing certain stories, the teller invites listeners to try on new perspectives, thereby giving them an opportunity to picture what it is like to walk in someone else's shoes. Human traits such as affection, compassion, tenderness, generosity, courage, trust, and forgiveness are regularly modeled, especially through the telling of the world's great stories (whether literature, history, or biography), which have moral wisdom embedded within. And in the very act of sharing stories we provide one another with positive regard, giving our full attention and praise, and affirming the importance of what is being said and who is saying it.

Like the valves of the heart, these four interactions ensure that the steady flow of experience that comes through us every day continues to nourish our empathic awareness. But if we expect to keep alive those traits that make us truly human, empathy — like the heart muscle itself — must be exercised regularly in order to retain its function and vitality.

Restoring the oral tradition

When we restore the oral tradition to our relationships, families, and schools, we also restore the conditions needed to foster empathy. To do so requires we make a concerted effort to protect our intimate moments together and reduce those distractions that keep us apart. By reducing the amount of time for watching TV, surfing the internet, playing video games, watching movies, and visiting arcades, there will be more time available for sharing stories. Parents, teachers, and school administrators must look carefully at the cost of substituting genuine human contact with the conveniences of depersonalized media.

While reducing our dependency on media, we must also refocus attention on ways of sharing our lives and feelings more intimately.

Storytelling itself is obviously an excellent way to exercise all of the various actions associated with empathic rapport. Because it is interpersonal and direct, storytelling lets us ask and answer questions. It conveys mood and resonates with emotional vitality. It dwells on sensibility and nurtures the imagination. In and of itself, storytelling helps us learn to give unconditional positive regard by focusing our awareness, requiring us to make good eye-contact, and giving ample opportunity for praise (from smiles to standing ovations!).

Resonant stories

Every story exercises the imagination. Not all stories, however, strike an emotional chord or promote moral behavior. Researchers have found that children develop a repertoire of empathic responses by seeing how others react (especially when someone else is distressed), by making word associations with certain feelings, and by imitating what they see. Certain stories, which Charles Smith calls "resonant stories" in *From Wonder to Wisdom: Using Stories to Help People Grow*, contain important benefits when used as source material by parents and teachers.

Resonant stories awaken and reinforce the sensibilities of the heart. They display powerful metaphors that appear repeatedly throughout history and throughout the world's many cultures and religions. These stories continue to thrive because they contain *empathic archetypes* — emotionally realistic descriptions of universal human experiences involving empathy and the other human traits that arise as a consequence of empathic concern. Children of all ages have always resonated with the truth that these stories have to tell. For this reason, Joseph Campbell, the noted scholar of world mythology, referred collectively to these stories as the wisdom-lore.

Resonant stories come in all shapes and sizes — myths, legends, fairytales, fables, poems, parables, songs, dramas, biographies, comedy, even personal anecdotes. They can be fiction or non-fiction. But what they have in common is that they all contain characters who —

- Ask questions to gain another's perspective
- Search for truth and remain faithful to a quest despite disappointments or setbacks
- Show emotion, especially sorrow
- Use a change of perspective (often through humor) to defuse a confrontation, settle a conflict, or help others reach a new level of understanding
- Possess humility
- Shelter the weak or inexperienced, and comfort those in need
- Learn from wise elders and others (such as wizards, fairies, and animals) who possess "magic" (e.g., deeper insight into the nature of things)
- Are generous and love others unconditionally
- Use self-discipline and restraint as a means to attain goals and avoid distressing consequences
- Listen carefully to what others say
- Respect the diversity of life
- Exhibit righteous indignation (or "empathic anger") as a positive emotional source for energizing a defense or fighting for the rights of others
- See that their actions are linked with the actions of others

- Experience the world through the eyes of a child, i.e., with awe, wonder, bewilderment, trust
- Place an emphasis on cooperative problem-solving when it is necessary to tap into resources outside themselves
- Show understanding of and emphasize the distress caused to someone by hurtful behavior
- Act compassionately or express concern for another's plight
- Praise others and celebrate good fortune

Opportunities

We can offer young people many opportunities to expand their awareness and knowledge of the human condition, take part in experiences that deepen their sensitivity to others, and express what they think and how they feel. For example, we can establish programs at libraries, civic organizations, and after-school clubs where storytelling and creative use of the imagination are encouraged. Young people can learn about puppetry, poetry, and composing songs or participate in local theater productions.

Many performing art guilds and folk festivals exist throughout the U.S. to encourage the oral tradition. One enthusiastic group created a festival specifically designed to perpetuate the oral tradition and foster an appreciation for resonant stories. Keepers of the Lore: The Joseph Campbell Festival of Myth, Folklore & Story is an annual New England event that brings together storytellers, poets, puppeteers, folk artists, and other bearers of the oral tradition to "celebrate the great stories of wisdom and tales of wonder from around the world." The popularity of this and other community festivals reflects the growing desire to create and sustain cultural initiatives that counter the encroachment of electronic media and give people an opportunity to gather and share their stories.

Restoring the oral tradition in our lives provides two additional benefits. It gives teachers, parents, and young people a model they can use to create a non-threatening, positive environment for sharing feelings, honoring differences, resolving conflicts, avoiding violence, and developing innovative solutions. It also serves to build a supportive community of people interested in focusing their energies on fostering empathy and continuing the development of a more civil society. Telling stories can reinvigorate our hope for a future filled with promise and possibilities.

Bibliography

Recommended by our Authors and Friends

MANY STORYTELLERS HELPED to shape this collection of recommended reading and stories. Thanks go to the authors of the articles and stories in both volumes of *The Healing Heart*. We also received recommendations from members of the Healing Story Alliance and their Healing Story listserv (www.healingstory.org), the Storytell Discussion List sponsored by Texas Women's University (www.twu.edu/cope/slis/storytell.htm), members of the National Storytelling Network (www.storynet.org/index.htm) and the Storytelling and Diversity Discussion Group listserv. We extend our gratitude to the tellers and listeners we have met along the way who shared their experiences, favorite books and the special stories that provide pathways to healing.

Please respect the copyright of the books recommended in this bibliography. The literary stories can be used as a guide for shaping your own stories or you can seek permissions for oral retellings from the author or publisher.

Abuse and Domestic Violence

Abuse and domestic violence — Selected stories

Barchers, Suzanne I., ed. "The Tale Of The Oki Islands" in *Wise Women: Folk and Fairy Tales from around the World*. Englewood, CO: Libraries Unlimited, 1990.

Chase, Richard. "Like Meat Loves Salt" in *Grandfather Tales*. Boston: Houghton Mifflin, 1990.

Czarnota, Lorna. "Moth To A Flame" in *Crossroads*. New York: Self published, 1999. Phone: 716-837-0551.

Estes, Clarissa Pinkola, "Skeleton Woman," "Sealskin, Soulskin," "The Red Shoes," and "The Handless Maiden" in *Women Who Run With The Wolves*. New York: Ballantine Books, 1992.

Evetts-Secker, Josephine. "The Waterfall of White Hair" in *Mother and Daughter Tales*. New York: Abbeville Press, 1996.

Justice, Jennifer., ed. "The Story Of A Pumpkin" in *The Ghost and I*. Cambridge, MA: Yellow Moon Press, 1990.

Martin, Rafe. *The Rough Face Girl*. New York: G.P. Putnam's Sons, 1992.

Minard, Rosemary., ed. "Cap O' Rushes" in *Womenfolk and Fairy Tales*. Boston: Houghton Mifflin, 1975.

Monaghan, Patricia. "By the Fountain at the Edge of the Sky" in *Wild Girls: The Path of the Young Goddess*. St. Paul, MN: Llewellyn Publications, 2001.

Ransome, Arthur. "The Stolen Turnips" in *Old Peter's Russian Folktales*. Toronto: Thomas Nelson and Sons, 1967. As the author suggests, you can switch the roles of the husband and wife.

Stone, Merlin. "Hina," "Songi," "Lia," and "PoHaha" in *Ancient Mirrors of Womanhood: A Treasury of Goddess and Heroine Lore from Around the World*. Boston: Beacon Press, 1979.

Wolkstein, Diane. "I'm Tipingee, She's Tipingee, We're Tipingee Too" and "The Magic Orange Tree" in *The Magic Orange Tree and other Haitian Folktales*. New York: Schocken Books/Random House, 1997.

Yolen, Jane. "The Boy Who Drew Unicorns" in *The Faery Flag*. New York: Orchard Books, 1989.

———,ed. "The Spirit of the Van" and "The Seal Skin" in *Favorite Folktales From Around The World*. New York: Pantheon Books, 1988.

———. "The Tree's Wife" in *Dream Weaver*. New York: Philomel Books, 1989.

———. *The Boy Who Had Wings*. New York: Ty Crowell Co., 1974. A father shuns his son due to the boy's unique qualities.

Abuse and domestic violence — Personal stories

Wood, Wendy, and Leslie Ann Hatton. *Triumph Over Darkness: Understanding and Healing The Trauma of Childhood Sexual Abuse*. Hillsboro, OR: Beyond Words Publishing, 1993. Poetry, art, and personal stories of 70 women recovering from childhood sexual abuse.

Adoption and Foster Families

Ashabranner, Brent, and Russell Davis. "The Lion's Whiskers" in *The Lion's Whiskers and Other Ethiopian Tales*. North Haven, CT: Linnet Books, 1997.

Burch, Milbre. "Odilia and Aldaric" in *Saints and Other Sinners*. Chapel Hill, NC: Kind Crone Productions, 1990. (Audio recording) Contact author for purchase. See website <http://www.kindcrone.com>.

Estes, Clarissa Pinkola. *Warming the Stone Child: Myths and Stories About Abandonment and the Unmothered Child*. Boulder, CO: Sounds True, 1997. (Audio recording)

MacDonald, Margaret Read. "The Bear-Child" in *Look Back And See*. New York: H.W. Wilson, 1991.

Minard, Rosemary. "The Stolen Bairn and the Sìdh" in *Womenfolk and Fairy Tales*. Boston: Houghton Mifflin, 1975.

Ransome, Arthur. "The Little Daughter of the Snow" in *Old Peter's Russian Tales*. Toronto: Thomas Nelson and Sons, 1967.

Spellman, John W. "The King's True Children" in *The Beautiful Blue Jay and Other Tales of India*. Boston: Little, Brown & Company, 1967.

Synge, Ursula. "Odilia and Aldaric" in *The Giant at the Ford and Other Legends of the Saints*. New York: Atheneum, 1980.

Wolkstein, Diane. "One, My Darling, Come to Mama" in *The Magic Orange Tree and other Haitian Folktales*. New York: Schocken Books/Random House, 1997.

Wyndham, Lee. "Once There Was and Once There Was Not" in *Tales the People Tell in Russia*. New York: J. Messner, 1970.

Yolen, Jane. *Greyling*. New York: Philomel Books, 1991.

Books About Storytelling

Baker, Augusta, and Ellin Greene. *Storytelling: Art and Technique*. New York: R. R. Bowker, 1987.

Barton, Bob. *Tell Me Another*. Markham, ON: Pembroke, 1986.

Dailey, Sheila. *Putting the World in a Nutshell: The Art of the Formula Tale*. New York: H.W. Wilson, 1994.

de Vos, Gail, Merle Harris, and Celia Lottridge. *Telling Tales: Storytelling in the Family*. Edmonton: University of Alberta Press, 2003.

Livo, N. and S. Rietz. *Storytelling: Process and Practice*. Littleton, CO: Libraries Unlimited, 1986.

MacDonald, Margaret Read. *The Storyteller's Start-Up Book: Finding, Learning, Performing, and Using Folktales, Including Twelve Tellable Tales*. Little Rock, AR: August House, 1993.

Pellowski, Anne. *The World of Storytelling: A Practical Guide to the Origins, Development, and Applications of Storytelling*. New York: H.W. Wilson, 1990.

Yolen, Jane. *Touch Magic: Fantasy, Faerie and Folklore in the Literature of Childhood*. New York: Philomel Books, 1981.

Community Building Resources

Kretzmann, John P., and John L. McKnight. *Building Communities from the Inside Out: A Path Toward Finding and Mobilizing a Community Assets*. ACTA Publications, 1997.

Mattessich, Paul, and Barbara Monsey. *Community Building: What Makes It Work? A Review of Factors Influencing Successful Community Building*. St. Paul, MN: Amherst H. Wilder Foundation, 1997.

Some, Malidoma Patrice. *Ritual: Power, Healing and Community*. Portland, OR: Swan Raven and Company, 1993.

Taylor-Ide, Daniel. *Just and Lasting Change: When Communities Own Their Futures*. Baltimore, MD: Johns Hopkins University Press, 2002.

Zipes, Jack. *Creative Storytelling: Building Community, Changing Lives*. New York: Routledge, 1995. Creating community in the classroom.

Coping With Illness

Coping with illness — Selected stories

Aardema, Verna. *Who's In Rabbit's House? A Masai Tale*. New York: Dial, 1990. Talking back to fears.

Hodges, Margaret. *Buried Moon*. Boston: Little, Brown & Company, 1990. Importance of a support system.

Holt, David and Bill Mooney., eds. "Little Burnt Face" in *Ready-To-Tell Tales: Sure-Fire Stories from America's Favorite Storytellers*. Little Rock, AR: August House, 1994.

MacDonald, Margaret Read. "Let's Go On A Bear Hunt" in *The Parent's Guide to Storytelling: How to Make Up New Stories and Retell Old Favorites*. Little Rock, AR: August House, 2001. Great participation story for children who are going through difficult experiences.

Coping with illness — Personal stories

Remen, Rachel Naomi. *Kitchen Table Wisdom: Stories That Heal*. New York: Riverhead Books, 1996.

———. *My Grandfather's Blessings: Stories of Strength, Refuge and Belonging*. New York: Riverhead Books, 2000.

Rybarczyk, Bruce, and Albert Bellg. *Listening to Life Stories: A new approach to stress intervention in health care*. New York: Springer Publishing Company, 1997.

Coping with illness — Additional resource

Kuner, Susan, Carol Matzkim Osborn, Linda Quigley, and Karen Leigh Stroup. *Speak the Language of Healing: Living With Breast Cancer Without Going to War.* Berkeley, CA: Conari Press, 1999. Describes stages of breast cancer as "impact, chaos, choices, community, and spirit."

Deconstructing Prejudice

Deconstructing prejudice — Selected stories

Bryan, Ashley. "Why the Frog Never Plays with the Snake" in *Beat the Story Drum, Pum Pum.* Minneapolis, MN: Econo-Clad Books, 1999.

McKissack, Patricia. "The Woman In The Snow" in *The Dark Thirty.* New York: Knopf, 1992.

Rylant, Cynthia. "Slower Than The Rest" in *Every Living Thing.* New York: Aladdin Books/Macmillan, 1985.

Surat, Michele Maria. *Angel Child, Dragon Child.* Milwaukee, WI: Raintree Publishers, 1983. A Vietnamese girl in the U.S. is tormented by a boy at school because she is different.

Swope, Sam. *The Araboolies of Liberty Street.* New York: Random House, 1989.

Wilkes, Sybella. "The Party" in *One Day We Had To Run.* Brookfield, CT: Millbrook Press, 1994. Refugee children tell the story of the bat who just wants to find somewhere to belong.

Deconstructing prejudice — Personal stories

O'Halloran, Susan, Antonio Sacre, and La'Ron Williams. *Tribes and Bridges at the Steppenwolf Theatre.* Chicago: Angels Studio SVD and O'Halloran Communications, 2000. Available through the website <www.race-bridges.net/sue>.

Elder Tales

Elder tales — Story collections

Chinen, Allan B. *In The Ever After: Fairy Tales and the Second Half of Life.* Wilmette, IL: Chiron Publications, 1989.

Meade, Michael. *The Second Adventure of Life: Reinventing Mentors and Elders.* Pacific Grove, CA: Oral Tradition Archives, 1998. (audio cassette).

Thomas, Ann G. *The Women We Become: Myths, Folktales, and Stories About Growing Older.* Rocklin, CA: Prima Publishing, 1997.

Yolen, Jane. *Gray Heroes: Elder Tales from Around the World.* New York: Penguin, 1999.

Elder tales — Encouraging remembrance

Akeret, Ed, and Robert U. Akeret. *Family Tales, Family Wisdom: How to Gather the Stories of a Lifetime and Share Them With Your Family.* New York: Henry Holt and Company, 1992.

Crimmens, Paula. *Storymaking and Creative Groupwork with Old People.* London/ Bristol, PA: Jessica Kingsley Publishers, 1998.

Greene, Bob, and D.J. Fulford. *To Our Children's Children.* New York: Doubleday, 1993.

Kaminsky, Marc. *The Uses of Reminiscence: New Ways of Working with Older Adults.* New York: Haworth Press, 1984.

Kindig, Eileen Silva. *Remember the Time?: The Power and Promise of Family Storytelling.* Downers Grove, IL: Intervarsity Press, 1997.

Meyerhoff, Barbara. *Remembered Lives: The Work of Ritual, Storytelling and Growing Older.* Ann Arbor, MI: University of Michigan Press, 1992.

Rainer, Tristine. *Your Life as Story: Discovering the "New Autobiography" and Writing Memoir As Literature.* New York: J.P. Tarcher/Putnam, 1998.

Elder tales — Working with Alzheimer's disease

Bridges, Barbara J. *Therapeutic Caregiving: A Practical Guide for Caregivers of Persons with Alzheimer's and Other Dementia Causing Diseases.* Mill Creek, WA: BJB Publishing: 1995.

Feil, Naomi. *The Validation Breakthrough: Simple Techniques for Communicating with People with "Alzheimer's-Type Dementia."* Baltimore, MD: Health Professions Press, Inc., 1993.

Mace, Nancy L., and Peter V. Rabins. *The 36-Hour Day. A family guide to Alzheimer's disease, related dementing illness and memory loss in later life.* New York: Warner Books, 2001.

Environmental Tales

Environmental tales — Story collections

Altman, Nathaniel. *Sacred Trees.* San Francisco: Sierra Club Books, 1994.

Brody, Ed, Jay Goldspinner, Katie Green, Rona Leventhal, and John Porcino., eds. *Spinning Tales, Weaving Hope: Stories, Storytelling, and Activities for Peace, Justice and the Environment.* Gabriola Island, BC: New Society Publishers, 2002.

Caduto, Michael. *Earth Tales from Around the World.* Golden, CO: Fulcrum Publishing, 1997.

Caduto, Michael, and Joseph Bruchac. *Keepers of the Animals: Native American Stories and Wildlife Activities for Children.* Golden, CO: Fulcrum Publishing, 1991.

———. *Keepers of the Earth: Native American Stories and Environmental Activities for Children.* Golden, CO: Fulcrum Publishing, 1988.

Dean, Jana. *Sound Wisdom: Stories of Place.* Olympia, Wa: Puget Sound Water Quality Authority, 1993. Available from the author at deanjana@hotmail.com.

DeSpain, Pleasant. *Eleven Nature Tales: A Multicultural Journey.* Little Rock, AR: August House, 1996.

Elliott, Doug. *Wildwoods Wisdom: Encounters with the Natural World.* New York: Paragon House, 1992.

———. *Wild Roots.* Rochester, VT: Healing Arts Press, 1995.

Gersie, Alida. *Earth Tales: Storytelling In Times Of Change.* London: Merlin Press, 1992.

Hamilton, Virginia. *In the Beginning: Creation Stories from Around the World.* San Diego: Harcourt, 1988.

MacDonald, Margaret Read. *Earth Care: World Folktales to Talk About.* North Haven, CT: Shoe String Press, 1999.

McVickar Edwards, Carolyn. *Sun Stories: Tales from Around the World to Illuminate the Days and Nights of Our Lives.* New York: HarperCollins, 1995.

Milord, Susan. *Tales of the Shimmering Sky: Ten Global Folktales With Activities.* Charlotte, VT: Williamson Publishing, 1996.

Moroney, Lynn. *Moontellers: Myths of the Moon from Around the World.* Flagstaff, AZ: Rising Moon, 1995.

Pellowski, Anne. *The Hidden Stories In Plants.* New York: Macmillan Publishing, 1990.

Strauss, Susan. *Coyote Stories for Children: Tales from Native America.* Hillsboro, OR: Beyond Words, 1991.

———. *Wolf Stories: Myths and True-Life Tales from Around the World.* Hillsboro, OR: Beyond Words, 1994.

Yep, Laurence. "We Are All One" in *The Rainbow People.* New York: HarperCollins Juvenile Books, 1992.

Environmental tales — Selected stories

Arkhurst, Joyce Cooper. "How Spider Got a Thin Waist" in *The Adventures of Spider: West African Folk Tales*. Boston: Little, & Company, 1992.

Frankel, Ellen. "Ibn Ezra's Bad Luck" from *The Classic Tales: 4000 years of Jewish Lore*. London: Jewish Publication Society, 1998.

Gillham, Charles E. "How the Little Owl's Name was Changed" in *Beyond the Clapping Mountains: Eskimo Stories from Alaska*. New York: Macmillan, 1944.

Ginsburg, Mirra. "Which Eye is Blind" in *Three Rolls and One Doughnut: Fables from Russia*. New York: Dial Press, 1970.

Heady, Eleanor B. "The Big Fire" in *Sage Smoke: Tales of the Shoshoni-Bannock Indians*. Chicago: Follett Publishing, 1973.

Parker, Arthur C. "The Owl's Big Eyes" in *Skunny Wundy: Seneca Indian Tales*. New York: Syracuse University Press, 1994.

Rohmer, Harriet, and Octavio Chow., eds. *The Invisible Hunters: A Legend from the Miskito Indians of Nicaragua/Los Cazadores Invisibles: Una Leyenda De Los Indios Miskitos De Nicaragua*. San Francisco: Children's Book Press, 1987.

Seuss, Dr. *The Lorax*. New York: Random House, 1971.

Shannon, George. "The Frog" in *More Stories to Solve: 15 Folktales from Around the World*. New York: Greenwillow Books, 1990.

Strauss, Susan. *The Passionate Fact: Storytelling in Natural History and Cultural Interpretation*. Golden, CO: North American Press/Fulcrum Publishing, 1996.

———. *When Woman Became the Sea: A Costa Rican Creation Myth*. Hillsboro, OR: Beyond Words, 1998.

Martinez, Alejandro, and Rosalma Zubizaretta-Ada. *The Woman Who Outshone the Sun: The Legend of Lucia Zenteno/La mujer que brillaba aún más que el sol: La leyenda de Lucia Zenteno*. San Francisco: Children's Book Press, 1991.

Exploring Alternative Sexual Identities

Exploring alternative sexual identities — Story collections

Cashorali, Peter. *Fairy Tales: Traditional Stories Retold For Gay Men*. San Francisco: HarperSanFrancisco, 1995.

———. *Gay and Fairy and Folk Tales: More Traditional Stories Retold for Gay Men*. Boston: Faber and Faber, 1997.

Donahue, Emma. *Kissing The Witch: Old Tales In New Skins*. New York: HarperCollins Publishers, 1997. Literary retelling of 13 fairy tales, told through the eyes of the unique women in these stories.

Thomas, Marlo. *Free to Be, You and Me*. Philadelphia: Running Press, 1998. Stories, poetry, songs, dialogues, essays that introduce the more serious realities of sexism to young children, but will be enjoyed by all ages.

Exploring alternative sexual identities — Selected stories

Chinen, Allan B. "The King has Goats Ears" in *Beyond the Hero*. New York: Tarcher/Putnam, 1993. The power of secrets.

DeHaan, Linda, and Nijland Stern. *King and King*. Berkeley, CA: Tricycle Press, 2002. A prince searches for his perfect match and finds another prince.

Exploring alternative sexual identities — Additional resource

Connor, Randy, Mariya Sparks, and David Hatfield Sparks. *Cassell's Encyclopedia of Queer Myth, Symbol and Spirit: Gay, Lesbian, Bisexual and Transgender Lore.* Continuum International Publishing Group, 1998.

Grahn, Judy. *Another Mother Tongue: Gay Words, Gay Worlds.* Boston: Beacon Press, 1990. Combines history, folklore, and personal stories to offer a history of gay culture.

Grief and Loss

Grief and loss — Story collections

Estes, Clarissa Pinkola. *Radiant Coat: Myths and Stories About the Crossing Between Life and Death.* Boulder, CO: Sounds True, 1993. (Audio recording)

Gignoux, Jane Hughes. *Some Folk Say: Stories of Life, Death and Beyond.* New York: Foulketale Publishing, 1998.

Henderson, Joseph L., and Maud Oakes. *The Wisdom of the Serpent: The Myths of Death, Rebirth, and Resurrection.* Princeton: Princeton University Press, 1963.

Livo, Norma. *Who's Afraid...? Facing Children's Fears with Folktales.* Greenwood Village, CO: Teacher Ideas Press, 1994.

Rosen, Gail. *Darkness and Dawn: One Woman's Mythology of Loss and Healing.* Pikesville, MD: Self published, 1997. 721 Howard Road Pikesville, Maryland 21208. (Audio recording)

———. *Listening After The Music Stops, Stories of Loss and Comfort.* Pikesville, MD: Self published, 1998. 721 Howard Road, Pikesville, Maryland 21208. (Audio recording)

Simms, Laura. *Stories To Nourish The Hearts Of Our Children In A Time Of Crisis.* New York: Holland and Knight, 2001.

Williamson, Duncan, and Linda Williamson. *May the Devil Walk Behind Ye!* Edinburgh: Cannongate, 1989. Traditional stories reflecting a Scottish outlook on death.

Grief and loss — Selected stories

Alexander, Sue, and Jim Trelease., eds. "Nadia the Willful" in *Hey! Listen to This: Stories to Read Aloud.* New York: Penguin Books, 1992.

Ashabranner, Brent, and Russell Davis. "The Lion's Whiskers" in *The Lion's Whiskers and Other Ethiopian Tales.* North Haven, CT: Linnet Books, 1997.

Cavanaugh, Brian. "A Cure for Sorrow," "Telling One's Own Story," "The Sorrow Tree," "Story to Heal," "The Face in the Window," "I Created You," "Grains of Caring," "Heaven and Hell," "Attitude at Work," "Merchant of Death," and "Find Someone in Need" in *The Sower's Seeds.* New York: Paulist Press, 1990.

Courlander, Harold, and George Herzog. "The Cow Tail Switch" in *The Cow Tail Switch and Other West African Stories.* New York: Henry Holt and Company, 1986.

DeSpain, Pleasant. "Grizzly Bear Feast" in *Eleven Nature Tales: A Multicultural Journey.* Little Rock, AR: August House Publishers, 1996

Estes, Clarissa Pinkola. *The Gift of Story: A Wise Tale About What Is Enough.* New York: Ballantine Books, 1993. Triumph of love over loss.

Feldman, Christina, and Jack Kornfield, eds. "The Mustard Seed" and "Blessings and Disasters" in *Soul Food: Stories to Nourish the Spirit and the Heart.* San Francisco: Harper, 1996.

Holt, David, and Bill Mooney., eds. "La Muerta: Godmother Death" in *Ready-To-Tell Tales: Sure-fire Stories From America's Favorite Storytellers*. Little Rock, AR: August House, 1994.

McVickar Edwards, Carolyn. "Kali, Dancer On Gravestones" in *The Storyteller's Goddess: Tales of the Goddess and Her Wisdom from Around the World*. San Francisco: HarperSanFrancisco, 1991.

Schram, Peninnah, and Jacob Aaronson. "Elijah's Mysterious Ways" in *Jewish Stories One Generation Tells Another*. Northvale, NJ: Jason Aronson, 1987.

Stone, Merlin. "Mawu" in *Ancient Mirrors of Womanhood: A Treasury of Goddess and Heroine Lore from Around the World*. Boston: Beacon Press, 1990.

Williamson, Duncan, and Linda Williamson. "Death in a Nut" in *A Thorn in the King's Foot: Folktales of the Scottish Traveling People*. Harmondsworth, England: Penguin, 1987.

Yolen, Jane., ed. "The End Of The World" in *Favorite Folktales From Around The World*. New York: Pantheon Books, 1988.

Grief and loss — Personal stories

Ajjan, Diana. *The Day My Father Died: Women Share Their Stories of Love, Loss and Life*. Philadelphia: Running Cliffs, 1994.

Canfield, Jack, Mark Hansen, Patty Aubery, and Nancy Mitchell. *Chicken Soup for the Surviving Soul*. Deerfield Beach, FL: Health Communications, 1996.

Grief and loss — Therapeutic storytelling

Cameron, Julia. *The Artist's Way: A Spiritual Path to Higher Creativity*. New York: G. P. Putnam's Sons, 1992. Methods for recovering your creativity when blocked by limiting beliefs, fear, self-sabotage, jealousy, guilt, addictions, and other inhibiting forces.

Gersie, Alida. *Storymaking and Bereavement: Dragons Fight in the Meadow*. London: Jessica Kingsley Publishers, 1991.

Harvey, John. *Embracing Their Memory: Loss and the Social Psychology of Storytelling*. Needham Heights, MA: Allyn and Bacon, 1996.

Rooks, Diane. *Spinning Gold out of Straw: How Stories Heal*. St. Augustine, FL: Salt Run Press, 2001.

Young-Eisendrath. Polly. *The Gifts of Suffering: Finding Insight, Compassion, and Renewal*. New York: Addison-Wesley, 1996.

Grief and loss — Additional resources

Callanan, Maggie, and Patricia Kelly. *Final Gifts: Understanding the Special Awareness, Needs and Communications of the Dying*. New York: Bantam Books, 1992. A study of the symbolic language of the dying.

Kubler-Ross, Elisabeth. *The Wheel of Life: A Memoir of Living and Dying*. New York, Simon and Schuster, 1997.

Levine, Steven, and Ondrea Levine. *Who Dies? An Investigation of Conscious Living and Conscious Dying*. New York: Doubleday, 1982. Personal stories illustrate the immensity of living with death while participating fully in life.

Miller, Sukie. *After Death: How People Around The World Map The Journey After We Die*. New York: Simon and Schuster, 1997. A cross-cultural overview on death.

Rico, Gabriele. *Pain and Possibility: Writing Your Way Through Personal Crisis*. New York: G.P. Putnam's Sons, 1991. Using creativity to achieve healing and growth.

Health Promotion

Health promotion — Story collection

Livo, Norma J. *Story Medicine: Multicultural Tales of Healing and Transformation*. Englewood, CO: Libraries Unlimited/Teacher Ideas Press, 2001. Forty tales from all over the world on healing the self, relationships, the community and the earth.

Health promotion — Selected story

MacDonald, Margaret Read. "Not Our Problem" in *Peace Tales: World Folktales to Talk About*. Hampden, CT: Linnet Books, 1992.

Homelessness

Vanderstaay, Steve. *Street Lives: An Oral History of Homeless Americans*. Gabriola Island, BC: New Society Publishers, 1992.

Wild, Margaret. *Space Travelers*. New York: Scholastic, 1992. A boy and his mother live in a jungle gym in the park while they search for a home.

Wilkes, Sybella. "The Party" in *One Day We Had To Run*. Brookfield, CT: Millbrook Press, 1994.

Lap Rhymes, Lullabies, and Finger Plays for Babies through Toddlers

Brown, Aaron J. *A Child's Gift Of Lullabies*. Nashville, TN: Someday Baby/JABA Records, 1987. (Audio recording)

Carpenter-Davis, Sandra. *Bounce Me, Tickle Me, Hug Me*. Toronto: Parent-Child Mother Goose Program, 1997.

Defty, Jeff. *Creative Fingerplays and Action Rhymes: An Index and Guide to Their Use*. Phoenix, AZ: Oryx, 1992.

Denton, Kady MacDonald. *A Child's Treasury of Nursery Rhymes*. Toronto: Kids Can Press, 1998.

Jaeger, Sally. *Lullabies and Lap Rhymes*. Toronto: Self-published, 1993. Write: Sally Jaeger, 105 Voctor Ave., Toronto, ON Canada M4K 1A7. (Audiocassette) This tape teaches rhymes, songs, and lullabies to play and say with babies.

———. *Mr. Bear Says Hello*. Toronto: 49 North Productions, Inc., 1997. Write: Sally Jaeger, 105 Voctor Ave., Toronto, ON Canada M4K 1A7. (Audiocassette) Rhymes, fingerplays, songs, games, and lullabies to play with children from one to four.

———. *From Wibbleton to Wobbleton*. Toronto: 49 North Productions, 1998. To order, call 49 North Productions, (416) 461-4327. (Video) Forty minutes of 38 rhymes, tickles, bounces, gallops, and lullabies.

Lee, Dennis. *Jelly Belly*. Toronto: Macmillan, 1983.

Lines, Kathleen. *Lavender's Blue*. New York: Oxford University Press, 1991.

Lottridge, Celia. *The Moon is Round*. Toronto: Parent-Child Mother Goose Program, 1992.

———. *Mother Goose: A Canadian Sampler*. Toronto: Groundwood Books, 1994.

Opie, Iona. *My Very First Mother Goose*. Cambridge: Candlewick Press, 1996.

Opie, Iona, and Peter Opie. *The Oxford Nursery Rhyme Book*. New York: Oxford University Press, 1955.

———. *The Puffin Book of Nursery Rhymes*. Baltimore: Penguin Books, 1999.

———. *Tail Feathers from Mother Goose*. London: Walker Books, 1988.

Stetson, Emily, and Vicky Congdo. *Little Hands,*

Fingerplays and Action Songs: Seasonal Activities and Creative Play for 2 To 6-Year-Olds. Charlotte, VT: Williamson Publishing, 2001.

Men's Issues

Men's issues — Story collections

Bly, Robert. *Iron John: A Book About Men.* New York, Addison Wesley, 1991.

Bruchac, Joseph. *Flying With Eagle, Racing With the Great Bear.* Mahwah, NJ: Troll Medallion, 1993. Many stories of boys from Native American folklore.

Campbell, Joseph. *The Hero With A Thousand Faces.* Princeton, NJ: Princeton University Press, 1972.

Chase, Richard. *The Jack Tales.* Boston: Houghton Mifflin, 1993.

Chinen, Allan B. *Once Upon a Midlife: Classic Stories and Mythic Tales to Illuminate the Mythic Years.* New York: G.P. Putnam's Sons, 1992.

Chinen, Allan B., and Dan Keding. *Beyond the Hero: Classic Stories of Men in Search of Soul.* Little Rock, AR: August House, 1993. (Audio recording)

Hillman, James, Michael Meade and Robert W. Bly. *Men and the Life of Desire.* Pacific Grove, CA: Oral Tradition Archives, 1998. (audio cassette).

Meade, Michael. *Off With the Rat's Head: Tales of the Father, Son & King.* Boston: Yellow Moon Press, 1990. (audio cassette).

Meade, Michael. *Men and the Water of Life: Initiation and the Tempering of Men.* San Francisco: HarperCollins, 1993.

Men's issues — Selected stories

Holt, David, and Bill Mooney., eds. "The Black Prince" in *Ready-To-Tell Tales: Sure-Fire Stories from America's Favorite Storytellers.* Little Rock, AR: August House, 1994.

Wolkstein, Diane. *The Red Lion: A Tale of Ancient Persia.* New York: Ty Crowell Co., 1977.

Zolotow, Charlotte. *William's Doll.* New York: HarperTrophy, 1985.

Men's issues — Additional resource

Pollack, William. *Real Boys: Rescuing Our Sons from the Myths of Boyhood.* New York: Henry Holt and Company, 1999.

Oral History

Baker, Holly Cutting, Amy J. Kotkin, and Steven J. Zeitlin. *A Celebration of American Family Folklore.* Cambridge, MA: Yellow Moon Press, 1992. Includes section about collecting your own family stories.

Brecher, Jeremy. *History From Below: How to Uncover and Tell the Story of Your Community, Association, or Union.* New Haven, CT: Advocate Press. 1986.

Ives, Edward D. *The Tape-Recorded Interview: A Manual for Field Workers in Folklore and Oral History.* Knoxville, TN: University of Tennessee Press, 1980.

Lichtman, Allan J. *Your Family History: How to use oral history, personal family archives, and public documents to discover your heritage.* New York: Random House. 1978.

Moore, Robin. *Awakening the Hidden Storyteller: How to Build a Storytelling Tradition in Your Family.* Boston: Shambhala Publications, 1991.

Preserving Our Culture

Baltuck, Naomi. *Apples from Heaven: Multicultural Folk Tales About Stories and Storytellers.* Hampden, CT: Linnet Books, 1995.

Cole, Joanna., ed. *Best-Loved Folktales of the World.* New York: Doubleday, 1992.

Curry, Lindy Soon. *A Tiger by the Tail and Other Stories from the Heart of Korea.* Englewood, CO: Teacher Ideas Press/Libraries Unlimited, 1999.

DeSpain Pleasant. *The Emerald Lizard: Fifteen Latin American Tales to Tell in English and Spanish.* Little Rock, AR: August House, 1999.

———. *Thirty-three Multicultural Tales to Tell.* Little Rock, AR: August House, 1993.

Dooley, Norah. *Everybody Cooks Rice.* Minneapolis: Carolrhoda Books, 1991.

Faulkner, W. *The days when the animals talked: Black American folktales and how they came to be.* Lawrenceville, NJ: Africa World Press, 1993.

Forest, Heather. *Wonder Tales From Around the World.* Little Rock, AR: August House, 1995.

Goss, Linda, Marion Barnes, and Henry Louis Gates Jr.., eds. *Talk That Talk: An Anthology of African American Storytelling.* New York: Simon and Schuster, 1989.

Gunn Allen, Paula., ed. *Spider Woman's Granddaughters: Traditional Tales and Contemporary Writing by Native American Women.* New York: Ballantine Books, 1989.

Hamilton, Virginia. *The people could fly: American Black folktales.* New York: Knopf, 1985.

Johnston, Tony. *The Quilt Story.* New York: G.P. Putnam's Sons, 1985.

Lester, Julius. *The Tales of Uncle Remus: The Adventures of Brer Rabbit.* New York: Dial Books, 1987.

Pijoan, Teresa. *White Wolf Woman. Native American Transformation Myths.* Little Rock, AR: August House, 1992.

Rosen, Michael. *South and North, East and West: The Oxfam Book of Children's Stories.* Cambridge, MA: Candlewick Press, 1992.

Shah, Idries. *The Subtleties of the Inimitable Nasrudin.* London: Octagon Press, 1989.

Sherman, Josepha. *Rachel The Clever and Other Jewish Tales.* Little Rock, AR: August House, 1993.

Spagnoli, Cathy. *Asian Tales and Tellers.* Little Rock, AR: August House, 1998.

———. *Jasmine and Coconuts: South Indian Tales.* Englewood, CO: Libraries Unlimited, 1999.

———. *Terrific Trickster Tales from Asia.* Fort Atkinson, WI: Highsmith Press, 2001.

———. *A Treasury of Asian Stories and Activities for Schools and Libraries.* Fort Atkinson, WI: Highsmith Press, 1998.

Vigil, Angel. *The Corn Woman: Stories and Legends of the Hispanic Southwest.* Englewood, CO: Teacher Ideas Press/Libraries Unlimited, 1995.

Webber, Desiree, and Dee Ann Corn. *Travel the Globe: Multicultural Story Times.* Englewood, CO: Teacher Ideas Press/Libraries Unlimited, 1998.

Wichman, Frederick B. *Kaua'i: Ancient Place-Names and Their Stories.* Honolulu: University of Hawaii Press, 1998.

Yolen, Jane. *Favorite Folktales from Around the World.* New York: Pantheon Books, 1988.

Resiliency

Resiliency — Story collection

Nelson, Annabelle. *Storytelling for Prevention.* Colorado: The WHEEL Council, (www.wheelcouncil.org), 1998.

Resiliency — Selected stories

Holt, David, and Bill Mooney., eds. "Little Burnt Face" in *Ready-To-Tell Tales: Sure-Fire Stories from America's Favorite Storytellers.* Little Rock, AR: August House, 1994.

McCall Smith, Alexander. "A Blind Man Catches a Bird" in *Children of Wax: African Folk Tales.* New York: Interlink Books, 1991.

Miller, Teresa, Anne Pellowski, and Norma Livo. "Freedom Bird" in *Joining In: An Anthology of Audience Participation Stories and How to Tell Them.* Cambridge MA: Yellow Moon Press, 1991.

Storm, Hyemeyohsts. "Jumping Mouse" in *Seven Arrows.* New York: Ballantine Books, 1985.

Resiliency — Additional resources

Benard, Bonnie. *Fostering Resiliency in Kids: Protective Factors in the Family, School and Community.* Portland, OR: Northwest Regional Educational Laboratory, 1991.

Garbarino, James. *Children in Danger: Coping with the Consequences of Community Violence.* San Francisco: Jossey-Bass, 1992.

Muller, Wayne. *Legacy of the Heart: The Spiritual Advantages of a Painful Childhood.* New York: Simon and Schuster, 1992.

Noddings, Nel. *The Challenge to Care in Schools: An Alternative Approach to Education.* New York: Teachers College Press, 1992.

Werner, Emily, and Ruth S. Smith. *Overcoming the Odds: High-Risk Children from Birth to Adulthood.* Ithaca, NY: Cornell University Press, 1992.

Wolin, Steve, and Sybil Wolin. *The Resilient Self: How Survivors of Troubled Families Rise Above Adversity.* New York: Villard Books, 1993.

Spiritual Healing

Spiritual healing — Story collections

Bausch, William. *Storytelling: Imagination and Faith.* Mystic, CT: Twenty-Third Publications, 1984.

de Mello, Anthony. *One Minute Wisdom.* New York: Doubleday, 1985.

———. *The Song of the Bird.* New York: Doubleday, 1982.

Forest, Heather. *Wisdom Tales from Around the World.* Little Rock, AR: August House, 1996.

Feldman, Christina, and Jack Kornfield. *Stories of the Spirit, Stories of the Heart: Parables of the Spiritual Path From Around the World.* San Francisco: HarperCollins, 1991.

Houston, Jean. *The Search for the Beloved: Journeys in Mythology and Sacred Psychology.* Los Angeles: J.P. Tarcher, 1987.

Kornfield, Jack, and Christina Feldman. *Soul Food: Stories to Nourish the Spirit and the Heart.* San Francisco: HarperSanFrancisco, 1996.

Kurtz, Ernest, and Katherine Ketcham. *The Spirituality of Imperfection: Storytelling and the Journey to Wholeness.* New York: Bantam Books, 1994. An anthology of tales for those in recovery.

Pearmain, Elisa. *Doorways to the Soul: Fifty-Two Wisdom Tales from Around the World.* Cleveland: Pilgrim Press, 1998.

Simpkinson, C., and A. Simpkinson., eds. *Sacred stories: A Celebration of the Power of Stories to Transform and Heal.* San Francisco: HarperSanFrancisco, 1993.

Swami Prakashananda. *Don't Think of a Monkey and other Stories my Guru Told Me.* Fremont, CA: Sarasvati Productions, 1994.

Theophane the Monk. *Tales of the Magic Monastery.* New York: Crossroads, 1992.

Spiritual healing — Specific traditions
Buddhist/Hindu

The Panchatantra. Arthur W. Ryder, translator. Chicago: University of Chicago Press, 1964.

Jewish

Buxbaum, Yitzhak. *Storytelling and Spirituality in Judaism.* Northvale, NJ: Jason Aronson, 1994.

Epstein, Lawrence J. *A Treasury of Jewish Inspirational Stories.* Northvale, NJ: Jason Aronson, 1993.

Lipman, Doug. *The Forgotten Story: Tales of Wise Jewish Men.* Cambridge, MA: Yellow Moon Press, 1988. (Audiocassette)

Schram, Peninah., ed. *Chosen Tales.* Northvale, NJ: Jason Aronson, 1995.

Shamanism

Van Deusen, Kira. *Raven and the Rock: Storytelling in Chukotka.* Seattle: University of Washington Press, 1999.

———. *The Flying Tiger.* Women Shamans and Storytellers of the Amur. Montreal/Kingston: McGill-Queens University Press, 2001.

Sufi/Muslim

Downing, Charles. *Tales of the Hodja.* New York: Henry Z. Walk, 1965.

Shah, Idries. *Exploits of the Incomparable Mulla Nasrudhin.* New York: Simon and Schuster, 1966.

———. *The Way of the Sufi.* London: Octagon Press, 1980.

Merton, Thomas. *The Wisdom of the Desert: Sayings from the Desert Fathers of the Fourth Century.* Boston: Shambhala Publications, 1994.

Zen

Reps, Paul. *Zen Flesh, Zen Bones: Collection of Zen and Pre-Zen Writings.* Boston, MA: Shambhala Publications, 1994.

Martin, Rafe. *One Hand Clapping: Zen Stories for all Ages.* New York: Rizzoli International Publications, 1995.

Storytelling — How To Tell

How to tell — Teaching storytelling

Hamilton, Martha, and Mitch Weiss. *Children Tell Stories: A Teaching Guide.* Kaytona, NY: Richard C. Owens Publishers, 1990.

Holt, David, and Bill Mooney. *The Storyteller's Guide: Storytellers Share Advice.* Little Rock, AR: August House, 1996.

Kinghorn, Harriet, and Mary Helen Pelton. *Every Child a Storyteller: A Handbook of Ideas.* Greenwood Village, CO: Teacher Ideas Press, 1991.

Lipman, Doug. *Improving Your Storytelling: Beyond the Basics for All Who Tell Stories in Work or Play.* Little Rock, AR: August House, 1999.

Lipman, Doug, and Jay O'Callahan. *The Storytelling Coach: How to Listen, Praise, and Bring Out People's Best.* Little Rock, AR: August House 1995.

Lottridge, Celia Barker. *You Can Tell a Story: A Handbook for New Storytellers.* Toronto: The Parent-Child Mother Goose Program, 2002.

Mellon, Nancy. *Storytelling with Children.* England: Hawthorn Press, 2000.

How to tell — Story collections

Hamilton, Martha, and Mitch Weiss. *How and Why Stories: World Tales Kids Can Read and Tell.* Little Rock, AR: August House.

Holt, David, and Bill Mooney., eds. *Ready-To-Tell Tales: Sure-Fire Stories from America's Favorite Storytellers.* Little Rock, AR: August House, 1994.

———. *More Ready-To-Tell Tales from Around the World.* Little Rock, AR: August House, 2000.

MacDonald, Margaret Read. *The Storyteller's Start-Up Book: Finding, Learning, Performing, and Using Folktales, Including Twelve Tellable Tales.* Little Rock, AR: August House, 1993.

Pellowski, Anne. *The Story Vine: A Source Book for Unusual and Easy-to-tell Stories from Around the World.* New York: Aladdin Books/Macmillan, 1984.

Sawyer, Ruth. *The Way of the Storyteller.* New York: Penguin, 1998.

How to tell — Personal stories

Atkinson, Robert. *The Gift of Stories: Practical and Spiritual Applications of Autobiography, Life Stories and Personal Mythmaking.* Westport, CT: Bergin and Garvey, 1995.

Arthur, Stephen, and Julia Arthur. *Your Life and Times: How to Put a Life Story on Tape.* Baltimore, MD: Genealogical Publishing Company, 1987.

Davis, Donald. *Telling Your Own Stories: For Family and Classroom Storytelling, Public Speaking, and Personal Journaling.* Little Rock, AR: August House, 1993. Celebrating remembrance.

Maguire, Jack. *The Power of Personal Storytelling.* New York: J.P. Tarcher/ Putnam, 1998.

Moore, Robin. *Awakening the Hidden Storyteller: How to Build a Storytelling Tradition in Your Family.* Boston: Shambhala Publications, 1991.

Nelson, Annabelle. *The Storytelling Project: How to tell your story to impress others and find your voice.* Colorado: The WHEEL Council, (www.wheelcouncil.org), 1999.

Stone, Elizabeth. *Black Sheep and Kissing Cousins: How Our Family Stories Shape Us.* New York: Penguin, 1989.

Taylor, Daniel. *Tell Me A Story: The Life-Shaping Power of Our Stories.* St Paul MN: Bog Walk Press, 2001.

Storytelling For Parents

Storytelling for parents — Collections

Baltuck, Naomi. *Crazy Gibberish and other story hour stretches from a storyteller's bag of tricks.* Hampden, CT: Linnet Books, 1993.

DeSpain, Pleasant. *Twenty-Two Splendid Tales to Tell (Volumes 1 and 2).* Little Rock, AR: August House, 1990.

Forest, Heather. *Wisdom Tales From Around the World.* Little Rock, AR: August House, 1996.

Fujita, Hiroko and Fran Stallings. *Stories to Play With: Kids' Tales Told With Puppets, Paper, Toys and Imagination.* Little Rock, AR: August House Little Folk, 1996.

Lottridge, Celia Barker. *Ten Small Tales.* Toronto: Groundwood, 1993.

MacDonald, Margaret Read, Jen Whitman, Nat Whitman, and Wajuppa Tossa. *Shake-It-Up Tales! Stories to Sing, Dance, Drum, and Act Out.* Little Rock, AR: August House, 2000.

MacDonald, Margaret Read. *Tuck-Me-In Tales: Bedtime Stories from Around the World.* Little Rock, AR: August House Little Folk, 1996.

———. *Twenty Tellable Tales: Audience Participation Folktales for the Beginning Storyteller*. New York: H.W. Wilson, 1986.

Mayo, Margaret. *The Book of Magical Tales*. New York: Doubleday, 1988.

Rockwell, Anne. F. *The Three Bears and 15 Other Stories*. New York: Crowell, 1975.

Sierra, Judy. *Multicultural Folktales: Stories to Tell Young Children*. Phoenix, AZ: Oryx Press, 1991.

Sierra, Judy, and Bob Kaminski. *Mother Goose's Playhouse: Toddler Tales and Nursery Rhymes, with Patterns for Puppets and Feltboards*. Ashland, OR: Bob Kaminski Media Arts, 1994.

Storytelling for parents — Selected stories

Ata, Te, and Lynn Moroney. *Baby Rattlesnake*. San Francisco: Children's Book Press, 1993.

MacDonald, Margaret Read. "Let's Go On A Bear Hunt" in *The Parent's Guide to Storytelling: How to Make Up New Stories and Retell Old Favorites*. Little Rock, AR: August House, 2001.

McGovern, Ann. *Too Much Noise*. Boston: Houghton Mifflin 1967.

Substance Abuse Issues

Substance abuse issues — Story collections

Kurtz, Ernest, and Katherine Ketcham. *The Spirituality of Imperfection: Storytelling and the Journey to Wholeness*. New York: Bantam Books, 1994. An anthology of tales for those in recovery.

Nelson, Annabelle. *Storytelling Powerbook*. Arizona: The WHEEL Council, (www.wheelcouncil.org), 1997

Substance abuse issues — Selected stories

Bennett, William J.., ed. "The Magic Thread" in *The Book of Virtues: A Treasury of Great Moral Stories*. New York: Simon and Schuster, 1993.

Caduto, Michael, and Joseph Bruchac. "The Boy and the Rattlesnake" in *Keepers of the Animals: Native American Stories and Wildlife Activities for Children*. Golden, CO: Fulcrum Publishing, 1991.

Cole, Joanna., ed. "The Fisherman and His Wife" in *Best-Loved Folktales of the World*. New York: Doubleday, 1992.

Dutton, Cheryl. *Not In Here, Dad!* Hutchinson, London: Children's Books, 1992. A story with an anti-smoking message. Have the audience join in on "Not in here, Dad!"

Ellis, Rex. "Bennie" and "Cocaine" in *The Ups And Downs of Being Brown: Traditional and Contemporary African-American Stories*. Little Rock, AR: August House, 1997. (Audio recording)

Kronberg, Ruthilde, and Patricia McKissack. "Bundles of Troubles and Bundles of Blessings" in *A Piece of the Wind and Other Stories to Tell*. San Francisco: HarperCollins, 1990.

Ransome, Arthur. "Misery" in *Old Peter's Russian Tales*. Toronto: Thomas Nelson and Sons, 1967.

Rylant, Cynthia. "Drying Out" in *Every Living Thing*. New York: Aladdin Books/Macmillan, 1985. This book contains 12 short stories about changing perspective through the inspiration of animals.

Smith, Mary Carter. "Two Little Birds" in *Mary Carter Smith...Nearing Seventy-five*. Baltimore: Aframa Agency, 1993. (Audio recording)

Taylor, Clark. *The House That Crack Built*. San Francisco: Chronicle Books, 1992.

Van Der Post, Laurens. "The Man Who Had Black And White Cows" in *The Heart of the Hunter*. New York/San Diego: Harcourt Brace (Harvest Books), 1980. Breaking Trust.

Teach Your Children Values

Teach your children values — Story collections

Barchers, Suzanne. *Fifty Fabulous Fables*. Greenwood Village, CO: Teacher Ideas Press, 1997.

Campbell, Joseph. *Myths to Live By*. New York: Viking, 1972.

Creeden, Sharon. *Fair as Fair: World Folktales of Justice*. Little Rock, AR: August House, 1997.

DeSpain, Pleasant. *The Books of Nine Lives: Tales of Wisdom and Justice*. Little Rock, AR: August House Little Folk. 2001.

Forest, Heather. *Wonder Tales From Around the World*. Little Rock, AR: August House, 1995.

Gellman, Rabbi Marc, and Monsignor Thomas Hartman. *How Do You Spell God? Answers to the Big Questions From Around the World*. New York: William Morrow/Junior Books, 1995.

Flack, Jerry. *From the Land of Enchantment: Creative Teaching with Fairy Tales*. Greenwood Village, CO: Teacher Ideas Press, 1997.

Kraus, Anne Marie. *Folktale Themes and Activities for Children: Trickster and Transformation Tales*. Greenwood Village, CO: Teacher Ideas Press, 1995.

Norfolk, Bobby, and Sherry Norfolk. *The Moral of the Story: Folktales for Character Development*. Little Rock, AR: August House, 1999.

Smith, Charles. *From Wonder to Wisdom: Using Stories to Help People Grow*. New York: Penguin, 1989.

Stotter, Ruth. *The Golden Axe and Other Folk Tales of Compassion and Greed*. Stinson Beach, CA: Stotter Press, 1998.

Teach your children values — Selected stories

Bennett, William J.., ed. "The Bundle of Sticks" and "The King and His Hawk" in *The Book of Virtues*. New York: Simon and Schuster, 1993.

Cole, Joanna., ed. "The Fisherman and His Wife" in *Best-Loved Folktales of the World*. New York: Doubleday, 1992.

Evetts-Secker, Josephine. "The Waterfall of White Hair" in *Mother and Daughter Tales*. New York: Abbeville Press, 1996.

Rodanas, Kristina. *Dragonfly's Tale*. New York: Clarion Books, 1992.

Yolen, Jane., ed. "The Old Woman Who Lived in a Vinegar Bottle" in *Favorite Folktales from Around the World*. New York: Pantheon Books, 1988.

Therapeutic Storytelling

Bettelheim, Bruno. *The Uses of Enchantment: The Meaning and Importance of Fairy Tales*. New York: Vintage, 1989.

Brett, Doris. *Annie Stories*. New York: Workman Publishing, 1986. Design stories to aid children in coping with fears, loss, pain, siblings, and other challenges.

Brun, Brigitte, Ernst Pedersen, and Marianne Runberg., eds. *Symbols of the Soul: Therapy and Guidance Through Fairy Tales*. London/Philadelphia: Jessica L. Kingsley Publishers, 1993.

Dieckmann, Hans. *Twice Told Tales: The Psychological Uses of Fairy Tales*. Wilmette, IL: Chiron Publications, 1986.

Estes, Clarissa Pinkola. *Women Who Run With The Wolves*. New York: Ballantine Books, 1992.

Feinstein, David, and Stanley Krippner. *Personal Mythology: The Psychology of Your Evolving Self*. Los Angeles: Tarcher, 1988.

Frank, Arthur W. *The Wounded Storyteller*. Chicago: University of Chicago Press, 1995.

Franzke, Erich. *Fairy Tales in Psychotherapy: The Creative Use of Old and New Tales*. Lewiston, NY: Hans Huber, 1989.

Gersie, Alida. *Reflections on Therapeutic Storymaking: The Use of Stories in Groups*. London: Jessica L. Kingsley Publishers, 1997.

Gersie, Alida, and Nancy King. *Storymaking in Education and Therapy*. London: Jessica L. Kingsley Publishers, 1990. Therapeutic work with folktales and myth.

Gordon, David. *Therapeutic Metaphors: Helping Others Through the Looking Glass*. Cupertino, CA: META Publishers, 1978.

Heuscher, Julius E. *A Psychiatric Study of Myths and Fairytales: Their Origin, Meaning and Usefulness*. Springfield, IL: Charles Thomas, 1974.

Houston, Jean. *The Search for the Beloved: Journeys in Mythology and Sacred Psychology*. Los Angeles: Tarcher, 1987.

Kast, Verena. *Folktales as Therapy*. New York: Fromm International Publishing Corporation, 1995.

Keen, Sam, and Anne Valley-Fox. *Your Mythic Journey: Finding Meaning in Your Life through Writing and Storytelling*. New York: G.P. Putnam's Sons, 1989.

Larsen, Stephen. *The Mythic Imagination: Your Quest for Meaning Through Personal Mythology*. New York: Bantam, 1990.

Meade, Erica Helm. *Tell It by Heart: Women and the Healing Power of Story*. Chicago: Open Court, 1995. Combines myth and personal story with therapeutic examples.

Meade, Erica Helm. *The Moon in the Well*. Chicago: Open Court, 2001. 63 wisdom tales along with reflections and therapeutic applications

Mills, Joyce C., and Richard J. Crowley. *Therapeutic Metaphors For Children and The Child Within*. New York: Bruner/Mazel, 1986.

Simpkinson, C., and A. Simpkinson., eds. *Sacred stories: A Celebration of the Power of Stories to Transform and Heal*. San Francisco: HarperSanFrancisco, 1993.

Stone, Richard. *The Healing Art of Storytelling: A Sacred Journey of Personal Discovery*. New York: Hyperion, 1996. How personal stories heal through the telling.

Von Franz, Marie-Louise. *The Psychological Meaning of Redemption Motifs in Fairytales*. Toronto: Inner City Books, 1980.

———. *The Interpretation of Fairy Tales*. Dallas: Spring Publications, 1970.

———. *Shadow and Evil in Fairytales*. Zurich, Switzerland: Spring Publications, 1974.

Wallas, Lee. *Stories for the Third Ear*. New York: W.W. Norton and Company, 1985.

Violence Prevention/Peace Initiatives

Violence prevention/Peace initiatives — Story collections
Bauman, Elizabeth Hershberger. *Coals of Fire*. Scottdale, PA: Herald Press, 1982. True stories of people who returned good for evil.

Brody, Ed, Jay Goldspinner, Katie Green, Rona Leventhal, and John Porcino., eds. *Spinning Tales, Weaving Hope: Stories, Storytelling, and Activities for Peace, Justice and the Environment.* Gabriola Island, BC: New Society Publishers, 2002.

Dass, Ram, and Paul Gorman. *How Can I Help? Stories and Reflections on Service.* New York: Knopf, 1990. Stories about compassion, suffering, listening, anger, conflict, burnout, and healing.

Durrell, Ann, and Marylin Sachs., eds. *The Big Book of Peace.* New York: Dutton, 1990.

Lehn, Cornelia. *Peace Be With You.* Newton, KS: Faith and Life Press, 1980. Fifty-nine stories of peace heroes throughout the ages.

Simms, Laura. *Stories To Nourish the Hearts of Our Children In a Time of Crisis.* New York: Holland and Knight, 2001.

Stotter, Ruth. *The Golden Axe and Other Folk Tales of Compassion and Greed.* Stinson Beach, CA: Stotter Press, 1998.

Violence prevention/Peace initiatives — *Selected stories*

Collier, Kenneth W. "How Coyote Lost His Songs, Music and Dance" in *Our Seven Principles in Story and Verse.* Boston: Skinner House Books, 1997.

Davar, Ashok. *The Wheel of King Asoka.* Chicago: Follett Publishing, 1977. True story of an Indian ruler who abandoned war for peace.

DeSpain, Pleasant. "All Things Are Connected" in *Eleven Nature Tales: A Multicultural Journey.* Little Rock, AR: August House, 1996.

Kronberg, Ruthilde, and Patricia McKissack. "The Rabbit And The Elephant" in *A Piece of the Wind and Other Stories to Tell.* San Francisco: HarperCollins, 1990. Dealing with a bully.

Leichman, Seymour. *The Boy Who Could Sing Pictures.* New York: Holt Rhinehart and Winston: 1973. A king realizes how war hurts his people when a boy sings of the sadness he sees.

MacDonald, Margaret Read. "War Between the Sandpipers and the Whales" and "Holding Up the Sky" in *Peace Tales: World Folktales to Talk About.* Hampden, CT: Linnet Books, 1992.

Maruki, Toshi. *Hiroshima No Pika.* New York: Lothrop, Lee and Shepard, 1980. The effects of the bombing of Hiroshima on one family.

Pomerantz, Charlotte. *The Princess and the Admiral.* New York: Feminist Press; 1992.

Zolotow, Charlotte. *The Hating Book.* New York: Harper Trophy, 1989.

———. *The Quarreling Book.* New York: HarperTrophy, 1982.

Violence prevention/Peace initiatives — *Additional resources*

Credle, Ellis. "How To Grow Hot Peppers" in *Tall Tales From The High Hills.* New York: Nelson, 1957. Good for discussions about anger.

Fredericks, Linda, and the Colorado School Mediation Project. *Using Stories to Prevent Violence and Promote Cooperation.* Boulder: Colorado School Mediation Project, 1996.

———. *Healing Wounds with Words: A Guide to Conflict Resolution Through Storytelling.* Boulder: Colorado School Mediation Project, 2000.

Frum, Thomas F. *The Magic of Conflict.* New York: Simon and Schuster, 1987. Stress reduction and conflict resolution based on Aikido. The book contains non-fiction stories and traditional tales.

Fry, A. Ruth. *Victories Without Violence*. Santa Fe, NM: Ocean Tree Books, 1986.

Glassman, Bernie. *Bearing Witness: A Zen Master's Lessons in Making Peace*. New York: Bell Tower, 1998.

Women's Issues

Carter, Angela., ed. *The Old Wives' Fairy Tale Book*. New York: Pantheon Books, 1990.

Chinen, Allan B. *Once Upon a Midlife: Classic Stories and Mythic Tales to Illuminate the Mythic Years*. New York: Putnam, 1992.

———. *Waking the World: Classic Tales of Women and the Heroic Feminine*. New York: Putnam, 1996.

Creedon, Sharon. *In Full Bloom: Tales of Women in Their Prime*. Little Rock, AR: August House, 1999.

Estes, Clarissa Pinkola. *Women Who Run With The Wolves*. New York: Ballantine Books, 1992.

Evetts-Secker, Josephine. *Mother and Daughter Tales*. New York: Abbeville Press, 1996.

Gunn Allen, Paula., ed. *Spider Woman's Granddaughters: Traditional Tales and Contemporary Writing by Native American Women*. New York: Ballantine Books, 1989.

Hastings, Selina. *Sir Gawain and the Loathly Lady*. Lothrop, Lee and Shepard, 1985.

Haven, Kendall. *Amazing American Women: 40 Fascinating 5-Minute Reads*. Greenwood Village, CO: Teacher Ideas Press, 1995.

Holmes, Kenneth L., ed. *Covered Wagon Women: Diaries and Letters From the Western Trails, 1852, The California Trail*. Lincoln, NE: University of Nebraska Press, 1985.

McVickar Edwards, Carolyn. *The Storyteller's Goddess: Tales of the Goddess and Her Wisdom from Around the World*. San Francisco: HarperSanFrancisco, 1991.

Meade, Erica Helm. *Tell It by Heart: Women and the Healing Power of Story*. Chicago: Open Court, 1995.

Monaghan, Patricia. *Wild Girls: The Path of the Young Goddess*. St. Paul, MN: Llewellyn Publications, 2001.

Phelps, Ethel Johnston. *Tatterhood And Other Tales*. New York: The Feminist Press, 1978.

———. *The Maid Of The North: Feminist Folktales from Around The World*. New York: Holt, Rhinehart and Winston, 1982.

Ragan, Kathleen., ed. *Fearless Girls, Wise Women, and Beloved Sisters: Heroines in Folktales from Around the World*. New York: W.W. Norton and Company, 1998.

San Souci, Robert, and Brian Pinkney. *Cut From The Same Cloth: American Women Of Myth, Legend and Tall Tale*. New York: Philomel Books, 1993.

Seagraves, Anne. *Soiled Doves: Prostitution in the Early West*. Hayden Lake, ID: Wesanne Publications, 1994.

Simms, Laura. *Moon On Fire: Calling Forth The Power Of The Feminine*. Cambridge, MA: Yellow Moon Press, 1987.

———. *Women and Wild Animals: Howl the Morning Welcome*. Minocqua, WI: Northword Press, 1992 (available from the author at www.laurasimms.com).

Stanley, Jo., ed. *Bold in Her Breeches: Women Pirates Across the Ages*. San Francisco: Pandora Books, 1995.

Zipes, Jack. *Don't Bet On the Prince: Contemporary Feminist Tales in North America and England*. New York: Routledge, 1989.

Youth On The Edge

Youth on the edge — Story collections

Czarnota, Lorna. *Crossroads*. New York: Self published, 1999. Phone: 716-837-0551.

Meade, Erica Helm. *The Moon in the Well: Wisdom Tales to Transform Your Life, Family, and Community*. Chicago: Open Court, 2001.

Meyers, Walter Dean. *Sweet Illusions*. New York: Teachers and Writers Collaborative, 1986.

Simon, Solomon. *The Wise Men of Helm and their Merry Tales*. Springfield, NJ: Behrman House, 1996. Coping through humour.

Youth on the edge — Selected stories

Barchers, Suzanne. "The Stolen Bairn and the Sìdh" in *Wise Women: Folk and Fairy Tales from Around the World*. Englewood, CO: Libraries Unlimited, 1990. Excellent story for teen mothers.

Chinen, Allan B. "The King has Goats Ears," in *Beyond the Hero*. New York: Tarcher/Putnam, 1993. The power of secrets.

Colum, Padraic. *The Girl Who Sat By the Ashes*. New York: Macmillan, 1968.

Hastings, Selina. *Sir Gawain and the Loathly Lady*. New York: Lothrop, Lee and Shepard, 1985.

Holt, David, and Bill Mooney., eds. "The Black Prince" in *Ready-To-Tell Tales: Sure-Fire Stories from America's Favorite Storytellers*. Little Rock, AR: August House, 1994.

Kimmel, Eric A., and Leonard Fisher. *The Three Princes*. New York: Holiday House, 2000.

MacDonald, Margaret Read. "The Lion's Whisker" in *Peace Tales: World Folktales to Talk About*. Hampden, CT: Linnet Books, 1992.

McDermott, Gerald. *Musicians of the Sun*. New York: Aladdin Books, 2000.

Meade, Michael. "The Half-Boy" from Throw Yourself Like Seed. Pacific Grove, CA: Oral Tradition Archives, 1996. (audio cassette).

Storm, Hyemeyohsts. "Jumping Mouse" in *Seven Arrows*. New York: Ballantine Books, 1985.

Wolkstein, Diane. "I'm Tipingee, She's Tipingee, We're Tipingee Too" in *The Magic Orange Tree and other Haitian Folktales*. New York: Schocken Books/Random House, 1997.

Zeman, Ludmilla. *Gilgamesh The King*. Minneapolis, MN: Econo-Clad Books, 1999. Destructive power is tamed by friendship and reconciliation with an enemy.

Youth on the edge — Additional resource

Hillman, James, Michael Meade and Malidoma Some. *Images of initiation*. Pacific Grove, CA: Oral Tradition Archives, 1992. (audio cassette).

Mahdi, Louise Carus, Nancy Geyer Christopher and Michael Meade. *Crossroads: The quest for contemporary rites of passage*. Chicago: OPen Court, 1996.

Mahdi, Louise, Steven Foster, and Meredith Little, eds. *Betwixt and Between: Patterns of Male and Female Initiation*. Peru, IL: Open Court Publishing, 1987. Rites of passage.

Author biographies and contact information

David H. Albert (Editor) holds degrees from Williams College, Oxford University, and the Committee on Social Thought, University of Chicago, but says, "the best education he ever received he gets from his kids." He writes a regular column — "My Word!" — for *Home Education Magazine.* He is author of two books on homeschooling — *And the Skylark Sings with Me: Adventures in Homeschooling and Community-Based Education* (New Society Publishers, 1999) and *Homeschooling and the Voyage of Self-Discovery: A Journey of Original Seeking* (Common Courage Press, 2003) As founder of New Society Publishers, he was also publisher of *Spinning Tales, Weaving Hope: Stories of Peace, Justice, and the Environment,* to which he contributed, and which has recently been reissued in a 10th anniversary edition. David lives in Olympia, Washington with his partner Ellen and two wonderful daughters, Aliyah (age 15) and Meera (12). When he is not learning with and from his kids, writing or telling stories, making music, or raising funds for child welfare or community development projects in India, he serves as senior planning and policy analyst for the Washington State Division of Alcohol and Substance Abuse. David is also an active member of the Religious Society of Friends (Quakers).

1717 18th Ct. NE Olympia, WA 98506
Phone: (360) 352-0506
E-mail: shantinik@earthlink.net
Website: www.skylarksings.com

Allison M. Cox (Editor) has a Masters degree in counseling psychology and a graduate certificate in public health. She has worked as a mental health therapist, social worker, health educator, health promotion specialist, and prevention specialist —and for the past 20 years, storytelling has accompanied her along these many paths. Allison's health-related storytelling projects have included parent/baby groups, the Adolescent Pregnancy Prevention Project, substance abuse prevention/intervention efforts, training volunteers for the Asthma and Allergy Prevention Project, women's health issues, the Ethnic Elder Health Promotion program, and using story in community assessment and development in her work for the Tacoma Pierce County Health Department. She was the chair for the Storytelling for Prevention Conference in Fife, Washington, in 1998 and is the vice chair and a founding board member of the Healing Story Alliance Special Interest Group of the National Storytelling Network. She is the editor and graphic artist for the Healing Story Alliance journal, *Diving In The Moon: Honoring Story, Facilitating Healing.* Allison has performed as a professional storyteller across Canada and the U.S., offering concerts and workshops on storytelling as a healing art, and also performs storytelling concerts just for the fun of it! She lives on Vashon Island in Puget Sound with her family and her gardens in the woods. (see over).

25714 Wax Orchard Rd., SW,
Vashon Island, WA 98070 USA
Phone: (206) 463-3844
Fax: (206) 463-2026
E-mail: allison@dancingleaves.com
Website:
http://www.dancingleaves.com/allison

Jan Andrews uses the power of quiet and containment to touch audiences deeply. She has a particular interest in epic stories, as well as in traditional folktales and fairytales. Past national coordinator for Storytellers of Canada/Conteurs du Canada and producer of Ottawa's Stories From the Ages, she has organized complete tellings of *The Odyssey* and *The Iliad* at her lakeside home. Jan has written nine published books for children and young adults, and is director of SC/CC's StorySave website, featuring elder tellers.

R.R. #2
Lanark, ON
K0G 1K0 Canada
Phone: (613) 256-0353
E-mail: jandrews@magma.ca

JoAnne Banks-Wallace, RN, PhD, writes: Two distinct but overlapping groups have profoundly shaped my life. I was blessed to be born into and nurtured by powerful God-fearing, card-playing families and communities. Stories shared by card-table philosophers and Bible-quoting sages continuously help me find my way in the world. My life is dedicated to passing on the lessons learned. I am currently working on the development of group storytelling as the cornerstone for culture-based interventions to promote physical activity among women.

MU Sinclair School of Nursing S-324,
University of Missouri-Columbia

Columbia, MO 65211 USA
Phone: (573) 882-0283
Fax: (573) 884-4544
E-mail: Banks-WallaceJ@health.missouri.edu

Sandra Carpenter-Davis is a versatile storyteller who captures the imaginations of children and adults alike. Whether telling folktales or family stories; using rhymes, songs, and stories to enrich the parent-child relationship; or teaching storytelling workshops, her ultimate goal is to infect everyone with the "Storytelling Virus." Sandra is the collector/editor of *Bounce Me, Tickle Me, Hug Me*, a multicultural rhyme collection. She is also a founding member of the Canadian Association of Storytellers for Children. She lives in Toronto.

15 Graham Gardens
Toronto, ON,
M6C 1G6 Canada
Phone: (416) 653-6475
E-mail: aubrey.sandra@sympatico.ca

Kevin Cordi is a professional storyteller and teacher at Hanford High School and California State University, Fresno. Even though he has a Masters degree in storytelling and education, he believes his real learning comes from his parents, who told stories to Kevin and his five siblings every day, seated on an old couch. Kevin knows that true learning comes when students are empowered to be part of the process. He is the co-author of *Raising Voices: Storytelling Youth Groups and Troupes* (Teacher Ideas Press).

PO Box 1066
Hanford, CA 93230 USA
Phone: (559) 587-0309
E-mail: Kctells@youthstorytelling.com
Website: www.youthstorytelling.com

In her roles as adoption specialist, parent trainer, storyteller, and sister of the earth, **Reneé Díaz de León Harvey** has melded her desire to help children and families with her passion for nature by sharing stories in a public agency and local venues that guide the listeners to self discovery and solutions for healing, honoring, and restoring ourselves, our relationships, and our planet. Reneé is co-founder of the Mount Tahoma Guild and has performed and presented workshops nationally that incorporate her Hispanic roots.

2715 N. 31st Street
Tacoma, WA 98407 USA
Phone: (253) 752-2757
E-mail: earthsister_storyteller_renee@hotmail.com

Nancy Duncan, MFA, was born in IN, raised in IL, reared in GA, awakened in IA, and settled in NE. She tells stories for all ages and venues including personal, folktales and fairytales, coyote stories with tribal members' approval, and literary tales. Duncan teaches graduate storytelling courses every summer in Nebraska and Iowa. Her most popular residency is STORYBUDDIES — an interactive oral history project linking senior citizens to school students, celebrating and building community.

1803 S. 58th St.
Omaha, NE 68106-0225 USA
Phone: (402) 551-4532
E-mail: storygalore@cox.net
Website: www.storygalore.com

Tom Farley is a writer, actor, and children's bookseller. He usually tells in tandem with his wife, Sandy, as Spontaneous Combustion Storytellers. They are co-authors of *Earthcare for Children: A First Day School Curriculum*, published by Friends Committee on Unity with Nature in 1998. Tom has organized children's programs for Quaker gatherings and is active in environmental, parenting, disability, and Balkan refugee projects. An earlier version of "I Don't Want To Talk About It" appeared in the April 1999 issue of *Friends Bulletin*.

1301 Himmel Avenue
Redwood City, CA 94061-3507 USA
Phone: (650) 366-1818
E-mail: farley@spont.com

Joan Fleitas, EdD, RN, PhD, is associate professor of nursing at Fairfield University (Connecticut) and has been interested in children with medical problems for a long time. The Band-Aides and Blackboards Project began as part of her dissertation for a doctorate in health education. She has been teaching college nursing students how to work with children for the past 29 years.

School of Nursing, Fairfield University
Fairfield, CT 06340 USA
E-mail: Fleitas@fair1.fairfield.edu
Website:
www.faculty.fairfield.edu/fleitas/contents.html

Linda Fredericks is a writer and storyteller who has lectured throughout the United States on the link between storytelling and human development. She has created a popular training for AmeriCorps and VISTA programs on "Using Storytelling to Develop Literacy and Critical Thinking Skills" and has written two books on storytelling and conflict resolution for the Colorado School Mediation Project. She was formerly a college administrator and director of a national non-profit focusing on health promotion for students. She currently directs Weaving Futures Consulting in Boulder, CO.

E-mail: lindaf@indra.com.

Michale Gabriel is a Parent's Choice award-winning performer, recording artist, corporate consultant, and inspirational speaker. She coaches corporate leaders, including those of the Boeing Company, on how to communicate vision and values in story form. Michale founded the Storytelling Residency Program at Children's Hospital in Seattle, where she specialized in storytelling as a healing art. She has traveled repeatedly to Russia, where she shared stories as part of a cross-cultural peace initiative. Michale offers coaching and training services for corporations and organizations, workshops, performances, and custom keynotes.

1975 Bellevue Way NE #477
Bellevue, WA 98004 USA
Phone: (425) 823-3656
E-mail: michalegabriel@bigplanet.com
Website: www.MichaleGabriel.com

Merle Harris has always been fascinated by stories. She is a freelance storyteller and has been a facilitator/trainer for the Parent-Child Mother Goose Program since 1994. She has told stories in schools, libraries, seniors homes, women and juvenile detention centers, on the radio, and at festivals across Canada. She was also resident storyteller at Fort Edmonton Park. A revised edition of Merle's *Telling Tales: Storytelling in the Family*, co-authored with Gail de Vos and Celia Barker Lottridge, is forthcoming from the University of Alberta Press.

6223 186 Street, Edmonton, AB
T5T 2T3 Canada
Phone: (780) 444-7214

Fax: (780) 487-0249
E-mail: merle@merleharris.com
Website: www.merleharris.com

Debra Harris-Branham has been sharing stories to delight, treasure, and tickle the funny bone of Northwest audiences for over 18 years. She specializes in weaving tales from her African American culture in an animated, rhythmic style. Besides working as an elementary school librarian in Renton, Washington, Debra appears as a professional storyteller, offering workshops and concerts.

5514 S. Juniper
Seattle, WA 98178 USA
Phone: (206) 772-0415
E-mail: dharris-branham@renton.wednet.edu

Randy Landenberger lived in Hawaii for eight years, until his neighbor inspired him to move to San Diego, CA, to study for his current profession — echocardiography, using ultrasound to image the heart. He currently lives, works, writes, and tells stories in the Monterey Bay area of the California coast. He returns to Hawaii as often as possible to relax, refresh, and rejuvenate his spirit among the showers and rainbows, mountains, ocean, and friends.

Phone: (831) 384-1149
E-mail: artistic2@earthlink.net

Hazel Lennox grew up in Scotland surrounded by stories. She believes that stories hold kernels of truth that transcend the boundaries of time as well as culture. Hazel's repertoire of tales from many lands have been spun in schools, festivals and celebrations in Britain, Canada and the United States for the past 15 years. As a writer, musician and performer, Hazel offers workshops in literacy, team building and self-empowerment.

Her performances include music, drama and invariably a lot of laughs.

735 Ninth Street
Courtenay, BC
V9N 1P1 Canada
Phone: (250) 334-2352
E-mail: spinningtales@telus.net

Doug Lipman became aware of the healing power of storytelling one day in 1970, when he accidentally entranced 70 "emotionally disturbed" children in the school where he taught. Since then he has told stories and coached on four continents, using the power of storytelling to teach, empower, and connect. He specializes in supportive coaching — and in training corporate executives to use storytelling for personal and organizational transformation. He offers a free e-mail newsletter, "eTips from the Storytelling Coach," via his website.

PO Box 441195
West Somerville, MA
02144 USA
Phone: (781) 391-3672
Fax: (781) 391-6341
Toll-free: (888) 446-4738
E-mail:
healingstory@storydynamics.com
Web page:
http://www.storydynamics.com

Celia Barker Lottridge has been a storyteller in libraries, schools, and community settings for many years. She was one of the founders of the Storytellers School of Toronto and teaches workshops and courses in storytelling. Celia helped to develop the Parent-Child Mother Goose Program from its beginning in 1984 and was director of the program from 1991 to 2001. She is also the author of many children's books

including several retellings of folktales based on her storytelling experience.

42 Vermont Ave.
Toronto, ON
M6G 1X9 Canada
Phone: (416) 531-6072
E-mail: celialottridge@yahoo.com

Margaret Read MacDonald works as a children's librarian at the Bothell branch of the King County Library in Seattle, WA, where she shares her tales with over 15,000 listeners every year. She has told stories and offered workshops in storytelling around the world. Margaret holds a PhD in folklore and is the author of over 30 books — many of which have become the favorite story collections of veteran storytellers. Margaret has pulled her repertoire from folktales around the world and encouraged many to give storytelling a try.

11507 NE 104th Street
Kirkland, WA 98033 USA
Phone/Fax: (425) 827-6430
E-mail: margmacd@kcls.org

Tom McDermott has worked as a minister and social worker, and has devoted the last 11 years of his life to sharing stories and songs that empower children of all ages. Each year Tom tours the U.S. and Canada to present concerts to over 60,000 students in schools, churches, hospitals, and medical camps. Tom teaches workshops on storytelling to students, parents, educators, ministers, health care professionals, and storytellers. He is a member of Celebration Shop — a nonprofit organization that produces award-winning CDs of songs and stories for children with chronic illnesses. Tom is a founder of the Tarant Area Guild of Storytellers. At the 2001 Texas Storytelling Festival, he was awarded the John

Henry Faulk Award for excellence in, and contribution to, storytelling in the Southwest.

PO Box 470593
Fort Worth, TX 76147 USA
Phone: (817) 738-TALE
E-mail: Uketeller425@cs.com

Paul Nelson is an author, educator, and consultant who holds a Masters degree in counseling psychology from the Harvard Graduate School of Education In 1993 he founded Keepers Of The Lore, a non-profit organization created to preserve and perpetuate the world's wisdom-lore through educational events and media. Among its activities, the organization sponsors the annual Joseph Campbell Festival of Myth, Folklore & Story. Paul lives in Wilton, NH, with his wife and three daughters.

PO Box 453
Milford, NH 03055 USA
Phone: (603) 654-5944
E-mail: story@tellink.net

Susan O'Halloran has worked as a dance teacher, DJ, TV host, scriptwriter, film maker, stand-up comic, instructional designer, diversity consultant, and storyteller. She is the author of several books and a diversity curriculum for high schools and has recorded many of her stories and songs. Since 1976, Sue has managed her own communications firm, writing for radio, schools, theater, media, business, medical institutions, and social service agencies. Her work focuses on many social issues such as racism, political activism, sexual abuse prevention, drug abuse prevention, aging and the workplace, detecting depression, and violence prevention. With humor and creativity, Susan encourages others to help shape a compassionate world.

PO Box 5170
Evanston, IL 60204 USA
Phone: (847) 869-4081
Fax: (847) 869-8184
E-Mail: superoh@aol.com
Website: http://www.racebridges.net/sue

Rose Owens writes: Once upon a time there was a little girl named Rose. Below her freckled nose was a happy smile. In her heart she cherished the dream that when she grew up she would be a story princess. Thirty years ago, she became a volunteer storyteller at her children's school and the students named her "The Story Lady." Rose specializes in educational storytelling and especially likes to include audience participation stories. She tells in the San Francisco Bay area, Utah, and Idaho.

E-mail: storylady@civprod.com
Website:
http://www.Rosethestorylady.com

Elisa Pearmain, MEd, MA, is a professional storyteller, a licensed mental health counselor, and the award-winning author of *Doorways to the Soul: Fifty-two Wisdom Tales from Around the World* (Pilgrim Press 1998). She lives in Lincoln, MA, with her husband and daughter.

PO Box 634
Lincoln, MA 01773 USA
Phone: (781) 259-0492
E-mail: Elisa@wisdomtales.com,
Website: http://www.wisdomtales.com.

Maureen Pedone has been telling stories ever since she was a child … and professionally since 1986. She developed a program using storytelling to address risk factors, increase developmental assets, promote positive values, encourage cultural pride, and promote literacy that is now used in eight elementary schools in

Vancouver, WA. She adapted E.T.A. Hoffman's *Nutcracker* for Oregon Ballet Theatre and wrote *The King Who Learned His Lesson*, an environmental fairytale, which was published by the City of Vancouver for its urban forestry education program. Maureen also started a literacy project and book distribution with the Native American Education Program.

Good Medicine Storytelling
8318 NE 14th Street
Vancouver, WA 98664 USA
Phone: (360) 699-4937
E-mail: geotale@pacifier.com

Melanie Ray approaches storytelling as an art and as a traditional key to a good community. She has been telling stories professionally since 1984, doing programs for audiences of all ages all across Canada. Her eclectic repertoire includes medieval legends, history, folktales, and literature. It often features women. Melanie has at times been supported in her work by the Canada Council for the Arts, and she is an active member of the Vancouver Society of Storytelling and Storytellers of Canada/Raconteurs du Canada.

4432 Walden St.
Vancouver, BC
V5V 3S3 Canada
Phone: (604) 874-3519
E-mail: melanieray@telus.net

Deborah Robins is an Australian teacher-librarian and mother of a 14-year-old son with Duchenne Muscular Dystrophy. Deborah is inspired by an American, Pat Furlong of Parent Project Muscular Dystrophy (www.parentdmd.org). PPMD's mission statement is "Research, Treatment, Hope," and the organization was instrumental in obtaining the first major children's health bill of the 107th U.S. Congress — the first public law in history to address muscular dystrophy. "In my mind," says Deb, "I see Pat waiting anxiously on the riverbank for our children to survive."

E-mail: garobin@tpg.com.au

Rico Rodriguez is a storyteller, drag artist, and percussionist. He is also a youth counselor, teacher, facilitator, and a consummate master of ceremonies. He tells folktale, fairytales, fables, and legends from the rich and diverse Latino and Hispanic cultures. He also writes and tells stories about his life and his family. He tells in English, Spanish and Spanglish. His easy style and his masterful use of humor, even in the most painful of situations, draw audiences young and old. A challenging but humorous exploration of equity issues and social change recurs throughout his telling.

595 Dovercourt Rd.
Toronto, ON
M6H 2W5 Canada
Phone: (416) 588-8442 or
(647) 293-RICO
E-mail: rico_lucy@hotmail.com
Website: www.storytellingtoronto.org
(see Directory/Rico Rodriguez)

Diane Rooks works with The Compassionate Friends, hospice, bereaved children, alternative schools, and other groups dealing with loss and transition. She gives speeches, tells stories, and leads workshops that encourage others to negotiate change to find healing and growth. Diane tells folktales and personal stories, develops historical characters, teaches storytelling and memoir collecting, and provides coaching for organizations and individuals. She is the author of *Spinning Gold out of Straw: How Stories Heal* and is secretary of the Healing Story Alliance. (see over).

151 Santa Monica Ave.
St. Augustine, FL 32080 USA
Phone: (904) 829 1754
E-mail: diane@storyjourney.com
Website: www.storyjourney.com

Gail Rosen is a storyteller, bereavement facilitator, and educator who tells stories about the "big questions" — life, death, and meaning. With humor, honesty, and insight, she works in grief support groups, retreats, and memorial services and provides training and support for professional and lay caregivers. She has presented at conferences including the National Association for Death Education and Counseling and the National Storytelling Association. Gail is the founder of the Healing Story Alliance Special Interest Group of the National Storytelling Network. Audiotapes are available.

721 Howard Road
Pikesville, MD 21208 USA
Phone: (410) 486-3551
Fax: (410) 486-5976
E-mail: gailstory@aol.com
Website: www.gailrosen.com

Nancy Schimmel presents traditional and original stories with verve, wit, and audience participation. She has performed and taught storytelling in libraries, schools, and colleges throughout the United States since 1976. Nancy is the author of *A Sourcebook For Storytelling, Just Enough To Make A Story*, which has become a classic reference among storytellers. A musician as well as a storyteller, Nancy has made many recordings for children.

1639 Channing Way
Berkeley, CA 09473 USA
E-mail: nancy@sisterschoice.com

Laura Simms, storyteller and author, is the founder/director of The Gaindeh Project, an international storytelling initiative for youth in crisis. *Stories to Nourish the Hearts of Our Children in a Time of Crisis* was published in 2001. She is writing a multicultural story and healing book for Mercy Corps, Inc. Laura teaches at New York University, the University of Milwaukee, Naropa University, and the EcoVersity in New Mexico. She tells stories throughout the world and is an award-winning author. *Robe Of Love: Secret Instructions of the Heart* (fairytales for adults) will be published by Codhill in fall 2002.

814 Broadway
New York, NY 10003 USA
Phone/Fax: (212) 674-3479
E-Mail: storydevi@earthlink.net
Website: www.laurasimms.com

Leslie Slape is a full-time reporter for a small daily newspaper (since 1979) and feels that her storytelling has vastly improved her writing. Leslie writes her humor columns in an oral voice so that people will read them to each other. Leslie tells stories to entertain, teach, and touch people's hearts. Storytelling has caused her to look deeply within herself. She performs folktales, literary works, original stories, and music throughout the Northwest at storytelling festivals and gatherings.

74283 Fern Hill Road
Rainier, OR 97048 USA
Phone: (503) 556-4048
Fax (360) 577-2516
E-mail: leslie@tdn.com
Website:
www.storyteller.net/tellers/lslape/

Cristy West, PhD, is trained as a creative arts therapist and has also completed her doctorate in arts in education, with a focus on storytelling.

She was one of the founding board members of the Healing Story Alliance. A longer version of this piece appeared in *Diving in the Moon: Honoring Story, Facilitating Healing*, Issue 2 (summer 2001), available from Healing Story Alliance.

2720 Brandywine St. NW
Washington DC 20008 USA
Phone: (202) 966-7746
E-mail: cristywest@aol.com

If you have enjoyed *The Healing Heart*, You may also enjoy the following title from New Society Publishers

SPINNING TALES WEAVING HOPE

Stories, Storytelling and Activities for Peace, Justice and the Environment

Edited by Ed Brody, Jay Goldspinner, Katie Green, Rona Leventhal and John Porcino
Foreword by Holly Near

The second edition of this much-loved storytelling sourcebook features 29 wondrous children's stories from around the world. From the mythic and the fantastic, to the silly and the serious, these timeless tales encourage conflict resolution, compassion, and sensitivity to the Earth and all living things. An incredible sourcebook for storytellers, teachers, parents and healers, each story is followed by suggested activities and exercises, storytelling tips, and resources, all designed to deepen the storytelling experience. Includes an Age Suitability Index, a Thematic Index, and a Directory of Contributors. A new introduction focuses on storytelling in education.

The editors are all dedicated storytellers and members of the Stories for World Change Network, founded by Ed Brody. They all live in Massachusetts.

296 pages 8.5 x 11"
Education & Teaching / Folklore / Fiction Anthology
ISBN 0-86571-447-9
US$24.95 / Can$33.95

If you have enjoyed *The Healing Heart ~ Families* you might also enjoy other

BOOKS TO BUILD A NEW SOCIETY

New Society Publishers' mission is to publish books that contribute in fundamental ways to building an ecologically sustainable and just society, and to do so with the least possible impact on the environment, in a manner that models this vision.

Our books provide positive solutions for people who want to make a difference.
We specialize in:

• **Sustainable Living • Ecological Design and Planning •**

• **Natural Building & Appropriate Technology • Environment and Justice •**

• **New Forestry • Conscientious Commerce • Resistance and Community •**

• **Nonviolence • Progressive Leadership • Educational and Parenting Resources •**

For a full list of NSP's titles, please call 1-800-567-6772 or check out our web site at:
www.newsociety.com

New Society Publishers

ENVIRONMENTAL BENEFITS STATEMENT

New Society Publishers has chosen to produce this book
on New Leaf EcoBook 100, recycled paper made with 100% post
consumer waste, processed chlorine free, and old growth free.

For every 5,000 books printed, New Society saves the following resources:[1]

37	Trees
3,370	Pounds of Solid Waste
3,708	Gallons of Water
4,836	Kilowatt Hours of Electricity
6,126	Pounds of Greenhouse Gases
26	Pounds of HAPs, VOCs, and AOX Combined
9	Cubic Yards of Landfill Space

[1] Environmental benefits are calculated based on research done by the Environmental Defense Fund and other members of the Paper Task Force who study the environmental impacts of the paper industry.

For more information on this environmental benefits statement, or to inquire about environmentally friendly papers, please contact New Leaf Paper – info@newleafpaper.com – 888•989•5323.

NEW SOCIETY PUBLISHERS